SHORE FISHING

SHORE FISHING

John Darling

Ward Lock Limited · London

© John Darling 1982

First published in Great Britain in 1982
by Ward Lock Limited, 82 Gower Street,
London WC1E 6EQ, a Pentos Company.

Designed by Viv Harper
House editor Helen Douglas-Cooper
Text filmset in Monophoto Apollo
by Servis Filmsetting Limited, Manchester.

Printed and bound in Hong Kong by
Lee Fung Asco Printers Limited.

British Library Cataloguing in Publication Data

Darling, John
    Shore fishing.
    1. Saltwater fishing
    I. Title
    799.1 ′2   SH457
    ISBN 0-7063-6088-5

Acknowledgments

The author would like to thank Keith Roberts for contributing the
chapter on baits, Ron Preddy for that on cod and related species, and
Alan Yates for those on flatfish and small bottom-feeders and match
fishing.

Photographs by John Darling

Line drawings by Nils Solberg

Contents

Introduction

The front cover picture of Ray Brewster surf fishing for bass tells a story that typifies the approach of this book. Rather than repeat the mass of technical information that abounds in most other sea fishing books, we decided to start with the fish, not the tackle.

The secret of successful fishing lies in understanding the behaviour of fish. This accounts for 80 per cent of the winning formula. The other 20 per cent is made up of technical know-how like casting, knot-tying and so on. The process extends to bait collecting, too.

So the story behind that cover shot is simple. The weather blew fair with a force 5 breeze, setting up a steady surf. Low tide was at dusk and the time of year was ideal for a strong inshore migration of bass. By reading the signs, Ray and I wound up in the right place at the right time with the right bait. We would have caught fish even if we had been using hand lines rather than rods and reels.

Much understanding can be gained from reading about fishing. But in the end, results are in proportion to the amount of time an angler spends along the shoreline and in analysing the wealth of new data each session brings. Armchair anglers catch few fish, but can think out the reasons why they succeed or fail. Even so, some people are better at interpreting signs than others.

This book contains detailed guidelines along which to let your thoughts run. By thinking like a fish and like an angler, the process becomes more logical and results improve as understanding increases. I believe that this is more important than detailed instruction on how to make a drop-net from an old cycle wheel — a pre-occupation of my predecessors.

Naturally no angler can be expert — or even interested — in everything. So I asked Ron Preddy of Brighton to pen the chapter on cod fishing; Alan Yates of Dover to write about match fishing (at which he's notoriously good) and the flatfish tribe; and Keith Roberts, the wormarium whizz-kid from Colwyn Bay, to contribute the chapter on baits.

I would also like to thank the scores of anglers I've met on my travels from whom I've learnt a snippet of inside information here, a technical trick there. Only the other day I was shown an effective line-stop made by winding fine telephone wire in tight, touching turns around the leader.

Thus knowledge accumulates, which is how Ray Brewster and I took five bass between us to 7 lb in two hours. Bites were also missed. While taking the series of shots from which this picture was selected, I was using my neck as a rod-rest. Twice the rod was bent across it by enthusiastic takers.

With the proliferation of uncontrolled commercial fishing, stocks are seriously threatened. Nowadays it is vital that slow-growing species like bass be conserved if results are to be fair in the future. Anglers put fish back. Fishermen kill everything.

Ray and I put back three school bass, but then we intend to be fishing sunset surfs for many years to come — with or without hand-lines!

John Darling,
Seaford, Sussex.
December 1981.

Watch out for the flooding tide!

1
The marine environment

The tides

The sea is one of the most powerful forces on earth. Pounding waves and rushing tides have shaped our coastline. Long ago they washed away the fragile causeway that once linked England to Europe. Look at a map of the west coast of Scotland or of south-west Ireland, and it is obvious how only tough rocks have been able to withstand the relentless battering of Atlantic storms. View the chalk cliffs of southern England and you can see how soft rock is easily sculpted to form the boulder-strewn, shallow reef areas so beloved by bass.

All marine life is governed by the tides. The winkles that cling to inter-tidal rocks have adapted to suit an environment that is exceptionally harsh. One day, at low tide, a fierce sun may evaporate the water in the rock pools, increasing the salinity of what is left behind. Another day, torrential rain will dilute it until it is merely brackish. And on another, a freezing nor'easter will sear the fore-shore. Winkles have much to contend with.

The shore fisherman has to understand the tidal environment before he can predict when and where he will be able to gather bait or catch fish. Because the tides are so important an influence on the marine ecosystem, the shore angler learns, early in his career, the ways in which fish respond to their influence. Some species react with almost clockwork precision to the tides. They'll be feeding at area A at low water, then they'll come on in area B as the tide begins to flood. They then may go off the feed until high water, but group up in area C and feed hard until a couple of hours before low tide, when they'll move out, making their way towards deeper water where they wait for the new flood.

Different species in different areas react in different ways. Knowledge of what they're up to at any specified state of tide comes with experience. It is just one facet of that fund of lore known as 'local knowledge'. This book will not tell you when to go and where. Much depends on the area you intend to fish, on the weather conditions prevailing and on the tactics you plan to use. Nowadays local knowledge is less freely imparted than of yore. There is much competition for fishing space and stocks of fish are too slender to allow much generosity. Anglers fear for the fish they seek. They have no love for the trammel netsman, and if they tell too much, there's a good chance that the next time they visit a productive beach, they'll find a string of trammels spread along it and the fish they came to catch trapped by the gills, drowned and undignified.

This chapter will tell you the basic rules that have been followed for generations. Fish don't alter their behaviour to adjust to the predations of man, as rats and mice can. The bass that feed around marks like The Dragon's Teeth have being doing so on the early flood tide for over a century. This knowledge has been handed down from grandfather to father to son. As long as there are bass along that coastline and the environment doesn't change, they'll come to that mark on seven tides out of ten during the relevant season of the year.

True, there are exceptions to all rules. Somebody will have a good catch when the regulars don't expect to find fish there. By all means take note of this, but reflect that it was an unusual influx of fish, and not to be counted on for consistent results. I once caught a 10-lb bass long after I should have packed up and gone home. It was a freak, a straggler after the main shoals had passed through, and a feat I have yet to repeat, despite hours of trying.

The tides are caused by the gravitational pull of the sun and moon on the oceans. As the earth rotates, a mound of water — a tidal wave — travels across the Atlantic (and other oceans), building up where it meets the land, and then decreasing. You can observe this oscillation in your bath. By creating a wave that sloshes up around the taps, the other end of the bath experiences a low tide. The wave then races back past your yellow rubber duck and builds up at the other end. Back to the sea. If this mound of water reaches a funnel, like the Bristol Channel, it builds up to an exceptional degree, which is why Cardiff has a range of over 40 ft between high and low tides. The same effect can be observed in a rock gully: a wave will swill up it, building up at the far end, the water appearing to hang there for an instant before roaring back out again.

Other irregularities cause other effects. Headlands constrict the movement of this tidal mound and cause the water to accelerate, producing fierce currents. Extreme shallows muffle the effect. If the Thames Estuary were to face into the tide, London wouldn't exist. Because it faces east, the tidal mound has to pass through several narrow passages before filling the estuary. The tidal mound moving up the western Solent has barely started to ebb when a similar mound that has carried on eastwards, round the Isle of Wight, floods up the eastern Solent and produces a double high tide.

At both full and new moons, the sun and moon pull on the water almost in a straight line, resulting in an increased mounding up of the tidal wave. We call these 'spring' or 'long' tides. This terminology has nothing to do with the time of year, even though spring tides are largest at the equinoxes (21 March, 21 September), when both sun and moon are pulling in an exact straight line. Because the sun and moon are not in such direct co-operation around mid-June and mid-December, the spring tides during those periods are not so marked.

For seven days after a new or a full moon, the angle between sun and moon increases, thereby decreasing the potency of their combined gravitational pull. Hence 'neap' or 'short' tides, when the water doesn't come in very far and doesn't go out very far either. As the angle between sun and moon closes again after neap tides, so we get 'rising springs' — the tides are building again towards spring tides. These are often the best of all for fishing.

Although shore anglers have to keep moving their tackle further up the beach as the tide makes, this only means that the water out there is deepening as the tidal mound moves through. The currents move along the shore, not in towards it as old-timers used to believe.

With this mound of water moving round the coast, high tide occurs at different times at different places. It also occurs at different times each day, twice a day. If the tide is high at London Bridge at mid-day, it will occur at one o'clock at Leith, two o'clock at Hartlepool, three o'clock at Bridlington, four o'clock at Grimsby, five o'clock at Weymouth, and at six o'clock at Aberdovey it will be low water. The movement of the water is regular enough for scientists to predict both times of tide and 'tidal constants' — the different times a tide will peak at specific ports. Thus you can turn up the relevant column in a daily paper, or obtain a tide

chart from a tackle dealer, or cut out a chart from a coastal local newspaper.

However, only machines can be predicted to the nearest minute. The movement of thousands of billions of gallons of water can't be so accurately foretold. Even so, the times on most charts are accurate to around fifteen minutes on most days. But strong winds with or against the tide may affect the timing. Estuaries pose other problems. When fishing for mullet several miles up from the sea, high tide up there may occur two or three hours later than advertised for the open sea. But this is much more simple to work out than the tides several miles offshore, and along some stretches of shoreline where the current of the flood tide will continue to flow for a couple of hours after the tide has started to ebb. At Dungeness Point, for example, the current continues to flow towards Dover for two hours after high water. Then there's a two-hour spell of slack water. Then the ebb tide current flows westwards for four hours. Another two-hour spell of slack water occurs before the eastward current is felt — even though it has been running along Denge Marsh for two hours before it becomes noticeable at Dungeness Point, just round the corner. This is a simplification of the pattern, which varies from day to day.

Confusion can arise when one compares tide charts for different ports along a specific stretch of coast. Take two charts for two towns not so very far apart. On one specific day, the height of the tide at Rye Harbour is given as 3.1 metres, and at Newhaven as 6.1 metres. While the tide itself is very similar at both ports, the mode of measurement can differ. The height of a tide is measured from different points, normally a dock sill, a board on a pier or wall, or at a weir. These differ from place to place. The true difference in tidal range for any part of the world can be found in publications obtainable from the Hydrographer's Department at the Ministry of Defence.

The tides affect anglers in several ways. On short tides, bait beds may not become uncovered at low water, so a bait shortage is likely in the shops. Some fishing marks may be inaccessible. Or there's insufficient current to bring fish foraging around other marks. Or a mark may not be worth fishing because there's too little time to do anything before being cut off. On spring tides, bait beds are more readily available, but the currents may be too strong. Spring tides also move fast. The shallow gully behind you may be empty one moment, and the next time you look round a churning torrent of chest-high water may be raging through it. Take care; check up first. No angler's life is worth a brace of fish. On a broader scale, it appears that spring tides are migration times at sea and bring seasonal influxes of species.

For the shore fisherman, it is vital to know how his quarry reacts to the tides. He has to learn at what state of tide the fish will feed – even if they'll be around. Some species feed over grounds that were high and dry just a couple of hours earlier, while others feed when a tidal current starts to push through, or slow down. Most species like a bit of push in the current. Some will feed even when there's a heavy tide pouring along the beach. Others don't like such strong water and feed when it falls slack. Some respond to different strengths of current by gathering at specific places according to how strong the current is. Bass on a favourite rocky ledge will be out in the main channel as the tide starts to move, but once it has gathered speed, they move inshore where it is less fierce. Usually, the fiercest part of a tide is the middle three hours, but beware of local differences.

All this information may seem dauntingly tough to evaluate. Have courage. If you keep an eye on the operations of canny locals and bear in mind the various factors listed above, it is quite easy to work out a picture of what the water is doing and its effect on the marks

The continual battle between rock and sea, with man a transient spectator.

you're interested in. Once these conditions have been evaluated, you can rest assured that they're unlikely to change overnight.

The coastline

The British coastline varies between vast, shallow sand and mud flats and precipitous rocks. The different environments are favoured by different species of marine life. It often pays to look at the very basis of the food chain – the worms, molluscs and crustaceans on which many fish prey. Shingle shores are barren of all but sand-hoppers because the shifting stones are too unstable even for species like crabs. However, a more suitable environment is likely to exist below the low water mark, even on shingle shores.

Precipitous rocks are populated by mussels and barnacles, species that anchor their home-grown shelters of shell to the bare rock faces. More life exists in the sheltering jumble of boulders and fissures at the base of such cliffs. Shallow reef areas, provided they're not abraded with sharp sand in heavy seas, probably have

Keep an eye on the gulls – they are opportunists and can lead the way to fish.

the largest populations of small creatures as they offer so much shelter.

By contrast, worms require a stable shoreline characterized by heavy admixtures of mud to the sand because this is both meat and shelter to them. However, western surf beaches, facing into the prevailing winds, are frequently pounded by Atlantic-born swells even on windless days. They're populated by more mobile creatures like swimming crabs and shrimps. There is little mud in the sand – that was washed out years ago.

If you view a map of the world, it becomes obvious that the English Channel, the Irish Sea and the North Sea are mere creeks off the mighty Atlantic. The further up those creeks one goes, the more stable the environment is, even on exposed coasts. Estuaries and firths are the most sheltered areas of all, and are sometimes heavily populated by small life forms, which makes them ideal nurseries for infant fish – and larders for predators.

The food chain is rich and complex. Some species eat nothing but worms and crustaceans. Other species never come close inshore to feed. Blue sharks and the legions of migratory deep-water cod feed on smaller fish which either directly or indirectly (by preying on species that are plankton feeders) feed on plankton, that vast drifting food-store that is universal throughout the world's seas. From sprats, right through to whale sharks, each fish species preys on specific items of food. Some, like most of our inshore fish, are virtually omnivorous, so they do not compete too heavily for any one food species, reducing its stocks to perilously low levels. At the other extreme, mullet have their food supply entirely to themselves – mud, diatoms and algae.

There is little need for the shore angler to go through the whole deduction process to decide which fish should inhabit what areas. Fish populations are naturally cyclic, and human rapacity either spoils the environment or reduces fish stocks. Thus it is of little value any more to argue that because an estuary holds large populations of small flatfish, there will be packs of tope feeding on them. Man-made cracks have appeared in the food chain. The beginner can easily find out from published guides or from the angling press what species are worth fishing for in specific areas. The more advanced angler will already possess such knowledge, and can make sensible deductions about how to approach less well-documented areas of coastline. Even today, there are rocky ledges that have never felt an angler's boot.

Some fish biology

All fish are cold-blooded – their body temperature is roughly the same as that of the water they swim in. But some species don't like being too warm, while others dislike water that is too cold. If you think of a fish's stomach as a test-tube and appreciate that the chemical reaction of digestion speeds up or slows down according to the temperature, you can readily understand why bass, say, feed little during the winter months. Mammals convert about 80 per cent of their food into body warmth, and it is unwise to think of fish as being hungry for the same reasons as mammals. They feed more in warm water than in cold, simply because their digestive system takes less time to process food. They can go without food for weeks without ill effect during cold weather as their metabolic rate slows down. Some species become completely inactive during cold weather.

Early and late in the summer season, warmth-loving species stay offshore if a sharp wind chills the shore over which the tide will flood. With cool water near the beach, the fish stay beyond casting range. But the opposite effect obtains when the air is warmer than the sea. During a cold spell in autumn, estuary mullet will drop back down to the sea. However, if an Indian summer comes along, they'll move back up the estuaries to take advantage of the increased warmth. Cod, although active in cooler water, are extremely active offshore in summer, packing on weight fast. However, even though they may be numerous inshore around Christmas time, they'll all move off if a bitter nor'easterly causes temperatures to plummet. Such cold snaps frequently catch out conger eels. Even though most of them linger in relatively shallow water during the winter months, their metabolisms slow down to such an extent that they virtually cease to feed. In a sudden cold spell many become too torpid to look after themselves. Several commercial skippers have made money by circling round and gaffing aboard congers floating at the surface that, although alive, were too severely chilled to swim out to deeper, warmer water. This is why several monsters well over record size have been washed ashore after cold snaps.

'It's quite warm for the time of year', is a phrase you often hear. These are the best fishing days. Human beings haven't totally lost contact with their animal ancestry. Good fishing is to be had when the weather, although rough and rainy, is mild. Miserable weather that has you regretting your decision to leave home rarely produces sparkling sport.

Most fish are sensitive to salinity – the amount of salt in the water. We've all heard of osmosis – the diffusion of a fluid through a porous membrane. When a salt solution meets a less salty solution, fluid passes through the membrane to balance out the different strengths. The gills of fish consist of membranes that separate their blood from the surrounding water. Sea fish live in a medium that is more saline than their blood, so fluid is always being drawn out of them. However, they have adapted by drinking a lot, their kidneys (the brown matter lying underneath the back-bone) separating out the excess salt and returning it to the sea in their urine. If sea fish were to be placed in fresh water, the process would reverse and they would become waterlogged. The opposite would happen in the case of freshwater species.

However, bass, seatrout, salmon, mullet, flounders and the shads can adapt to different salinities, but they do so gradually. Therefore, when these fish are living in brackish water and the full salinity of a flood tide comes up the estuary, even these species prefer to run up ahead of it rather than stay where they are and adjust back and forth each time the tide ebbs and flows. Most sea fish can tolerate quite some latitude of salinity, which is understandable as several major rivers debouch into Britain's enclosed sea areas. However, if a heavy flood of fresh water comes down a river, most marine species will move out a little way until matters settle down to their liking.

No matter what species of fish the shore angler goes for, he must think logically about how he intends to appeal to them. All his actions must lead up to one point – informing the fish that a meal is awaiting their attention. The feeding senses of fish are more complex than our own. Like us, they have the senses of vision, hearing, taste and smell. Unlike us, they have an in-built sonar system and several species are equipped to pick up weak electrical fields.

The piscine sense of vision is not stereoscopic like our own, although most species can move their eyes to provide rudimentary stereoscopic vision. However, as each eye can be moved independently of the other, their vision covers almost 360°. This enables them to detect the flicker of a small fish darting from cover even after they have passed by, and to detect a predator sidling up from astern. They also have colour vision, which is why spinners of different colours work better on some days than on others. Even though the water absorbs light of different wavelengths at different depths, starting from the red end of the spectrum, it is simpler for the angler to assume that the fish see modified versions of the colours he sees, rather than try to work out what colours the fish see and represent those. Much depends on the clarity of the water and the depth at which the spinner is working.

Fish hear quite well. Because they live in water, they have no need for an opening from the inner ear out to the open water. Sound vibrations pass through the fish's body and are amplified when they meet the swim-bladder, that bag of air whereby fish regulate their bouyancy. These vibrations then pass to the inner ear via a chain of small bones.

Fish do not have to breathe in and out in order to smell. Their nostrils aren't needed for breathing because their gills separate dissolved oxygen out of the water. Instead, each nostril is formed with an inlet and an outlet. Thus water is continually flowing over a complex of tissues covered with sensory cells, enabling fish to follow the direction of a scent with extreme accuracy. The shark tribe has highly-developed nostrils. Each is widely separated from the other (and the hammer-head shark has taken this to an extreme). So they are better-equipped than us for detecting the direction from which a smell originates.

The taste sense of fish is more complex than ours. Fish have taste cells not just in their mouths, but on their lips, on barbels and, in the case of cod, pouting, gurnards, and so on, on the pointed rays of their pelvic fins. Cod, for example, swim close to the sea-bed with their pelvic fins pointing forwards. With such an array of taste cells it is not surprising that a fresh, bleeding lug-worm has so much appeal.

Along the flanks of fish is a line of sensory pores that also covers much of their head and chin. This is the lateral line system, their in-built sonar. It picks up vibrations from other fish and also vibrations caused by the fish's own swimming motion bounced back from objects in its path. The way in which it can differentiate between its own noise, the sound of surf, or an approaching predator is through the different tuning of the nerves inside these pores. Thus a fish may be spooked by a sinker thumping the surface, or it may vector in on the vibrations emitted by a spinner. This is how bass can move about in a choppy sea among rocks at night without bumping into things.

Members of the shark family, and the rays, also have electrical receivers built into some of these pores. They pick up weak electrical fields, like those emitted by buried flatfish. Some species, like the electric ray, can pack a punch from specially-arranged electrical cells along the top of their body that is powerful enough to stun prey – and incautious anglers.

With all these senses, it seems improbable that fish could be daft enough to take a baited hook. After all, once a bait has been located, a back-up system could check it out. However, fish are basic creatures, governed largely by involuntary reflexes to certain stimuli. Otherwise cod, a species equipped with a complete armoury of sensory systems, would never eat plastic cups. But these flutter in the tide and glitter like small fish.

Just by looking at a species of fish, much can be learned about how it feeds. Flounders lie half-buried in sand and mud with their eyes high on their head, scanning the sea-bed on each side for prey. No wonder a baited spoon arouses their curiosity. Pollack, with their

Wide-spaced dogfish nostrils find food very quickly. Tiny pores packed with sensory cells also locate grist for those sharp teeth.

huge eyes, obviously feed largely by sight – and in poor light. Lesser-spotted dogfish, with their widely-spaced, sensitive snouts are excellent at following up weak scents. Little wonder they're often first to a bait intended for a better fish.

Weather

Fish respond to water temperature in certain ways, as we have seen. They also respond to the water conditions caused by certain weather systems. Tope like calm seas and warm conditions. You can catch them when flat calms set the water glittering along favoured western surf beaches. But when the waves build up again, the tope move out and bass return to the surf. But bass don't like fierce surfs, those with clouds of gill-irritating sand in them. They, too, move out, well beyond casting range. They'll come back in when the surf subsides.

Cod along shallow eastern beaches react in a similar way. They'll feed hard on whatever food the waves dislodge. But if a full gale causes the beaches to seethe with surf, they'll move off a way, and return when conditions improve. Sometimes, when codding, it is wise to get down there the moment the wind drops, but fishing is hard to compartmentalize like this. Different species react in different ways to specific weather conditions along different shores – another facet of local knowledge. I've caught no cod on days when bait has been washed up in vast quantities by each breaking wave – and yet had cod three tides later.

Why should this be so? Well, fish are fish. They have their own logic, which often strikes the human brain as curious to the point of eccentricity. One point that the shore angler must come to terms with is that he learns more than he can understand. Certain factors produce the goods. It is easier sometimes to accept these things unquestioningly rather than try to reason why.

Proceed with caution, and then only after obtaining local advice.

2
Tackle

At one extreme, there's the man who takes everything with him on a fishing trip – just in case. At the other, there's the guy who carries a minimum of gear, sometimes even relying on others to fill any gaps that become apparent later. While the former approach often turns out to be a masochistic form of weight-training, the latter is practical only after years of experience.

A friend who totes a ruck-sack filled with enough gear to equip a well-prepared match squad once arrived at a promising rock gully after a sweating hike only to find he had left his hooks at home. The clued-in guy who carries minimal gear is unlikely to overlook any of the few essentials he has decided will be necessary. On the other hand, he invariably limits himself to one style of fishing and can do no more than watch with mounting frustration when the fish go on a sand-eel spree at a place where he has come prepared for crab fishing.

The middle road is followed by the angler who hedges his bets efficiently. There is a limit to the number of species likely to be found at any mark selected for a day's fishing, so a few extra items of tackle allow different methods to be employed without adding much to one's burden. If the frustrated crab fisher had packed a few spinners or red-gill sand-eels he would have arrived home with a smug grin of satisfaction, and wouldn't have kicked the cat.

Obviously much of what one takes on a fishing trip depends on what is expected, and this comes with experience. Even so, research will reveal what to expect on a trip to a strange shore. Charts, maps, phone-calls to tackle dealers and a dollop of common sense will slim down the load of gear required to cover every eventuality. Meanwhile our over-burdened masochist loads up with ten of everything and uses less than 20 per cent of it.

So what does one need? Not a vast amount. It is easy to justify the purchase of every new nick-nack, the latest in rods and reels and new designs of hook.

However, tackle design has reached such an advanced state of sophistication that not only is less required (each item being more versatile), but the cost of trading in one model reel for another doesn't justify the extra performance – some of which is real, but most of which is advertiser's hype.

No rod ever made either cast an inch or caught a fish; it's the bloke behind the rod who casts and fishes. Top anglers buy the best tackle on the market, and then learn how to use it. There are several 'best' makes of rod and reel, some from giant corporations, some from tiny two-man businesses. There is little to choose between different makes of line nowadays, and good hooks are easy to come by. Major new advances in basic tackle are unlikely to happen. Certain items of ancilliary gear are improved, and new ones are designed to make us wonder how we ever got by without them.

Never skimp on rods, reels, or other essential basic gear. Quality merchandise is expensive, but thorough maintenance will guarantee its longevity. The older a rod or reel grows in your company, the more familiar you will be with its performance under different weather and tidal conditions, and the more memories it will share with you. This sense of kinship is invariably more valuable than the gleaming varnish or lustrous side-plates of a new outfit, provided it is well-designed gear in the first place. On the other hand, this kinship is mere sentimentality if the tackle it relates to has serious flaws of character.

Plenty of anglers fish with junk tackle and suffer the problems inherent in its poor design, so by buying the best you won't be provoked into trading in a trashy outfit and losing out financially at a later date. For this reason, avoid those items of tackle aimed at beginners or boys. If the experts, with their vast fund of experience, require nothing but the best in order to make good catches, how can the tyro achieve anything but heartache with inferior tackle? A false logic pervades here. The idea is that if the boy decides he doesn't like fishing, then the cheap gear hasn't cost too much.

However, cheap gear has little trade-in value so, in fact, it works out more expensive than a respectable item that commands a good second-hand price.

Rods

The only rods worth using are built from glass-reinforced plastic or glass/carbon-reinforced plastic. No rods are built exclusively of carbon (also called graphite) because at present such a rod would snap. Glass fibre is required for lateral strength in a carbon rod. Glass is a heavier material than carbon, so rods built from it are heavier and thicker than those built with carbon.

A rod starts as a V shape of resin-impregnated glass-fibre or glass/carbon-fibre cloth that is tacked to a tapered mandrel. This cloth is then rolled round the mandrel, taped into position with a special tape that shrinks when heated, thus forming the outside of the mould, and is then cured in an oven. The tape and mandrel are removed and the result is a rigid tapering tube called a blank.

Often a handle of glass, carbon or dural is spliced to the end of this tube to increase the length of the finished rod. Much depends on what the blank is designed for. A ferrule is fitted mid-way on some models so that the rod can be broken down into two equal parts. Or the ferrule may be spliced to the handle so that the blank need not be cut, resulting in a slightly improved performance.

There are two types of ferrule. Older designs consist of a metal ferrule glued to the bottom of the tip section, which fits inside a tubular female ferrule glued to the top of the butt section. More modern rods have a glass or carbon spigot glued inside the butt section that fits up inside the tip. With this design, there should be a small gap at the junction of the two sections to allow for wear, and the ends of the blank should either be whipped tightly or fitted with metal collars to prevent the blank from splitting under pressure.

Blanks have different actions. A soft action means that the rod bends right down to a point near the handle, while a fast action, often built on a fast-taper blank, bends at the middle and tip only. Top shore fishermen prefer fast actions because they are better for long casting and have fine tips that show up bites well. The middle section of a fast rod is flexible enough to absorb the lunges of hooked fish and thereby prevent a taut line from being shock-loaded to breaking point. Rods used in high-velocity casting have totally rigid butts, as this is more efficient at transmitting casting energy to the rod-tip, causing the sinker to fly out faster and therefore further.

A good rod will have its reel fitting some 28 in up from the butt cap. In the old days this distance – or 'reach' – used to be some 36 in or more, resulting in abysmal casting technique. Some good casters prefer to hold the reel a few inches up from the butt even though such a position inevitably increases the leverage a hooked fish imposes on an angler.

The international firm of Fuji has brought out several excellent light-weight reel fittings and strong, light rings. Other firms are following suit. Blanks are now so delicate and precise that they should not be hobbled – crippled, even – through using inferior fitments on them.

Rod length for efficient casting need be no more than $11\frac{1}{2}$ft. Such a weapon is ideal for all styles of casting, including the pendulum style, although several experts who practise the less common South African and Yarmouth styles prefer slightly longer rods. But a long rod imposes leverage against the caster and many shore anglers over-rod themselves in the mistaken belief that extra length produces extra casting distance. In one sense it does. Extra length compensates for inefficient casting technique and poor style, but even so this advantage is very slender when compared to the results achieved by a practised performer of a powerful, efficient casting style like the pendulum when using the $11\frac{1}{2}$-ft rod. Some anglers argue that a long rod holds line above the water, away from plucking breakers and weed floating close in. Well, a shorter, lighter rod can be held with the tip high or put to rest in a long monopod rod-rest, thus achieving the best of both arguments.

Local custom and fishing conditions often dictate the rod to use. The man who frequently fishes for congers from piers is likely to prefer a much shorter rod. Those who fish the rocky shores of Yorkshire frequently employ rods that are extremely stiff, using them to winch tackle free of weed and boulder jungles or to hoist a fish up the side of a cliff.

For most British shore anglers, where 4–6-oz sinkers are needed to carry a big bait aloft or to push out a very long way, such a rod as outlined earlier will be quite adequate. This is the heavy artillery, for use when fishing for cod, conger, rays, tope and so on. It is at home on both piers and open shoreline. The angler who needs to cast lighter sinkers can buy a slimmer version to handle 3–4-oz sinkers. And the bass specialist will find that an even slimmer version that casts 2–3-oz sinkers will cope with virtually every bass-fishing situation – and several others where bass are not the quarry.

However, bass anglers use fairly big baits, but don't cast them very far. So such a rod is fine for a whole baby squid, a half side of mackerel, or a large peeler crab fished at short range (say, up to 70 yd), with $\frac{1}{2}$–2-oz sinkers, the total package weighing 6–8 oz.

Time for contemplation.

Modern blanks cope with a wide range of weights. Even so, they work best within a narrow loading band. Thus the big stick will cast a 5–6-oz sinker and a couple of lugworms like a rocket up to a possible 200 yd. The same rod couldn't cast a 7-oz sinker that far because it would be overloaded, while a 4-oz sinker wouldn't load the rod sufficiently to draw out its full potential. The limit is reached when a rod is loaded to excess by a combination of too much bait, too heavy a sinker and too powerful a casting style. Under extreme conditions it will snap. A rod can be overloaded if an angler holds it in an upright position while pulling out of a snag. This causes plenty of rods to snap each year. When snagged, reel in line until the rod is pointing along the line, then pull directly against the obstruction with all the pressure on the reel. Or, if heavy line is used, wind the line round a piece of wood so as to take the strain off both rod and reel.

Other rods will prove useful. You can get a spinning rod or two. While the bass rod is also ideal for paternostering a spinner, a proper spinning rod adds an extra dimension of sensitivity to a form of fishing that is often only as successful as the angler is skilful – in greater proportion than is the case with some other methods.

One spinning rod, 8–10 ft long, casting $\frac{1}{2}$–$1\frac{1}{2}$-oz lures will suffice for most situations, except where maximum fun is desired from mini-predators like school bass, small pollack, mackerel, mullet and garfish. A 7–9-ft rod casting up to $\frac{1}{2}$-oz lures will then provide best sport. Few shops stock such delicate weapons, so you may have to build one from a blank designed for fly fishing.

A reservoir-style fly rod rated for AFTM 9–10 lines can be employed to good effect in some areas, while a 13-ft freshwater match angler's rod is suitable not only for mullet fishing, but also for casting out light sinkers for whiting, pouting, school bass and flatfish where conditions and tides permit such a sporting approach. Again, carbon/glass blanks make the strongest, lightest and slimmest weapons.

Now that rings and reel fittings can be whipped into position with thread (nylon is strongest), many home builders construct a rod from a blank with butt and ferrule spliced in. Initially they hold the fittings in place with electrical tape until satisfied the design is right. When doing this, take one turn of tape round the blank alone before attaching the rings, so that the feet can bed into it and don't slip. Later the positions can be plotted in pencil and the rod whipped, varnished and finished off.

Today's glass and carbon rods are easy to maintain. The only damage likely to occur is scarring, through dropping them or letting them fall onto the beach or similar hard surfaces; the occasional broken ring (once more common, when tungsten carbide or welded stainless steel rings were used); and the inevitable scratching of varnish. All rods profit by the occasional wash. Frayed whippings should be replaced before the ring falls off – all simple enough. Care should be taken to keep sand from ferrules, where it will grind away at the material. Spigot ferrules are best lubricated by rubbing them with a wax candle. Hold a lighter underneath to melt the wax into the surface of the spigot, but before it sets hard wipe off the excess.

Reels

The job of any reel is to deliver line at a rate that matches the requirement of a flying sinker, to retrieve line, and to permit hooked fish to take back line under a safe, controlled pressure. Most shore fishermen prefer a multiplier reel for heavy work and a fixed-spool for spinning and mullet fishing. Some models of fixed-spool are designed for heavy work, but with modern rods becoming even lighter, such hefty reels are cumbersome, obtruding on the svelte sophistication of modern blanks. By comparison, multipliers are more compact, more adaptable, and more efficient.

Multipliers from the Ambassadeur range are tough little beasts, well designed and engineered. They boast a structural integrity that allows anglers to fish hard for a lifetime. The fast-retrieve Ambassadeur 6500C is so versatile that it is a favourite of both the light tackle bass-man and the long-range cod fisherman. When plenty of spare line is required, as when tope fishing, the Ambassadeur 7000 and the 8000 have adequate line capacity. Where fish like conger (and cod from rock tangle country) need to be bullied ashore, both the 8000 and the wider-spooled Ambassadeur 9000 are standard tools owing to their automatic two-speed gearing. There are other models on the market, some of which are fair mimics of ABU reels, and some cheaper models with plastic spools that distort or crack under pressure.

Where ruggedness is of less importance, as is the case when small fixed-spools are used, several firms make suitable models – ABU, Daiwa, Shakespeare and Mitchell. Fixed-spool reels are easy to use provided one remembers never to carry on winding the handle when the slipping clutch (drag mechanism) starts clicking. To continue winding after a fish has started to take line, or when the gear is snagged and no line is being retrieved, causes the reel to do no more than put lots of twists into the line. This causes casting problems and weakens the fragile connection between angler and fish.

A problem experienced by the tyro when learning to use a multiplier is variously known as a bird's-nest, over-run, back-lash and, ultimately, a crack-off or frapp-off. This condition is caused by the reel spool spinning faster than the flying sinker can drag line out through the rod-rings, or by failure on the angler's part to brake the spool when the tackle hits water. At its worst, several loose coils of line will tangle, causing the spool to stop abruptly. There is often sufficient energy in the sinker to pull hard at this tangle and snap the line. A really good crack-off leaves the spool looking like a nylon hedge-hog with loose ends poking out from a mass of twisted coils. Such a one requires surgery, cutting back to sound line. Don't lose your temper and tug savagely at the mess or matters will deteriorate. Always inspect line very carefully after a snarl-up and cut off any that shows signs of damage.

Most back-lashes are caused by a combination of incompetence and optimism. Multipliers should never be tuned up so that they are totally free-running. But anglers with poor casting styles frequently ignore all the controls of line flow built into a reel, in the hope that the sinker will fly out further. This is akin to driving with the accelerator down and no hands on the wheel. Anglers who spend lots of time sorting out bird's-nests rarely have a bait in the right place at the right time, and therefore fail to find action when the fish come through. Anglers who have mastered a powerful casting style make judicious use of the controls so that the reel feeds out no more line than the air-borne sinker requires.

Gone are the days when reels with wide, chrome-plated, brass spools were used for beach casting, spewing out line uncontrollably as they churned around like fly-wheels. It has been proved that slim spools made of light-weight alloy are easier to control during high-velocity casts. Hence the popularity of the Ambassadeur 6500C – and similar reels made by Daiwa and DAM (though these have yet to prove themselves in the tournament field). Such narrow spools rotate very fast when delivering line, making it easier to apply precise braking to compliment the natural braking of the spool. As the sinker slows down, so the line on the reel has been reduced, so the smaller the coil that is delivered by each revolution of the spool, requiring the reel to spin at the same RPM during the whole cast.

Adequate braking is achieved by the use of one or two brake-blocks, according to one's ability. A less consistent method is the use of heavy oil in spindle bearings. As an extreme measure, the spool's spindle can be squeezed by tightening the bearing cap at one end.

Level-wind systems also act as brakes. Such a system is detrimental when long-range casting with a 6500C. However, a reel like the 7000 has a wider, heavier spool that tends to fly-wheel slightly. Leave the level-wind on this reel because its drag reduces this effect. Some level-winds tend to pile up line at one end of the spool. Provided this is not caused by excess play between the

spindle and the bearing caps, this is rectified by adding or removing the shims inside those caps to realign the spool until the level-wind is loading the spool correctly.

Spool-braking control is vital when casting large air-resistant baits that cause the sinker to decelerate rapidly. So when large baits are in use, the removal of a level-wind is pointless. Indeed, it is sometimes necessary to keep a thumb feathering the spool during the cast for extra control.

When those extra yards are not necessary, a level-wind is a boon, spooling back line evenly, permitting the angler to concentrate exclusively on playing and landing the fish. When a level-wind is not used, there are times when the thumb is not so efficient and mounds and hollows appear. Just lob out and rewind evenly, else a crack-off is guaranteed for your next cast.

A feature of both fixed-spool reels and multipliers is a drag system that allows fish to take line at a tiring pressure. The fixed-spool also allows the angler to knock off the anti-reverse catch and back-wind the handle, playing the fish through the gears rather than using the slipping clutch. Many prefer this method. When fishing for non-fighters like cod, many anglers keep the drag screwed up fairly tight, loosening it only when the fish is close in and a sudden lunge wouldn't be absorbed by the elasticity of the line or rod tip. While landing a fish, it is wise to back the drag right off, applying any necessary pressure to the spool with a thumb or finger. This sensitive approach allows instant reaction to a sudden, panicky run or surging wave that might break the line.

When after tope and fish that fight, set drag tension between one third and one half of the breaking strain of the line, using a spring balance hooked to the line as a guide. But reflect that pressure increases if the tension is left at one setting while the level of line drops on the spool. It may be necessary to back off the drag a little after a fish has run a fair way.

Another feature of multipliers is a click mechanism that is used to warn that a fish is running with the bait. This is ideal for some forms of fishing where takes come with long intervals in between, or a fish needs to be allowed to run some way with a bait before it will take it properly. If tidal pressure causes the click to signal false takes, put the reel into gear, but wind off the drag to a point where the tide doesn't take line. This is the only method that can be used with a fixed-spool. No matter what, it is unwise to let a fish feel the check. The extra drag may spook it. So knock the reel into free spool and gingerly thumb the spool to prevent an over-run.

A word on fighting fish. At no time should it be allowed to snap the line – a sure sign of either a monster or of incompetence. Keep the rod tip high and use the rod tip and drag pressure to both cushion lunges and tire it out. However, when fishing for cod or other species that allow the angler to reel them in without registering protest until they're close to the beach, wrist strain is prevented by pointing the rod along the line and reeling it in as waves push the fish towards you. Be prepared to change methods the moment it takes fright.

When a big fish or weed exerts pressure, pump it in: wind down until the rod points along the line, then drag the fish in a few feet by raising the rod tip high. Reel in as you drop the rod tip again, and so on. An alternative is to walk backwards up the beach, reeling in while walking back down to the water's edge.

A well-made reel deserves proper maintenance, especially if required to cast far. Wipe it off after each trip and store it in a warm place to keep it dry. If salt water has penetrated into the works, rinse it with fresh water, then place it in the airing cupboard. Before a major expedition, and at the end of the season – and more frequently, as necessary – completely strip down a reel. Follow the exploded diagram for re-assembly, if you're nervous about this. Strip, clean and re-assemble each unit of the reel so that nothing is mislaid and no pieces defy relocation.

Alloy side-plates benefit from a thin film of silicone grease for protection. Use a suitable fine grease – thinly applied – on gears, but nothing on nylon cogs. Thin oil is suitable for level-winds – no more than three drips carefully placed. Don't overload bearings with oil. Never be heavy-handed with lubricants else they'll get where they didn't ought to. Neither should you completely encase the works in grease, as some old-timers used to do. Drag washers can be lubricated with graphite, or maybe candle wax, but should be kept free of grease. The best cleaner is petrol. Allow the sediment to sink after use, and pour the clear petrol into an old glass bottle for re-use, but be careful not to disturb sediments when pouring it out again. Use an old tooth-brush to clean all parts. Wipe them dry with kitchen paper when drained, and lubricate while reassembling.

A reel is a precision instrument. A multiplier spool spins in excess of 20,000 RPM during a high-velocity cast. Careful maintenance will guarantee longevity. Disregard for reel maintenance costs both fish, through drags freezing at moments of stress, and money, through excessive wear.

Line

Nylon (and other polymers) monofilament line is really the only type worth using from the beach. Braided Terylene or Dacron (the same, but different brand names) can be used where extra sensitivity to bites is required, but it abrades easily and needs a nylon leader to take the worst of the punishment.

Line is the only link between angler and fish. It must be strong, with no nicks and abrasions. Even so, cheap-skates skimp on line, making do with worn-out stuff, then grizzle when specimens break free.

Different types of fishing require different breaking strains (also called test strengths). Strong, carefully-tied knots are vital to retain full strength. After landing a big fish, test all knots and retie suspect ones. When spinning, retie the lure every twenty casts or so. Line wears out and finer stuff wears faster, being thinner, than heavy gauge, so change line frequently because broken line is a sign of incompetence. Huge fish are taken each year by the skilful on skinny lines.

Remember that the sea-bed is abrasive, and that spool-slip may singe line while casting. Heavy wear also comes from landing several fish or hauling lumps of weed – which is also abrasive. Spool off old line for casting practise.

Nylon absorbs water. Knots also reduce its strength by a combined total of around 10 per cent. If a knot fails to snug up neatly, cut it off and retie. Lines should be spooled on tightly to within $\frac{1}{8}$ in of the lip of the spool. Over-loaded reels produce tangles and bird's-nests, so don't be tempted to put on just a few extra yards to compensate for line lost due to wear during the first sessions of its life. It's not worth the trouble. Too little line is bad for casting and reduces the effectiveness of modern highly-geared reels, which, with small spools, require a full complement of line for efficiency. After a heavy session, make a few casts with just a sinker, retrieving line before it sinks in the water. Run it through a rag to remove dirt and it will then be ready for use next trip. Or wind it off at home, letting it dry before re-spooling. Never let *oil* get on line, or squirt WD40 and similar onto loaded reels.

When using big reels, like the 7000 and 9000, it is sometimes practical to leave a bed of old line on the reel permanently so that only 200 yd need be loaded each time the line is changed. The stuff near the spindle ends up crinkley and weak and is rarely used.

Where light line is desirable but heavy sinkers are required, knot on a casting leader (also known as a shock leader) to take the force of the cast. Leaders are also useful for controlling big fish awaiting the drop net while pier fishing and when a big fish needs to be dragged from surf on very steep beaches. A leader need be no longer than twice the length of the rod (for casting) and in strength – well, this depends on what you're doing with it. A useful formula is to allow 10 lb of test strength for 1 oz of sinker. Thus a 5-oz sinker requires a 50-lb shock leader. Tournament casters allow as much as 11 lb of test strength per 1 oz of sinker, while soft casters are unlikely to require a ratio of more than 1:7.

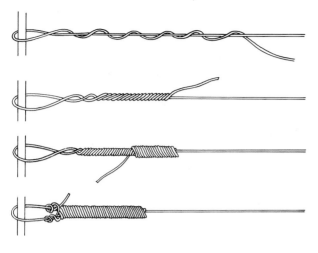

Bimini loop

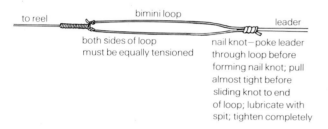

to reel

bimini loop

leader

both sides of loop
must be equally tensioned

nail knot—poke leader
through loop before
forming nail knot; pull
almost tight before
sliding knot to end
of loop; lubricate with
spit; tighten completely

Leader knot combination for full strength — Bimini loop and nail knot

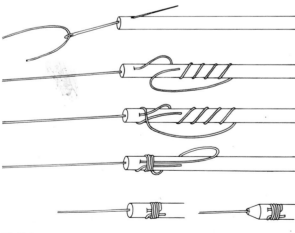

Nail knot

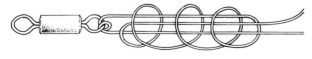

No-name knot

There is little to choose between various makes of line. Price is a reliable guide. Anglers who swear by one line express prejudice about another make that somebody else uses all the time. Some people are happy to use cheap, bulk line that others abhor. The only guidance worth following is this: find a make of line that you like, and stick to it. More is gained from familiarity with the characteristics of one specific make, than from wide experimentation with different makes.

There are two severe flaws in line. Firstly, shredding, when the outer skin breaks away, leaving the line feeling like twine, and secondly, excessive stretch, which builds up pressure that will crush, burst or distort reel spools. Line used for leaders should be the soft variety. Wirey leaders are an abomination. However, too soft line weakens quickly.

Now for some knots. Master these few because no others are likely to prove necessary. Always wet nylon with saliva before snugging knots up tight. Where possible, two turns of line are taken round swivel eyes, hook eyes, and so on, for added strength.

Bimini loop The strongest of all loop knots, even though it requires a special tool to tie it. A variation is to take two turns round the eye of a swivel, form the knot, then finish either with a whipping or with half-hitches around the swivel eye. This is technically not a knot, which accounts for its 100 per cent strength. The tyer is easily bent up from an old coat-hanger. A useful leader knot, again 100 per cent strong (every other system for joining thick line to thin is less than 70 per cent strong), is to form the loop in the main (thin) line, then tie on the leader to this with a three-turn nail-knot. This requires that the nail-knot be formed and tightened before being slipped along to the end of the loop, where it should be tightened completely. Remember to use saliva for lubrication.

Nail knot Use this for tying the leader to the Bimini loop, and for joining both leader and backing to a fly-line. For this latter use, poke a needle up inside the end of the fly-line, and back out again after $\frac{3}{16}$ in, heat the needle to soften the plastic line covering, dab it with saliva to cool it down and prevent the hole thus formed from closing again when the needle is removed. Insert nylon through this hole. Cut the end of thickish line to a neat diagonal for easy insertion.

No-name knot Very useful, and ideal for knotting unresponsive thick line. Take two turns around the swivel, etc., before forming — therein lies its strength. Remember that thick lines tied around swivels built from wire with a thinner diameter than the line will cut into the nylon and thus weaken it. Match swivel size to line diameter.

Blood knot A standard knot, tied with five turns here. But finer lines may slip, so six to seven turns may be

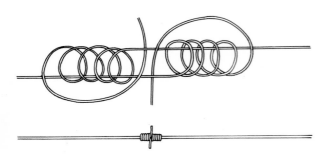

Blood knot

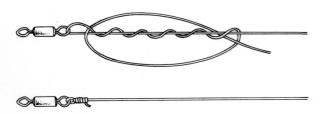

Tucked half-blood knot

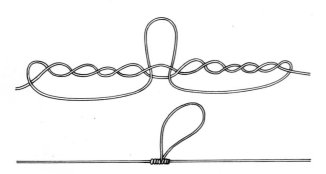

Blood loop

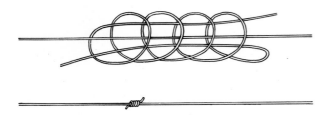

Stop knot

Braided wire join

needed when using 4–5-lb line. Always tuck the spare end twice, except when using thick line that doesn't like being knotted anyway. Never give this knot a heavy, final tug just to make sure – that will set up internal stresses that will weaken it.

Blood loop The only one for making a loop stand out from a leader, but it tends to strangle itself if subjected to full stress, and snap when least expected. Never use this when high-velocity casting because of this trait. It is ideal for making up strings of mackerel feathers. Use 8–10 turns for maximum strength.

Stop-knot Useful for setting floats fishing at a specific depth, yet generally used to stop a bead which stops the float, the knot itself being too small for most float eyes.

Braided wire join Use this when making wire traces. Take two turns around the swivel or hook eye (straight, ring eyes are best), slide on the first crimping ferrule and close it tight, then cut off the spare end shorter than the length of the second ferrule so that the sharp end is safely shrouded.

Other items of gear

Rod rests are vital at times. On rocks, use a tripod if there aren't suitable, natural rod rests about. On penetrable shorelines, use a monopod. A very good one can be built from a 4 ft length of $1\frac{1}{4} \times \frac{1}{8}$ in alloy angle and 4 in of 2 in alloy tube. Cut the tube in half. Cut one piece into a horse-shoe shape and bolt that to one end of the angle. Then drill straight through the other piece, and bolt that 24 in below the first piece. Cut the other end of the alloy to form a spike, and hey presto! Use wing-nuts, and the rest can be taken apart, the two cups fitting into the tackle bag while the length of angle fits inside a rod bag. The best way to persuade a rest to dig into a shingle beach is to work it in, moving it from side to side while leaning on it. Banging with hammers or stones is less effective.

Hooks: there are many good patterns about nowadays. Useless tackle dealers sell rotten hooks. Those who know their stuff sell good ones. I use Mustad Limerick size 5/0 for tope, conger, skate and other big fish with teeth or crushing jaws, and for heavy-water codding. The Sundridge Specimen Longshank in the same size is also good. For bass, small cod and much other fishing I use the Mustad 79510 in sizes 1/0 to 4/0. For whiting down to dabs, Mustad Aberdeen hooks between 1/0 and size 6 are adequate. Some people use Aberdeens for cod, but they tend to spring open, release the fish, then spring shut again. This can also happen on the take when a cod hits a bait very hard. Not recommended for big fish but lovely for small ones. Always buy good hooks. Sharpen them with a small triangular file. Smear the file with silicone grease to prevent rust, which will blunt it. Match hook size to bait and fish species pursued. Use strong hooks, but not heavy ones where thick metal is a substitute for inferior design or temper. There are many good hooks around nowadays. Few arrive so sharp that they dig into a thumb nail rather than skate over the surface. Shortish, sharp points and small barbs sink home easily.

Swivels are rarely necessary to eliminate twist from nylon, except when spinning. Their main function is as links between items of terminal gear. The strongest are those with the wire loop entering the swivel body in the shape of an omega, or, in recent designs, a triangulated omega. Split-rings can be used instead of swivels. They are cheaper, less reliable, and more fiddley to tie on. Swivels are best carried in an old 35-mm film pot. These are also good for smaller hooks. Some people carry boxes of hooks with them, but only a few are used in a session and the others are likely to become rusted before they are needed.

A small essential item is a lead-clip. This prevents line knotted to a lead's eye from banging against stones while being retrieved. This damages the join, and is the most common reason for nylon snapping at that point, which can be exceedingly dangerous in mid-cast. Lead-clips are cheap to buy, cheap to make, and should always be used if the sinker isn't to be sacrificed.

Bait-clips can be made from old flex cover and stainless steel wire. Take a $1\frac{1}{2}$ in length of wire, file both ends smooth and round, bend it two-thirds of the way along at a sharp angle. Slip the leader through a 1 in long piece of PVC cable sheathing, then force home the bent wire. Before casting, ensure that the tension is on the hook-link and re-adjust after each cast. Clips can be used where long traces are employed, because the hook

trace can be tied to the leader several feet up from the sinker, such a knot slipping easily through the rod rings. I have used such rigs with the trace partly wound onto the reel, so long has it been. Clips prevent baits from flapping about and ensure perfect bait presentation.

Elasticated thread – known as shirring elastic – is ideal for tying on baits, making stops and markers on line, and for some emergency repairs. Quick-setting epoxy glue and electrical tape are useful for small repairs or lash-ups. Super-glue can be used for locking up some knots, although that shouldn't be necessary, and for glueing delicate baits like tiny ragworms to small hooks, thus guaranteeing the liveliness of the worm.

Lighting can be provided by electric torches, or a head-lamp that can be bought with a battery pack. These packs are pretty useless. The best power sources are re-chargeable Nicad cells, or a six-volt motor-bike battery, which can be recharged cheaply. Keep the latter in a polythene bag, held with elastic bands, in case of acid leaks. The fewer junctions between bulb and battery, the better, because salt air corrodes terminals. Switches and terminals should be simple and kept in shape with silicone grease.

Paraffin pressure lamps are standard equipment nowadays. The Optimus lamps are best; Tilley lamps are less bright. The cheap Chinese Anchor lamp is good value, being an imitation of the Optimus. Service these regularly for best results, and never forget to take a couple of spare mantles. Pack them carefully – glasses become fragile with age. An extendable pole to hold the lamp high above the beach maximizes its efficiency. Even so, it is wise to paint rod-tops white or fluorescent yellow, or fit reflective tape over the top 18 in.

Clothing must be top quality. Helly Hansen, Functional and Damart make excellent warm underclothes and socks. Henri Lloyd and Functional (at Warrington), make the most efficient foul-weather gear. Experience has shown that heavy sweaters are useless for maintaining warmth. Clean, dry clothing and efficient weather-proof outer garments maintain body warmth and allow full mobility. Skee-tex (and other makes') boots are better in winter unless wading is essential. Waders should be hung upside down to prevent creases forming in the rubber, which lead to cracks.

For full warmth on a winter's night, I wear a Damart top, thick socks and ordinary underpants. On top of these I wear a one-piece Functional pile fibre suit, then a pair of bib-and-brace Functional overtrousers and a Functional coat; and a hat. More efficient gear is being designed each year. It is light, wind and rain proof, and a joy to wear. When digging bait, and if you are one of those people who get sand everywhere, buy a poly-thene dustbin liner (heavy gauge) and cut out arm and head holes. Thus a good coat isn't allowed to spoil. Always note maker's instructions about washing gear. Damart shrinks in too-hot water, and heavy soiling on outer garments should be soaked overnight in a biological powder which will eat out filth without damaging the fabric. Never remove tar with solvents because they dissolve waterproofing compounds. Scrape it off with a knife and try to rub off the rest with a dry rag, just leaving an unsightly – yet harmless – stain.

A coarse angler's umbrella is useful, with or without a draught-excluding sheet of polythene. Anchor brollies well, with a stake buried in shingle or the crown tied via a length of rope to a canvas bag filled with stones or sand. Poorly anchored brollies blow away! There is a new bubble being designed, a PVC inflatable beach shelter that should prove perfect. At the time of writing it is only in prototype form. Beach shelters protect you from the chill factor of bitter winds, and cold is a severe enemy of the fisherman.

Sinkers: use grapnel leads where very strong tides are encountered, as breakaway and other release-type leads don't work in severe currents. Bead-type breakaway leads are patent and are available in most shops. You can make your own, but not for sale. Band-type release leads are easy to make. Drill tiny holes straight

Dress up warm in winter and keep smiling.

through the mould, not across as is conventional, but parallel to each other, one pair each side of the nose. Insert thickish wire into each set of holes, pour in the lead, remove the wires (else the mould won't come apart), and when needed, put in 4–6-in lengths of stainless wire and bend them to shape. Half-hitch an elastic band to one wire else you'll lose a band each cast and may run out. Tension can be adjusted more efficiently with these than with breakaways, which sometimes require rubber bands in borderline situations. Plain leads, from 2–6 oz, are also useful. When moulding plain leads in a mould drilled for release leads, put match-sticks into the holes else they'll become plugged with lead that is very, very hard to get out. Bend the ends of sinker eyes inwards to prevent them pulling out when casting.

Apart from a range of major sinkers, like 5- and 6-oz grapnels and 2–5-oz release leads, you'll need drilled bullets for floats, split shot also for floats, and small bombs for light legering.

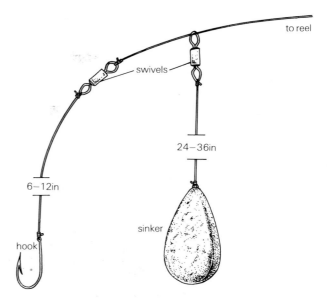

Running paternoster

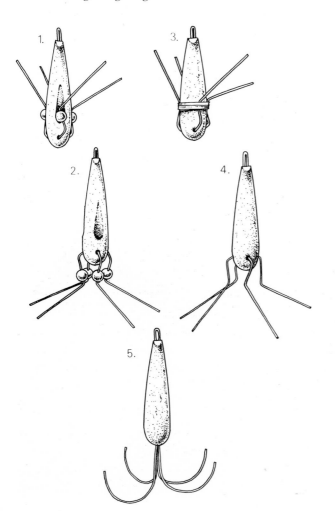

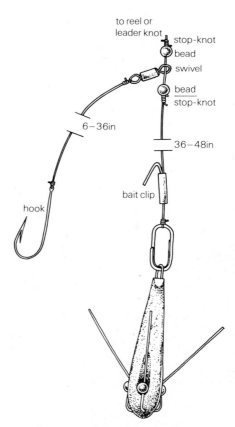

Fixed paternoster

Left: Grip leads. Bead breakaway 1. ready for use and 2. collapsed; elastic band break-out lead, 3. ready for use and 4. collapsed; 5. grapnel lead with in-built bait clip.

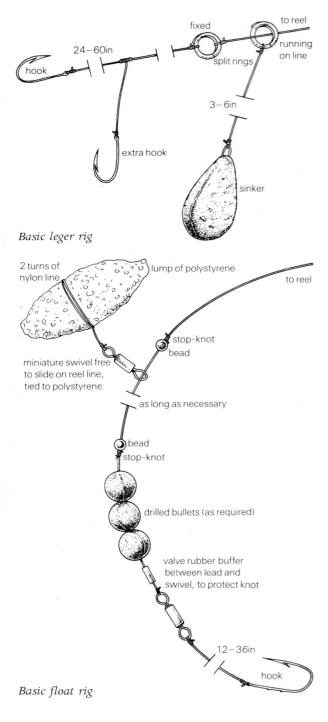

Basic leger rig

Basic float rig

You can also take a gaff (for congering, drill right through a gaff with a screw-in removable head and lock it up with a split pin); a landing net — cheap ones are made from orange plastic twine; a clonker to inflict terminal brain damage on fish intended for the table; bait buckets (drill these, if necessary, with red-hot knitting needles so they don't hold water as well as bait). Other things will occur to you as experience grows.

Terminal rigs

Contrary to what some believe, the fish are not impressed by complicated rigs. Provided heavy wire booms are not used — and some anglers still use them, terrible though they are — most rigs can be built from well-knotted nylon, one or two swivels, a lead-clip, a hook or two and some lead. How many hooks? Three are useful if different baits are necessary, as in match fishing. As a general rule, one hook is adequate when the fish are feeding. The important ingredient is the carefully-prepared bait. Terminal rigs are judged on their effectiveness at presenting the bait unobtrusively and at keeping the rodster informed of what is happening.

Running paternoster This is rigged so that the sinker precedes the bait. Even a $\frac{3}{4}$-oz bomb will therefore lead a big crab out to the fishing area. It is an excellent rig that doesn't tangle. The fish can take line and give good bite indication where water pressure on line between the swivels and the angler doesn't muffle this, as happens in long-range casting, when a fixed paternoster is more effective. Ensure the two swivels are of the same size, else the eye of one will jam in the eye of the other.

Fixed paternoster This is standard for all long-range fishing, because it is so stream-lined. The free swivel rotates in any direction, thus preventing a small fish from tangling the trace when spinning in the tide.

Basic leger rig This is simple, and useful for many types of fishing. If you like long traces (which tend to tangle, don't catch any more fish, muffle bite detection, and tend to catch around rock and weed stems) this is the best rig to use. In snaggy ground, tie a couple of inches of weaker line between sinker and swivels, but remember that this action prevents full-blooded casting — the lead will fly off.

Basic float rig No problem here. The float need be no more than a small piece of polystyrene, tied round with old nylon ending in a small swivel to run on the line. Cheap and easy to lose when wrasse fishing in snaggy areas — standard wrasse country.

Spinning paternoster More efficient than putting lead on the trace above the lure. This tends to drag the lure into snags. But the paternoster hampers seductive action to a lesser degree, while weak line to the sinker allows you to break free from obstructions and maybe not lose the lure. The addition of a boom sometimes prevents tangling, though it is rarely needed.

Other rigs will suggest themselves as experience grows. In a fast current, a paternoster dropped down from the edge of a pier will allow a pared-down ribbon of squid to flutter enticingly in the tide provided the lead-link and hook-link are both around 6 ft long.

3
Casting

There are several different styles of cast used around British coasts. Least powerful of all is the overhead thump, as practised by the majority of shore anglers. This style uses little more than the arms to put speed into the rod. It is excellent for accuracy, poor for distance.

Next there are the various styles of lay-back cast. These provide moderate distance, are adequately accurate, and are powered by the arms and the caster's shoulders. Swivelling of the trunk also adds some steam.

Then there are the three high-velocity styles. First, and most popular, is the pendulum style. Less widespread is the South African style, and the Yarmouth back-swing is used mainly by casters around the shallow East Anglian shore. These three long-range styles owe much to the fact that they employ the full body power of the caster, starting from the balls of the feet, flowing through the entire body to the arms. It is this more than anything else that makes high-velocity casting look so graceful and effortless, especially when compared to the strenuous, unscientific antics of those fishermen who attempt to stretch the overhead thump style to distances that it cannot reach.

There is something about anglers that seems to prevent them from following the example of golfers. When a tyro buys his first set of clubs, he generally watches the accomplished members of his club and seeks their advice. Better still, he obtains tuition from the local professional, regarding the money spent as an excellent investment against lost balls and tempers.

Not so the angler. Generally he buys an outfit, often on the strength of advertisements that trumpet the rod's or reel's performance on the tournament field, then goes to the beach for a few casts without any proper tuition at all. Around January time, at the end of the cod season, angling writers receive a spate of letters from these guys, bemoaning the fact that their casting is no good, that the bloke along the beach caught twelve while they stood biteless, and what rod or reel should they buy to rectify this. The tackle trade does well out

of this as would-be casters trade in their gear for another outfit, even though the original set was quite adequate – had the skill to use it been there.

Casting is an athletic exercise. It requires muscular co-ordination on the level of that required by field eventers who put shots, hurl javelins and send discoi spinning off into the distance.

Sadly, even though the act of casting is a marvellous photographic challenge, there must be but few shore anglers who have managed to translate all those pictures from the printed page and add the third dimension of reality with any success at all. It is impossible to become an accomplished caster merely by reading about it, even though the angling press has discovered in its surveys that articles on casting are very popular with their readerships. Indeed, it could be claimed that such articles are dangerous. All too often the reader goes out with only half of the ideas and ends up sending 6-oz leads skipping all over the place, and rarely in the intended direction. On three occasions, I have come close to being hit by amateurs in action. And on almost every occasion when I have observed an angler making a complete – and dangerous – mess of the pendulum cast, it has turned out that he is merely putting into action his interpretation of a printed page.

It is time that we had a few well-paid professional casting tutors in this country. There are some excellent casters, but this does not mean that they are able to impart their knowledge to others. Proper tuition would clear up a few grey areas in the realm of beach-casting. It would make anglers realize that it is they who cast, not their rods. Provided gear is of a certain acceptable standard, it will hurl a sinker 200 yd. Proper tuition would also eliminate much dangerous behaviour from beginners. And it would provide all those bonuses that would-be casters dream of, like an absence of crack-offs and bird's-nests, good bags of fish, and the satisfaction that everything is running smoothly.

Casting ability is more than being able to bang out a bait a long way. Alan Yates, in his chapter on match

UK casting champion Paul Kerry shows perfect stance (above) and technique (right).

fishing, mentions how pleasant it is to catch fish while those around are not. On those days when I have been catching while all around have not, I have felt as though I could hit the moon with a well-aimed 6-oz sinker.

It is often tempting to bang out a long way at all times. One rainy night at Orfordness I went along with two other expert casters. We took along with us a man who, although keen, had never handled a beachcaster in anger before, even though he sold plenty from his London shop. He was so embarrassed by his incompetence in the face of our expertise that he trudged along the beach for a quarter of a mile. Throughout the long night, we saw his lamp twinkling in the darkness. We were catching nothing, so none of us felt it would be profitable to wander along to see how Derek was getting on. But at dawn, I popped along to see how things were with him. He was sitting on his tackle box, holding his rod, completely surrounded by cod. His face was a happy ray of sunshine amid that drizzley, cold seascape. I rushed back to the others, and we too began lobbing baits into the gully that runs along the bottom of the shingle beach. We picked up a few stragglers, small stuff: the main run had passed through in the darkness.

Long-range casting enables the shore angler to reach distant hot-spots like banks and trenches that may or may not produce the goods, depending on the species sought and the locality. But when the bottom is of a relatively uniform depth, a bait placed at 140 yd enables him to command a zone beyond the competing baits of other anglers. Most anglers, for all their claims, can put out baits around 70 yd. This may be the edge of the runway along which the fish shoals will travel with the tide. The other side of that runway may be a mile away, or it may be as close as 180 yd. Thus the long-range bait is right in the middle, where it will attract most interest.

Some species of fish, like cod, swim close to the beach some days and far out at other times. The reason for our fiasco at Orfordness was due to the organizer of the trip catching plenty of hefty fish at long range on an earlier trip. That night the fish came in close. This is one reason why shore anglers often use two rods on specific beaches so that they can intercept fish travelling both routes. One bait lies fairly close in, the other well out. However, if the beach is crowded, both baits are hurled out a long way. If the fish come in close, nearby short casters will catch them and the observant angler will know to adjust his tactics.

There are, of course, many times when it pays not to cast out too far. Flounders and bass, for example, often work the very edge of the tide. Obviously there is only one rule about how far to cast – only as far out as the fish are feeding.

Technique

Watch a man like Paul Kerry in action, and you will appreciate that a high-velocity cast takes less than a second to execute. This doesn't take into account the time spent teeing up the sinker. Paul uses the pendulum style, where the sinker is teed up in the air. During that second, Paul probably uses every muscle in his body. Years of practice have programmed his subconscious mind to put together one glorious sequence of movements ranging from small inflections through to full-power muscle movements that culminate in his sinker whistling away from the rod at a frightening speed.

You can't learn this from books. But what you can learn is the general approach, how to build up power.

In the overhead thump style of cast, the rod is still compressing when the sinker is let fly. In high-velocity casts, the rod is compressed totally well before this point is reached. It is probably true that most long-range casters like to feel the rod go hard, becoming fully compressed, before they give it that final clout that makes the sinker zip through the air.

With the sinker following behind the rod-tip, it is obvious that its initial speed when it leaves the rod will be the same as the rod-tip itself is moving at. From that point on, the sinker begins to decelerate. This deceleration is caused by gravity, line/air friction, line/line friction on the spool, line/ring friction, and reel-bearing friction. Of these, gravity is the most serious. Most leads run out of steam through the necessity of towing a long length of line up the gradient of the cast's trajectory. This line is rubbing against the air, so it isn't surprising that the sinker whistles off at a great rate of knots then suddenly seems to become lethargic. So the faster it can be sent off, the further it will go before all these factors overwhelm it and it falls back to earth.

With a standard pendulum cast, the sinker is swung away from the angler, parallel with the beach, then is swung back high above his head. As it is coming up, the angler positions his arms and shoulders so that he is what casters call 'under' the rod, as though the rod is to be pushed round and up in the same way that a boxer gets behind a punch. The caster then clouts the rod as hard as possible, moving it round and up, then finally he pulls in with one hand and punches with the other. Ideally this should be against a fully-compressed rod, so that the sinker accelerates just that little bit more. So where has the power come from?

At the start, most pendulum casters transfer all their weight onto the foot that is away from the sea. Some beginners have trouble with this. The best way is to bend the leg a little and position the body-weight so that perfect balance can be held on that leg. The other foot lightly touches the ground, just to add support.

At this stage, the caster's shoulders are facing away from the sea. His left arm is away from his body, with the right arm bent close towards the shoulder. At the moment of hitting the rod, power comes from the swivelling of the shoulders and trunk, the straightening of the weight-bearing leg and from the transfer of weight from that leg to the other. When these reach a climax, the arms punch and pull. At the climax the butt of the rod ends up high in the caster's chest, the up-rod arm straight, and the shoulders following through that movement. All this takes a second to execute and can only be learnt through tuition and practice.

In the pendulum cast, a common fault is to hit the rod too soon. Now, if you are highly proficient at this cast and very fast at executing it, it is almost impossible to hit it too soon. The beginner, however, is advised to move into the cast slowly at first before giving it everything he has got. Until he reaches the higher classes he is likely to power the sinker into the ground or, worse still, have the sinker swing outside the arc of the rod and cause the reel spool to slip, thus burning the line, which will break and let the sinker zip off along the beach.

Another common fault is failure to get under or behind the rod. You have to imagine that you are little David and Goliath is leering down at you from up there, only today you left your sling behind. If the cast goes out of control, the cause is likely to be a failure to get underneath the rod – or behind it. It's a bit of both, really. One way of sorting out mistakes is to work backwards through the cast. Practise punching imaginary giants in the face, but do it with a rod-butt in order to co-ordinate both arms and shoulders.

A major fault, and a serious one, is the neglect of the left hand. Because this does not provide much power to the cast until the closing stages, many casters tend to neglect it. Keep it close to the body and you'll never get anywhere. The left hand should describe an exaggerated stirring motion while the cast is in progress, being kept about 16 in out, and at shoulder height and rising as the rod is brought around the body until the final push-pull. Most would-be casters keep it both too close to the body and too far down towards the waist. Keep it up and out. I recall a time when, as a rank beginner, I was having terrible trouble with my casting. John Holden, casting champion at that time, casually walked up to me and murmured 'Keep your left hand up and away from your body.' My troubles evaporated after that.

Obviously, while the rod is high after swinging the lead above the caster's head, the angler has to get his arms and shoulders into position prior to the big heave. This he does while the sinker is swinging up behind him. The heave starts when the sinker is at the apex of its swing.

There is, incidentally, just one problem with all this instruction. Every pendulum caster has his own interpretation. Go to a tournament run by the United Kingdom Surfcasting Federation, and you'll see different casters using noticeable variations on the basic theme. As most of these guys are hurling sinkers well over 200 yd – about three times the national average casting distance – who is to say which one is right and which one is wrong?

Any would-be caster is advised to join the UKSF and go to tournaments in order to pick up a few ideas. Membership is scattered throughout the British Isles, and there may be somebody close to your home who would be willing to provide you with tuition for a modest fee. All the top men have been through the mill. They know the misery of crack-off after crack-off. They can recognize mistakes quite easily, having made them themselves many, many times.

The plain fact is this: the only way to learn to cast is to integrate a course of tuition with plenty of practice. Find somewhere safe, take plenty of spare sinkers, a sharp knife to cut out heavy bird's-nests, and a bulk spool of line. The first few bulk spools will appear to have one hell of a lot of bird's-nests built into them. But persevere, things will get better.

The lonely road

When learning to cast, the tyro is advised to practise with a friend. Then you can criticize each other and point out faults the other may not be aware of committing. One of the most demoralizing things a caster can do is continue to practise on one of those days when nothing seems to go right. Pack it up for the day. Nothing is achieved by a dogged determination to put down just two good casts together before going home. Rarely do they come. It is much better to sit at home with a glass of whisky and think things out, maybe with a rod-butt to help recreate those unrewarding strokes. Everybody gets days like that – even top casters.

One sure-fire way of bolstering confidence is to make a measuring line. This is easily made from polypropylene string (the white, plasticy stuff) and curtain rings. Tie a ring to the base-line end, and fix it to the ground with an old screwdriver. Tie in another ring at 100 yd, and another every 10 yd up to 210 yd. These distances can easily be measured in the back garden. Poke a garden cane into the lawn and another an accurately-measured 10 yd away. Five times up and down is 100 yd. The rest is easy. Slip a length of waterproof tape through each ring and stick it to itself, then write on the measured distances. An old cable spool will hold the finished line.

Casting champion and top rod designer Terry Carroll explains away a bird's-nest. Nobody is immune to such tangles.

Gradually you will notice that distances creep upwards. Last week 153 yd was the maximum. Today you broke 160 yd and so on. You'll get stuck at certain points, while at the higher end you will discover that casting efficiency has to be improved dramatically just to add an extra couple of yards. What probably happens is this: an angler develops his style, then reaches the maximum that both his style and his build can produce. Only by building in additional components and by adjusting that style will progress be made after reaching that limit.

Never be tempted to run a reel without any braking, just to get a few extra yards. While dismembering the ensuing bird's-nest you will have time to reflect that only style and body speed put down good casts that remain attached. Incidentally, the measuring tape is excellent at keeping casters honest. It would be very profitable to receive a fiver for every lie that is told about casting distances. We have all met anglers who claim to be able to cast colossal distances. Curiously, they have never done so over a measured court. Perhaps they have small paces.

Now, how about the fixed-spool user? These ungainly monstrosities are quite undeservedly popular mainly because they offer an easy way out to anglers who can't quite get the hang of a multiplier. They are said to offer some advantages over the multiplier in strong on-shore blows, and some tournament men believe that the fixed-spool reel is the ultimate long-distance caster. But this book is about fishing, not tournament casting.

The major problem with a fixed-spool reel is the tendency for the spool to slip during the casting stroke, despite heavy drag pressure applied to prevent this. Thus fingers are burned. Some anglers use the thumb-button devised by Breakaway Tackle, though a slipping spool will cause the line to weld itself to the device in extreme circumstances. Others use a leather thong, though this can whip back and catch the line. Others use a glove, which is probably most popular of all. Whatever method is used, there are occasions when even the most ardent fixed-spool user must pause to reflect that his outfit offers none of the delicacy and refinement of the multiplier reel.

Other business

Match anglers, bass anglers, and others who specialize in the more sensitive branches of shore fishing are well aware that accuracy in casting is often paramount to success. A pod of fish may be grouped together in a very small area. Cast 2 yd to the left and the tackle lands among snaggy rocks, cast 3 yd to the right and it is among a kelp bed. Cast just so and it lands on the sandy

Tournament rods come in all sizes to suit different casting styles. The beginner cannot do much better than watch and learn from tournament casters.

floor of an intersection of gullies. There the bass will be hunting. Match fishermen cast to small depressions, freshwater springs and other features noticed during a low-tide recce trip.

At times it pays to stand at one place during a flooding tide and cast the same distance each time, especially if a marker of elastic thread has been coiled around the line. In this way, the same spot can be fished from low to high to low tide, if the feature warrants such exclusive attention. When spinning, it is often important to place a lure precisely and accurately ahead of a school of frenzied fish. They move so fast on occasions that a poor cast will result in groans and frustration as the fish go down or change direction before the lure reaches them. Or they may spook if the spinner lands right in their midst.

As in all shore angling matters, casting is just another skill, a weapon to be used to reap rewards for the diligent angler. There are many occasions when the difference between 100 lb of fish and a handful of tiddlers is measured in yards. But it is also a skill that is valuable in its own right. Many anglers come home happy after a day when the fishing was pathetic, but their casting was smooth and skilfully accomplished. Add a few rays of warm sunshine and a sackful of fish — especially when other anglers are scratching — and you have a recipe for one of the most glorious feelings of smugness known to man.

4
Baits

As far as anglers are concerned, baits can be classified as sighted, or scented, or both. To attempt to understand why a fish will take one particular bait and not another is difficult in view of the differences between the environments of fish and anglers. As explained in Chapter 1, a fish functions according to biological characteristics appropriate to its own environment. Only experience, observation and conclusions drawn from various sources can help you figure out why that fish won't take the luscious-looking morsel you are offering it.

Even with the finest tackle that money can buy and a well-proven venue, you need first-rate bait for success. First-rate bait means as much as is required, relevance to the area and as fresh as possible. There may sometimes be exceptions to the latter, when a smelly bait might entice the occasional fish, but Nature rarely provides putrifying food for predatory fish.

Nature's food

The sea, from the vast deeps to the splash zone, is inhabited by a large variety of creatures which, in some way or other, are interdependent for life. This is the food chain, the structure whereby sea creatures subsist on each other. To acquire the food they need, and to prevent themselves from becoming the targets of aggressors, sea animals require some means of attack or defence. Some seek refuge in sheltered places, others are armoured. Some are armed with teeth, pincers, spurs or spines. Camouflage is protection for others. Some species shed limbs quite easily to escape from predators. Others emit a screen of inky fluid to put off followers. Many anchor themselves firmly to rocks, while others drift aimlessly with the current.

Plankton forms the very basis of the food chain. It includes both plants and animals, some of which cannot be seen other than through a microscope. Either directly or indirectly, these form an important food source for most marine creatures. Many whales eat nothing else. The animal plankton consists of many forms of immature life together with animals which although minute, are completely formed. For example, copepods are so plentiful that they form the main food of the herring shoals on which other predators prey. Plankton also contains the eggs and larvae of the bulk of our bait species. During the early summer months there is a bloom of plankton, a massive proliferation of growth which later dies down. This bloom may turn the sea a dull greenish or a bright rusty colour and a scum may be formed that seems to deter the fish from feeding inshore. Dead plankton is extremely important as food for the lesser types of life on the beach.

One of the lowliest forms of inshore life is the worm. Because of its abundance, it is the most widely-used sea bait. There are many species, several of them too minute or too fragile to be of any use as bait. The most prolific and most widely sought-after species is the lugworm.

Lugworm

This worm graphically betrays its presence by forming neat coils of sand on the surface of the beach. In most cases a small indenture will be found nearby. The coil and pit mark each end of the U-shaped burrow in which the lugworm spends its life. It swallows sand, extracts the food, and extrudes the inedible remains on the surface. The much sought-after black, sewie, or yellow-tail lugs are generally found further down the beach, and their burrows may go down a yard or more to rich feeding strata. The more watery versions, known as the well worm, soft lug, red or blow lug, are found closer in. The bigger spring tides produce the better-quality black and leathery lugworm.

The coil-and-pit method of digging requires no more than location of the give-away marks. Digging mid-way

Overleaf: Digging for lugworm, a convenience bait that is spectacularly effective at times.

between them will locate the worm. Better still, follow the tunnel down from the coil until the worm is located. On many beaches the former method of location does not work because there is no indent. So dig out a spit of sand from slightly ahead of the coil and then dig directly down at the rear of the first spit, ensuring that you keep the burrow in view. As soon as the worm can be seen, it can be gently extracted from its tunnel. Don't pull at its soft tail as it will break off and the worm will be lost into the bowels of the sand. Only practice makes perfect with lug digging! While the professional digger may be seen to lift only about three spits of sand before extracting the worm it may take many more spits, plus extreme back-ache before the learner masters the art.

Trenching can also be a productive method but requires more energy to excavate mountains of sand before collecting the same amount of worm. Bait digging is hard graft so the less effort put into digging one worm, the longer the active life of the digger!

The orthodox long-bladed bait-digging spade is the most efficient tool to use. This design is improved by shortening it by 4 in and honing the edge to reasonable sharpness. It also improves digging technique. Whatever tools or methods you use, study those of the professionals. Such is the structural variety of British beaches that local preferences often make most sense.

There are various methods of storage both short and long term, but the first operation is to remove the gut by gently squeezing the worm's head and drawing the finger and thumb along the body towards the head. This prevents the outer skin from becoming soft and flabby. If the worms are for immediate use this gutting is counter-productive as it removes a valuable source of scent.

To store lugworms for only a couple of days, either mix them in dry sand or sawdust to absorb excess moisture or wrap them individually in newspaper. Keep them in a cool place. For storage up to six months or more, the easiest method is to place a folded sheet of newspaper on the floor, lay out the worms with plenty of space in between and parallel to each other, then roll the paper into a cylinder. Place these into a polythene bag and store in the deep freeze until required. I find that the worms look and feel as good as new when thawed. As with all frozen bait, the drier it is prior to freezing, the less mushy it will be when thawed. Commercial operators lightly salt lug prior to freezing to draw out excess water. Tanking live lugworms is very successful, though some anglers consider that they seem to lose flavour if kept for too long.

Lugworm catches most species of fish either on its own or in a cocktail with fish or shellfish. It must stay on the hook and look like a worm, not a sloppy bundle of jelly. It is a soft bait and the operation of casting tends to tear at it, so care must be taken in threading worms up the hook and over the eye or spade end lest you pierce the outer skin. The eye plus the knot help prevent the worm from slipping down to the bend. A two-hook Pennell rig is an excellent idea. It not only holds the bait firmly, but also improves catches of flatfish, which sometimes go for the wrong end. Many times I have caught dabs or flounders on the smaller secondary hook further up the trace.

For larger species of fish such as cod or bass, a number of worms may be threaded up the hook shank and on to the nylon, making sure that the lowest worm is well secured as an anchor for those upstairs. I don't subscribe to the view that a bunch around the gape of the hook provides a more attractive bait. Three worms threaded carefully up the snood give off the same amount of scent, look more like one worm, and are more likely to stay put during the cast and the bite. An important point to remember when baiting up, and this applies to all baits, is to relate the size of your bait and hook to the species of fish you expect to catch. A big cod will turn up its nose at $\frac{1}{2}$ in of lush lugworm on a size one hook which a dab will relish. Likewise a dab will be over-awed by, or maybe peck at, three or four worms on a 4/0 hook.

Ragworms

There are many species of ragworm. Most live in burrows and feed on planktonic matter extracted from the mud and water. Along each flank are projections which the worm uses to hold steady in the burrow, to produce currents in order to prevent the water going stale and to circulate feeding matter.

One species that burrows into sand or mud is the king rag, which grows to an enormous 2–3 ft long. It is tinted purple-green with a pinkish underside, but will turn an angry red and orange colour after removal from its hole.

It is probably the most sought-after ragworm and the easiest to locate. Shingle beds, mussel banks and estuarine conditions are the best places to find it. They can often be located by treading around the area – water will spurt from the mouth of their tunnels. Another method, particularly on a spring tide, is to ease over some of the larger stones. Very often the worm may be seen lying stretched along its run. Burrows are characterized by a distinctive coating of mud around them. Speed at digging is essential for this species. When they realize you have evil designs on them, they move extremely fast down into the clay or mud.

Half a king rag threaded nicely up a size 3/0 or 4/0 hook (and secured with either shirring elastic, cotton or a secondary small hook) frequently produces the most viscious bite from a passing bass.

White ragworm is the sea matchman's dream bait – so difficult to obtain, yet so effective. It averages 4–5 in long, and rarely exceeds 8 in. It is generally found by accident on most beaches whilst digging for lugworm, but larger colonies may be found on others. It is a superb bait for flatfish and ideally suited to fine-wire hooks. It wriggles well and there can be little doubt that its white colouration has something to do with its effectiveness. It fishes best in clear water, while dirty water conditions are best tackled by a cocktail of rag and lugworm – bait the hook with lug and tip off the point with white rag (which also acts as an anchor for the lug).

A related species, called the rock worm, is found in the green-weed and piddock zones of soft chalk. It requires a small pick or similar to harvest it. It is slightly greenish in colour during the summer, while winter rock worms are more brownish, like large harbour rag. Experienced users consider that fish disdain cocktails made with this worm.

Many of the ragworms look green during the spawning season. At this time they become free-swimming and can be caught with a muslin net once the worms have been attracted to a lamp suspended close to the water. However, spawn-filled rag seem to deter fish from eating them and, as a general rule, green spawny ragworms should not be used as bait. Fortunately plenty of non-spawny ones can be caught during the free-swimming season.

The harbour rag's name gives away its general location. It is a small worm around 3–4 in long, and of a brownish-green, slightly transparent hue with a blood-red line down its back. As it is more tolerant of fresh water it is found in the mud of harbours and estuaries. It lives near the surface, thus making it an easy target for the digger armed with a small garden fork or, in many places, bare hands. A worm suited to small and fine wire hooks, it is a killer bait for flatfish, wrasse, small pollack and thin-lipped mullet.

Storage is fairly straightforward with king rag, either short or long term, but the only sure way of keeping ragworm of any species in tip-top condition is to start right at the digging stage. Immediately, separate any damaged worms into a separate bucket so that the whole ones aren't wallowing in blood. It is a grave mistake to pile them all into the same bucket full of slime, blood and mud, then expect them to survive a two-hour journey home in the car boot. Immediately after digging, in the case of the king rag, wrap them in newspaper and inspect them daily for signs of excessive dampness, preferably changing their bed daily until all excess moisture has been absorbed. With this method the worms will stay healthy for at least a couple of weeks. The smaller versions of king rag will keep quite

happily in damp, but not wet, vermiculite or sand in the salad compartment of a fridge.

With white or harbour rag, the only effective method of keeping them alive and fresh is to dig them directly into a bucket of sea water which is aerated by means of a battery-operated air pump (available from pet shops and some tackle shops). Either transfer them into an aquarium, or use them immediately. Storage in tanks is comparatively easy and is the only successful long-term method. Alan Yates offers more advice on keeping white rag in chapter twelve. Ragworm will not freeze successfully, nor will it salt down. Forget about preserved rag in attractive-looking packets mounted on cards like peanuts, that's all they are worth as bait.

Crabs

What a superb bait we have in the shape of the much-maligned bait-stealer itself! Crabs are eaten by most species of fish, most invertebrates like octopus and cuttlefish, various sea birds, mammals like otters, seals and whales, and of course, man. In Britain anglers must account for many millions of shore crabs each season. There can be no better bait for inshore fishing than a succulent peeler or soft crab. But what is a peeler? Herewith a small biology lesson.

The rigid skeleton inside which a crab depends for support is non-living and cannot expand. The animal grows by a process of moulting or peeling. It builds up a supply of body-food reserves, lays down a new cuticle or skin, cracks off the old shell, blows itself up to a much larger size by the intake of water, and then the new cuticle hardens. Until this has hardened the crab is barely able to move and can't defend itself. Mortality is highest at this stage, particularly from predatory fish and anglers on collecting sorties. This is where Nature has dealt the crab a cruel blow. Before it is ready to moult it hides itself under a rock or in a muddy pool or under seaweed. But as soon as it has cast its shell, the fool moves from its hideaway to another one, be it only 1 ft or so away. This is when it is most vulnerable to hunting fish and, fortunately, why it is such a successful bait. Find a moulted shell with the gills a tell-tale honey colour, denoting freshness, and a thorough hunt nearby should reveal its owner.

The growth of body tissues and increasing food reserves, coupled with favourable conditions of temperature and light, stimulate the crab to peel. Hormones which emanate from the brain and the eyestalks also control the process.

Shore crab peelers can be expected in fair quantities from about the beginning of May onwards but the full flush of peeling does not really start until June. In sun-warmed lagoons and brackish estuary drains free from the cooling tides, shore crabs can be found as early as late March, depending on the weather. Peelers are found throughout the year along the south Devon and Cornish coasts. Much depends on the severity of the preceding winter.

The experienced gatherer is able to select the ripe ones at a glance just by looking at the colour of the underside and gently feeling the shell texture. There is a distinctive fading of the shell's pigment and it feels slightly soapy. The easiest way for the novice is gently to twist off the last segment of a leg, pressing the crab face down onto the thigh of his wader so as to prevent retaliation. The segment should reveal the new skin if it is a peeler; if not, then a white sinewy strand will be revealed. The best baits – especially among velvet swimming crabs – are those with the claw fully formed at the end of the new leg. A male carrying his mate may be robbed to obtain bait. Always replace the upturned stones where they come from so as not to expose the multitude of creatures which rely on their cover. Experience will show that certain rocks, crevices and gullies are regular moulting homes. Also, if a weed-strewn rock is heaved over onto its back, the weed will rot, produce a pungent smell and deter any other crabs from using that hideaway for the remainder of the season.

Take a large bucket containing weed to keep the crabs cool. Put peelers under the weed and softs on top otherwise the peelers will cuddle the softs to pulp. Never collect more than you will require for a couple of fishing sessions. Unless your keeping techniques are first class, they will be wasted.

For storage, it is imperative that they be kept in a cool environment, never in water unless aerated as they will drown through lack of oxygen. Peelers may be kept lightly chilled for up to three weeks as this lowers the body temperature, slowing down the peeling process. Softs will carry on with the hardening process until quite useless as bait and should be used up as soon as possible. Give them a reviver in sea water for a few minutes each day. The ultimate in peeler technology is the aquarium method of storage.

Fish are often packed full of hard crabs, which may tempt the angler to try these as bait, unfortunately without much success unless severely mangled to assist body juices to escape. Even then, they are less effective than peelers. Sight and lateral line sensitivity combine when a fish locates a hard crab. Place that same crab on to a hook and its movement is so restricted that it is virtually a static bait with no scent. Sometimes hard crabs work when float-fished, fixing the hook under a harness made from shirring elastic.

Opposite page: *King ragworm heads a family of juicy, wriggley baits suitable for many occasions.*

Left: *Fresh from the trawl, squid is a very versatile bait. Your own sense of smell is the best guide when buying it.*

Below: *Peeler crabs like this can charm fish from the sea when used correctly.*

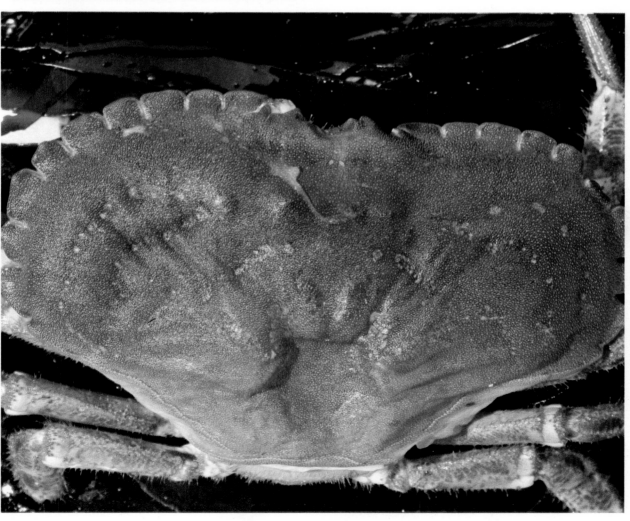

However, place a luscious piece of peeler crab which is oozing juices on to the hook and although it may not look remotely like a crab it will nevertheless have the tell-tale taste and smell that fish are tuned in to. I don't care what my peelers look like on the hook as long as they are well secured, with juicy body meat (looking like lumpy custard) oozing out, and the right size for the species I wish to catch. That is why I prefer to mount two halves on to a hook rather than one whole crab. Or to puncture the skin in several places with a knife point.

To be effective, the soft crab must be in a velvet soft condition, not partially hardened. A peeler needs to be undressed. First kill it by pressing firmly with finger and thumb between the eyes, gently lift off the back shell and peel the underside. Take off the legs and retain them, if required, for small baits. Legs and claws of large crabs like edibles can be peeled and tied into bunches. Hard leg sockets may be left on as a means of securing the hook. What remains is virtually a soft crab. Pass the hook through the body, out through a leg socket and repeat the process. Secure it with dress-maker's shir-ring elastic, available from any haberdasher (colour is totally unimportant). This prevents the bait flying off on the cast. It should be a cylindrical shape for fish to take without fiddling about. If bass are finicking, leave legs on the hook-eye side to encourage them to take from the point side.

Crab is a natural for rock fishing, in estuaries for flounders, and on sandy beaches for bass, cod, plaice, dabs and smooth-hounds. It is widely agreed that the most effective species are velvet swimming crab, edible crab and shore crab. Watch out when collecting velvets because of the phenomenal speed of their pincer-strike. This can result in a badly gashed finger while feeling around blindly under rocks in pools. Best idea is to strike faster when a velvet is cornered and press it hard against the ground to trap its claws, then manoeuvre a finger and thumb across its back and slightly under-neath it so that its claws can be pushed across the underside of its body. It can then only glare at you. A velvet swimmer so close to peeling that its shell crumbles away is irresistable to bass.

Shellfish

Shellfish baits include razorfish, mussels, cockles, gaper or soft-shelled clams, butterfish, slipper limpets, pid-docks and hermit crabs, which can also be included in this group. Shellfish baits come into their own after a violent storm on a beach where they live. They are also excellent stand-by baits in many situations either on their own or as cocktails with worms – mainly lug.

The razorfish is aptly named because of its shell's likeness to the old cut-throat razor. It must be the shellfish supremo. It will tempt bass, cod, rays, flatfish and many other species. It is not as easy to locate as most other shellfish, but its size makes up for this. It is worth the trouble it takes to find.

On most beaches empty shells are in evidence, particularly after a storm, but this does not necessarily mean that they are available to the collector – they may live below the low-water mark. A small member of this group of species is common fairly high up the tide line. However, there are accessible beds of the larger species around our coastline – on shallow sandy beaches, tidal flats and estuaries.

Razors are very sensitive to vibrations and will disappear well out of sight at the tread of a size ten wader, maybe sending up a mini-fountain of water. But all is not lost. There are two methods of extracting them from the burrows in which they move up and down with the tides, filtering water through their syphon for food particles.

Location is relatively easy since razors produce a distinctive keyhole-shaped aperture which is usually well worn and easy to see. Collection is easiest on a receding tide when they will be quite near the surface. One method – which can be a hit-or-miss job – is to make up a solution of salt and water in a washing-up liquid container and squirt this down the aperture. The razor should then hopefully rise to the surface to clear the solution from its syphon, whereupon it is quickly grabbed.

But the most effective method, and the one I have seen used to perfection by professional collectors on the French coast, is the art of spearing them. Incidentally, they don't collect them there for fishing bait but to eat. They are considered quite a delicacy. With the spear method the razors are not suitable for tanking as the spear usually pierces and kills the fish. Make yourself one from a length of $\frac{1}{4}$ in mild steel rod and get a friendly blacksmith to form a barbed point at one end, a handle at the other. Push it down the hole until the razor is located. Then push a little further, twist, and extract the fish. With a little practice it is amazing how many can be collected on a tide. Razor freezes excellently and will keep usable for up to a year. It is a tough bait which stays on the hook and casts well.

The gaper or soft-shelled clam is a close relation to the razor and is another highly delectable bait if used in the correct circumstances. Neither is much good under a flat calm sea where the fish aren't really looking for them. But on a storm beach in the teeth of a big wind then it's a different picture.

Mud flats and estuaries are the haunts of this species, which is spoon-shaped and grows to about 5 in long. Unlike the firm flesh of the razor, the clam has a soft body which does not stay well on the hook. It is safer to discard the body and be content with the syphon or shoe. This is covered by a thin brown skin which needs to be removed to reveal firm white flesh.

Digging for clams is done by location of the aperture and digging down, or by trenching in an area where many holes may be seen. Generally the clams are situated from 9 in to 2 ft down. They can't move through the sand so once located it's just a matter of digging. This bait is suitable for a variety of species and is particularly effective for cod if tipped with lugworm.

The mussel is a good stand-by bait, easily collected and stored in tanks, and is often a good tempter for shy-feeding fish when worms aren't effective. Mussel is a very soft bait and many shore anglers steer well clear of it because of its poor casting qualities. It is ideal for rocky ledge situations where casting isn't necessary, or for float fishing. Codling, pollack, coalfish, plaice and wrasse often go silly after mussel bait, so here is a method of hardening it for the hook.

First it has to be parted from its shell and the method I use is to hone down the business end of a teaspoon so that the front edge is quite sharp. The end of the handle is also reduced in thickness to be used as a lever when prising open the shell. The spoon is used to scoop the meat and muscle cleanly away from the shell.

The mussels are then placed in a sieve above a bowl and liberally sprinkled with household salt. After two or three hours in a cool place the salt will have drawn out the excess moisture, thus tightening up the meat and producing a firmer bait. Wrap them in newspaper to keep them firm. A couple of turns of shirring elastic will complete the exercise. A system of making cock-tails, where hard casting is vital to success, is to thread mussels on to the hook, lay black lug alongside and tie them with thread to the mussels like splints. The same method of preparation also applies to some of the smaller species of shellfish such as slipper limpets, scallops and carpet shells.

Among the other shellfish, a garden rake is a valuable tool for collecting cockles and others that live close to the surface of sand or mud shores. Piddocks require a hammer and chisel or pick to break them from rocks. Slipper limpets are found living along some shorelines, but are more easily gathered when washed ashore in their characteristic bundles after a storm. The mussel spoon is apt for them too. Whelks can be picked up or, if you have a boat, gathered in a whelk pot and sorted out with a hammer. Hermit crabs can be collected in some rock pools if large enough, scrounged from trawlermen, gathered from the shore after a storm, or captured in a baited drop-net from some piers. They lack the scent of a good peeler, though peeler or soft hermits are excellent. Most people mount their soft bodies on small hooks for flatfish or in bunches tied on with elastic thread for

larger fish. Incidentally, trammel netsmen often bring in whelks, bunches of mussels, peeler crabs and, in August and September, large numbers of peeler spider crabs. A suitable collusion can pay dividends.

Fish baits

Into this category we can place such species as sand-eels, sprats, mackerel, herring, and squid which, although a mollusc, is nevertheless a fishy type of bait. Although fish baits are generally stand-bys, many species are partial to a fish tea. The oily species are the most highly scented. Their attractiveness lies in the combination of sight and scent. A strip of mackerel is a deadly spinning bait and equally good fished statically.

A live sand-eel, lightly hooked through the top of its back, can be an absolute killer when free-lined from a rock ledge or jetty for bass, pollack and other mid-water predators. It is a very realistic bait. Many are foul-hooked while mackerel spinning and if care is taken to keep them alive in sea water they can be very effective. Fast-frozen eels, although not as effective under most circumstances as live ones, also work in similar con-ditions, but owing to the deterioration of the flesh through freezing they must be more firmly presented on the hook.

A baiting needle is a handy tool for threading the line through the mouth and down the spine before tying on the hook, which should be secured to the tail with either cotton or shirring elastic. Don't mutilate the little fish or cut it into bits because it must look realistic to be of any effect. A long flowing trace weighted with a jardine or spiral lead is often a most productive method of spinning for pollack, coalfish or bass. When re-trieved in a jerky fashion the bait will look like a distressed fish – a surefire way of conning a predator on to the hook.

Sand-eels are also effective legered or float-fished alive or dead, though the latter method requires a choppy sea to impart movement. When casting a long way, thread the hook through to the mouth from the tail and half-hitch the trace around the tail once or twice.

In some parts of the country the collection of sand eels is no trouble at all while other beaches do not produce. If you can locate the right beach, an easy and effective method of gathering them is to rake the surface of a sandy bank. They will be found hiding close to the surface. In other places, a seine net works best or a bladed scraping tool will bring them to the surface – but beware of weevers.

Whitebait may be used in a manner similar to sand-eels (and elvers, when hooked behind the head to prevent them squirming around the trace). These can very often be collected in their hundreds from the

shoreline after mackerel have trapped a shoal and forced it up on to the beach. Cast one back out for an instant take on ultra-light tackle.

The faithful old mackerel proves excellent at times. It must be frozen very fresh to last any length of time. It is an excellent stand-by species if you are a little hard up for baits, and has a place all of its own when fishing for congers, silver eels, bull huss, doggies and other species.

After a productive mackerel-bashing session, some may be frozen for later either whole, ungutted and singly in polythene bags or filleted and frozen individually (lay the fillets out on a sheet of polythene on a tray) and packeted for storage. It is important that no air can get to the fish while frozen otherwise the flesh will lose its texture and develop freezer burn. Make sure all baits are well-sealed in polythene bags.

Presentation is governed by which species you intend to fish for. Fishing for whiting or pollack with a chunk cut indiscriminately might attract a bite but may not hook the fish. But cut a neat thin lask from the tail and tidily pass the hook through a couple of times and you will likewise attract the same bite and succeed in hooking the fish. The relationship of bait size to species hunted gains greater importance with fish baits. Tail sections or whole fish when used for tope, conger, rays or bass must be secured so as to allow the hook to face outwards, otherwise many fish will be missed due to the hook being struck back into the meat and not into the fish. The needle is again useful for threading line through the bait.

Herrings are generally shop-bought and therefore slightly stale in even the best circumstances, so examine them well prior to purchase otherwise, if frozen, you may find yourself the owner of packeted mush when you arrive at the beach. Best bet is to buy direct from the boats that catch them. They freeze well and can be used like mackerel. Sprats, when dead, appeal mainly to scavenging fish but rarely predators, which have little difficulty in catching these slow-moving fish on the fin.

Squid is used for species under circumstances similar to those where mackerel or herring are used. One form is the smaller Californian (or Chinese, etc.) Kalamari (Calamar is the Spanish word for squid), which measures 4–6 in long, and makes an ideal hook-size bait. Another is the larger European species, best bought from the dockside, which may be sliced up or used as larger static baits or in boot-lace strips for spinning and float fishing. The freezer is the best storage system. Buy a large box and partially thaw its occupants for repacketing. When some shops do this, the squid are completely defrosted and start to decompose prior to re-freezing.

Mackerel: no other bait is such fun to collect.

The Kalamari must be presented as naturally as possible for maximum effect, in order that it may double as a sighted and scented bait. Pass the hook through the body and through the head between the eyes before tying on with elastic thread at the head. The hook must stand proud else it may be choked on the strike through the flesh catching on predatory teeth.

Shrimps and prawns

These easily-collected baits are particularly effective in clear water from rocks, piers or jetties. Shrimps can be amassed with a suitable net pushed along the low-water line of sandy shores. Select the larger ones and place them in a bucket of sea water which is aerated by a portable pump. Alternatively, change the water constantly. Live shrimps are far superior to dead ones.

Prawns may be collected from small rock pools with the aid of a net or from under seaweed fronds hanging from breakwaters and jetties. Another method is a baited drop-net or, where practicable, a prawn pot. Allow sufficient time for a quantity to collect in the net to feed, then lift it smoothly and swiftly.

Fished live these crustaceans are superb fish catchers, producing viscious bites from pollack and bass. Pouting bite the tails off. To present them alive, insert the hook point into a small V-shaped indentation among the legs close to the head. This avoids the vital area – the dark spot inside the body. They may also be hooked through the third or fourth body segment. For pier, drift and float fishing the head method appears more natural because the hook lies underneath. Smallish, fine-wire hooks are light enough to allow them to stay active for some time. The aquarium is ideal for long-term storage.

Aquaria

Any container is suitable for holding sea water provided no metal comes into contact with it. But in the long term an all-glass aquarium is a must. Aquaria can successfully be maintained indefinitely without messing about with constant water changes. Either natural sea water may be used or salts for making up a saline solution. This, and other items, can be obtained from an aquarist or some pet shops.

For long-term storage, forget about buckets because they are not biologically working units and can quickly become stale and turn into bait destroyers. An all-glass tank with dimensions of 2 ft × 18 in × 18 in will house up to forty shore crabs, forty to fifty king ragworm, or a similar number of lug – and any other live baits.

Baits may be maintained in peak condition for long periods provided the unit is working biologically correctly. The way to do this is to install an under-gravel filter which is simply a plastic corrugated sheet with vents. On top of this is placed about 4 in of sea-shore gravel – not sand as this clogs the vents. As well as acting as a filter, the gravel allows the inhabitants to bury themselves when feeling depressed about their fate.

An air pump operates the filter by passing small bubbles from the pump into the up-stands of the filter. The bubbles pull water with them when rising to the surface, thus drawing water and minute deposits down through the gravel and under the filter. After only a short time these deposits of silt and dead plankton will break down organically, providing a clean environment for the occupants. Once the unit is working correctly there should be no need to change the water for a year or more.

Such a system is essential for keeping edible or velvet peelers because both species will not survive out of water for longer than a few hours. The only setback is that they continue with the moulting process far more easily than if kept dry. This can be avoided by installing a separate chilling system to lower the metabolic rate and inhibit the peeling process.

Mine is a cooler of the type used in hotels to chill beer. Under normal operation the beer is forced through the cooler by means of gas. Anglers should install a circulating pump which sucks water from the tank, passes it through the cooler and back to the tank through a spray bar. This is a perfectly reliable system which also aerates the water. The pipes inside the cooler are of stainless steel, so there are no corrosion problems. The temperature can safely be reduced thermostatically to 6°C (42°F) so as to slow down the moulting process. Crabs of all species may be kept alive and in limbo for up to six weeks. There is a point of no return around this time when the crab must peel, but as the process is so slow it can be detected and the crab removed, either to be used immediately or transferred to the fridge for a few days.

Baits such as crab, ragworm, lugworm, all shellfish and sand-eels may be kept by this method quite successfully for very little cash outlay. An angler may spend upwards of £200 on his basic tackle and yet resort to using either frozen or preserved baits to catch fish. As the purchase of a tank and pump for less than £30 will ensure a ready supply of top-quality bait, it seems that priorities have become a little mixed up.

Lures

These are sighted baits (not forgetting vibrations, of course), which attract by colour, shape and movement. Lures are designed in a vast variety of shapes, colours and sizes and it is said that the majority are designed to catch the angler and not the fish. So care must be taken to place these items into perspective as to their possible effectiveness. The basic lures used in shore fishing are spoons, spinners, feathers and soft plastic sand-eels.

Selecting a useful spoon is not difficult. Remember that the difference between two spoons of equal weight, but of different size, is that the one with the smaller blade area will sink faster, work deeper, and cast easier against the wind. The spoon with the greater surface area will sink more slowly and swim higher in the water. A spoon is designed to wobble and flutter. You will have to judge the depth of water and correct speed of retrieval so that the lure is wobbling at fish level. This is acquired by experience.

There are times when a spinner will catch fish where a spoon will not – and vice versa. In some respects a spinner is more versatile because it can be relied on to fish more slowly as the blade offers more resistance to the water. So it can be used without snagging in knee-deep situations. The trick when using a spinner is to estimate where the fish are shoaling and then over-cast and bring the lure back to them. You can learn to have absolute control over a spinner, fishing at various speeds, holding it almost stationary against the current. Maximum water coverage is achieved by fanning casts across from right to left. By casting in a pattern of widening circles you can cover every inch of an area before moving on.

Don't forget that fish sense vibrations long before they sight a bait or lure. Movement is of more interest to the predator at the first moment of contact than the colour, shape or size. Selection of spinner designs is a matter of trial and error. The various colours of the well-tried Toby lure fill many situations. The general rule at sea is that long and slender lures fish best, imitating sand-eels. Suffice it to remember that the lure which works today may have no effect tomorrow.

Whilst the original coloured, feathered lures are still effective at catching fish, there are now on the market many variations on the theme which far outfish the feather. A range of fluorescent plastic tube and feather, silver ribbon, or sparkling mylar tinsel outfits have taken over as representations of shoals of fry. In all lure fishing, keep your ears and eyes open for effective patterns and watch the experts to learn how they fish them. Then try to understand wherein lies their effectiveness.

Plastic and rubber eels are proven fish catchers. The Red Gill and Eddystone designs, in various sizes, are very effective for all mid-water predators. Fish the smaller sizes in tandem on short snoods, or the larger ones on flowing-trace type rigs, which may be weighted above for casting. Or use a long-trace paternoster. A trolling situation from rock marks or jetties allows natural movement of this type of lure, which often works well when held steady in a current, with periodic upward sweeps of the rod to make it spurt forwards, then fall back. Colour is frequently most important. I have experienced total failure when using one colour and immediate success when changing to another.

For casting rubber eels on light line, weight them with split shot inside the body cavity. This may improve the motion through the water. There are other types of soft plastic fish with superb tail vibrations which are well worth testing. Some anglers have had success with long, slender silver plugs like the ABU Killer. If imitation is the sincerest form of flattery, then live sand-eels must surely blush at some of the imitations which are now available for the shore angler.

In conclusion, here's a reminder of all the important criteria: freshness; careful presentation; meticulous preservation; relevance to the area; relevance to the species fished for; size suited to size of species; matching hooks. The only exceptions to these rules are usually chance ones.

5
Bass

For most British shore fishermen, the bass is the premier summer fish. Some anglers catch plenty, others not enough, and some have never seen one. Those who live north of a line imagined between Anglesey and the Wash in England and between the mouth of the River Moy and River Boyne in Ireland see few bass. There are stragglers – and some good catches have been made from places like Yorkshire and Luce Bay – but the bassing isn't so consistent as it is down south.

Some biology

The bass we catch are the same species that hunt round the coasts of Portugal, Morocco and the Mediterranean Sea. But while specimens down there grow fast and don't live very long, UK fish grow slowly and live to a good age. It takes twice as long for bass to reach sexual maturity as it does cod, and that is a very good reason for slipping small fish carefully back into the water.

Spawning takes place between late April and early July round our coasts. While cod lay all their eggs in one blast, bass gonads ripen slowly so that the fish lay in batches over a period of time. Warm, settled weather conditions are vital to the success of spawning. Cold, rough water causes many eggs and fry to perish. This is why bass exhibit such startlingly different year classes. Some seasons are so poor that catches in later years will show that very few basslings survived the critical egg/fry period that year. But spawnings in hot, settled springs are generally so successful that maybe 50 per cent of all bass caught ten to fifteen years later will prove to have been born in one such year. All bass anglers hope for such summers – not just because the fishing is better, but because more fish will be available in later years.

Obviously the position of bass in our marine ecosystem is somewhat unstable. Another factor compounds this: bass populations tend to be somewhat localized. In some parts of the British Isles, the population may limit its wanderings to just a few miles of coastline. If commercial pressure seriously depletes that population, fish from elsewhere won't come and make up the numbers. This was demonstrated to me when I tagged a bass off a small rocky headland. Two months later it was recaptured just a few yards from where I returned it. In other areas the fish move around a little. It is suspected that fish from Wales move south while those from the south-east of England move south-west when the sea cools towards winter. Bass along the Atlantic shores of Ireland benefit from the more constant temperature of the Gulf Stream and move no further than deeper water in winter. Often, when the weather stays mild until early in the New Year, surf bassing around the Kerry coastline will be productive until after Christmas. Generally, however, nobody is very certain about what happens to bass in winter, so we had better leave this point alone!

One thing we do know is that bass from the Bay of Biscay run up to the outer Thames estuary and spend much of the summer there. It is suspected that they drop back south-westwards as autumn approaches. These fish are identifiable because they're faster-growing and younger for their size than our resident stocks. While our bass cease feeding when the temperature plummets in winter (although good specimens are landed from some areas up until Christmas), the Biscay fish return to warmer southern waters where they are able to feed for longer into the winter.

Bass are essentially inshore fish and are rarely caught beyond the ten fathom line. As fry, they inhabit the warm, brackish waters of estuaries and tidal lagoons. They then seem to disappear into the sea for a few years until they're about 1 ft long. These fish, and those up to about 3 lb, are termed school bass or schoolies. Rarely are they found on their own. Over breeding grounds, males form up into large schools. Although I once beached a 9 lb male for a colleague at Stradbally on Kerry's Brandon Bay, males are generally smaller than 4 lb. This was in March, and it liberally squirted my jacket with milt. Females grow much bigger, to a

Left: *Aberthaw (South Wales) power station outfall. Basslings in their thousands are slaughtered here by commercial rod-and-line fishermen.*

Below: *With perfect weather, tide, sea conditions, time of day, bait and tackle, this bass-man cannot fail to score. He later landed a seven pounder.*

possible 20 lb. Some people believe that bass over 15 lb are more likely to be Biscay fish, but here again evidence is lacking.

Surf fishing

March is the earliest one can open a bass season. In England, the first of the schoolies are caught from western estuaries by anglers fishing for flounders. These little fish are best ignored. The best March sport comes from Irish Atlantic storm beaches like those along Brandon Bay and at Inch in County Kerry. Many English visitors are fazed by the size of the surf there, but experience shows that it is less violent than at first seems true. Tackle need be no more powerful than a standard 11–12-ft fast-action bass rod, casting up to 3-oz sinkers. Sometimes a light cod rod is required with 3–4-oz leads in really wild surfs. But if such tackle is needed, the bass are unlikely to be around in force. Tumultuous surfs rarely produce good catches, but they may yield the odd monster fish. Find a sheltered corner, however, and the bass could be concentrated there.

The type of water to look for is a surf with a steady pattern of heavy breakers. Such a surf is likely to have been born way out in the ocean. At other times, a rising sea after a period of calm or a decreasing surf after a big storm can prove rewarding. Generally the bass will be inshore of the breaking waves and in the water tables, the spent waves rushing towards the sand. The tables push ahead of them small flatfish, shrimps, swimming crabs and similar grub, while the back-draw of the water carries this food seawards. Thus a band of food is created 60–120 yd out, and the bass will be there. In very heavy surf, the fish will be outside the breakers, while in weak surf they'll be scattered over a wide band. On Brandon Bay, with its wide curve, it is possible to find good surf at sheltered Fermoyle when Stradbally is seething with massive breakers. Provided there is no sand suspended in the clear water, bass should be there. And in March some very big ones are taken.

Clip a light reel to your rod, load it with 10-lb line, tie on a 25-lb casting leader and finish off with a standard paternoster. Long traces just get tangled. Bait the 2/0 hooks with rag, lug, squid strip, crab, razorfish, clam, fresh mackerel strip, live or dead sand-eel. Chest waders are helpful here, but as they're expensive you may prefer to extemporize with ordinary waders and over-trousers (not ones with side gussets permitting access to pockets), and keep the trouser ends closed tight to the boots with elastic bands or waterproof tape. Thus surging surf is prevented from filling your boots, even when a wave slops right up to your waist. Stand in the water rather than paddling at the edge – too much line out spoils bite detection. Remember that the back-draw of the water is sucking sand from under your feet. Every now and then you'll have to step up out of a small pit.

After casting out your 2–4-oz breakaway lead, wind in the slack line and note the angle it enters the surf. If a side-wind has caused it to belly to one side, walk along until your line enters the water at right angles to the surf. Thus the waves will run up the line rather than rolling it ahead of them. Bite detection will be easier. Bites vary from gentle tugs to full-blooded pulls and slack-liners. In all cases either run backwards to make the contact and set the hook, or wind until the fish is felt then bump the hook home. Instant action is required or the fish might move on. For the beginner, some experience will be needed to sort out bites from the sudden lifting of the sinker by a big wave and the plucks of the surf.

Playing the fish is easy enough provided you remember to fight the fish and not the surf. By reeling in and trotting backwards, or letting the fish take line when the back-draw takes it, you can use the surf to your advantage and beach the fish. Handsome, isn't she? Why not take a couple of photos, then slip her back?

Surf beaches may look somewhat featureless. In my experience it often pays to fish near any feature – be it a small stream entering the surf, or a lump of rock, or maybe you know where a tidal current licks the shore. The edges of surf beaches, among rocky, rubbly reef, often produce more fish than at the centre. Each beach has its own merits.

Because most surf fishing is practised on beaches that strip a long way with the tide, take a couple of spare leads, leader and trace line, hooks, elastic thread and other vital items out there in your pockets. A polythene bag in another pocket filled with enough bait for a few hours will obviate the long trudge back to the high water line and also rules out the necessity of moving tackle bags back with the tide. A rod rest is a nuisance and landing nets and gaffs are quite unnecessary.

Experience will prove that light tackle defeats heavy surf more efficiently than heavy gear. I recall one day at Kilcummin when I used a carp rod and 10-lb line to catch large fish that gave me a good run-around. Sandy surf-beaches are virtually snag-free, so unless snags are evident, 10-lb line is quite adequate with strong knots. Lateral tide run only enters the picture on some Welsh and Cornish surf beaches, but here again light gear presents less line surface for the water to work on.

The Irish surf beaches fish best early and late in the year. July and August find the surf as empty of bass as it is in January and February. The best surf fishing starts later and ends earlier in Wales and Cornwall. Successful surf fishing for bass can be found from many shallow beaches along the south and west coasts of England and Ireland. In south-east England, the best time is June, July and September/October. Such places are worth searching out, especially since the surfs are usually very much more tame than those along the Atlantic seaboard. But the water is generally clouded with silt (which the bass don't mind) and doesn't have the sparkling clarity of blue-water surfs.

Rock bass

When the crabs begin to peel in late May, through the peeling explosion of mid-June, and on towards mid-July, that's the best time of all for bass fishing. Or so rock bass men will tell you. These fish are generally of a high average size and are caught among some of the most beautiful scenery in England. The type of ground varies slightly. From Wales round to Ramsgate, shallow reefs, often smothered with bladderwrack and kelp, are the best places to fish. Steep rocks are less productive. Some bass reefs lie below the low-tide mark and are never seen except from a boat during spells of clear water. Some research has to be carried out as to the best places to fish. Bass men who fish this rough ground love it for its solitude and are rarely eager to provide strangers with free information. This is understandable. Rock bassers invariably burn the candle at both ends. They suffer periods of frustration. They tear their hands gathering crabs for bait. But the rewards of this effort make it all worthwhile. To my mind, the capture of an 8 lb reef bass under the towering cliffs of Beachy Head on a clear, still June morning is every bit as pleasant as the 7 lb bonefish that sets the reel sizzling on a Caribbean flat.

The would-be rock bassman has to learn some lessons well. The first is where to fish, how long to fish there, and what rocks he should watch as indicators of tide height. Bass shoals patrol certain parts of a reefy shoreline at specific states of tide. Most marks have a cut-off time, sometimes literally. When the water is lapping a specific rock, there's just time to gather up the tackle and slosh back to safety before a gully fills and cuts off retreat. Obviously only the super-confident or the foolhardy fish such ground alone at night.

The second lesson has to be how to gather crabs – not just the standard shore crab, but edible and velvet swimming crabs too. These make the best baits for rock bass, though some anglers use wrasse heads, kipper, mackerel strip, squid, and so on. Crab is the killer, and velvet swimmers bring in bass faster than any other bait – even if they're not usually found along that stretch of coast.

The third lesson is how to re-tackle fast. Rock bassmen are generally loners, or fish with one or two time-tested friends. This is because most shore anglers become very agitated if their tackle snags and they lose a hook, a weight, or a couple of swivels. It takes me just four minutes from total snap-out to when I cast back out with new terminal gear and a fresh bait. This could be reduced if I had baits ready-tied and traces pre-prepared.

On many reefs, the bass move through quite quickly. They'll be at mark A for half an hour. There's time for just one cast at spot B. Then, after a half-mile walk down the tide there's a chance of picking up two or three fish during the next hour, and so on. They will be at specific points, determined through observation, experience and good old eaves-dropping of other anglers' conversations. Time is very important and must not be wasted.

Standard rock bass tackle is an 11-ft rod weighing 16 oz or less in glass or carbon fibre. I prefer a fast action because it transmits bites to my hands better. Soft-tipped rods absorb the tiny taps that signal the interest of a shy fish. The ideal bass rod allows you to feel the tiny plucks caused by crabs tearing at a bait. (Incidentally, if you feel crabs, there are no bass around. But once the crabs go off, put on your best bait. Crabs sense when the bass are on the prowl.)

Use a light reel – a multiplier is my favourite weapon. If the reef is free of line-cutting barnacles and flints, I'll fish 10–15-lb line. But it is no joke to lean into a confident, dragging pull only to feel the line come taught then snap on a flint. Under such conditions 30-lb nylon is more suitable. True, it isn't nice to fish with. But I hate having fish escape with hooks in them. Often this heavy line comes back shredded for several feet where it has encountered a flint. But at least it didn't break.

Casting distance isn't important on most reefs. Bass are happy to forage wherever there is about 2 ft of water over their back. If such a depth exists just 10 ft out from your rock ledge, and the fauna suggests bass will hunt through there, try lobbing a crab out and keeping out of sight. You may be surprised. Bass will hunt right at the edge of a flooding tide. Do much rock bassing and the chances are that one day you'll see a bass cruising along the edge of a reef with its dorsal fin out of the water.

Specific marks at specific times of tide – ebb and flood – that's the story of bass fishing. Among the gibberish frequently repeated by the inexperienced is that fish prefer the top two hours of the tide. This is not so, for bass or any other species. Each area of coastline has its own times when fish of any species will feed. On many reefs, the top two hours of the tide are totally unproductive – the bass are 300 yd out, exploring the

A good bass, but many anglers are worried for the chances of others surviving the eighteen years required to reach this size.

bladder-wrack zone for its rich food life. The inshore area is often a poorly-stocked larder. One generalization, however, may be useful to the would-be reef bassman. The first two hours of the tide are often the best.

When reef fishing, the further you cast out, the more snags your tackle has to be brought back over. And the shallower the angle of line from the rod-top. Thus the rod cannot help by lifting the tackle off the sea-bed. 30–50 yd casts are generally the most productive. After all, there's little point casting out to a distant area if it proves impossible to retrieve tackle from it. Now, the shorter the cast and the slower the current, the lighter the leads you can use. I never use more than 2 oz for reef fishing, often as little as $\frac{3}{4}$ oz. Light leads bounce over rocks more readily and snag less frequently. Also, because plenty of sinkers are lost each season, the man who loses four $\frac{3}{4}$-oz sinkers loses as much as the guy who leaves behind just one 3-oz bomb. The lead should be tied on anyway with line of about 5–6-lb breaking strain; this is adequate for casting out the light sinkers and breaks readily if snagged.

Reef marks can be tiny – the productive area little larger than a standard living room. In fast tides bass – like river chub – move out of the current into the edge. The best place to fish is where there's a gentle pull of water. Watch a bonfire on a windy day. The smoke is quickly diffused over the fields. On a day of light breeze, a dense cloud of smoke goes down the wind. Likewise the body fluids of a peeler crab. Bass will follow that scent from a good way down-tide.

After casting out, very gingerly tighten the line until there's reasonable tension on it and you can feel the sinker. If you tighten too much, or drag the sinker to make sure it is not snagged, you'll pull it into a crevice and maybe tangle the hook around a weed stem, thereby ensuring complete failure. If no bites come, wind down the rod tip until it is pointing along the line, yet without shifting the sinker. Now strike smartly upwards, pulling the tackle off the sea bed and wind like hell. A high-speed reel is vital here to bring the gear to the surface and out of reach of the graunch.

Rock bass bites vary from tiny twitches to full-blooded pulls. Sometimes these pulls are from school fish. This can be most frustrating. You'll get take after take, with the rod bending to the fish. Strike hard, and nothing is there. Schoolies often run off with the bait held lightly between their lips. Just to make sure, drop down from a 4/0 to a 1/0 hook, tie on a small crab, but break off its legs on the side of the hook point. Leave the other legs sticking up the shank. A bass will then take from the bend side and is more easily hooked. Sometimes big bass play with a crab in this manner, running off with it, dropping it, running again, then just as you

strike, they drop it again. You need to be very lucky to make contact with these. Equally wierd is the bass that picks up the crab and shakes it, drops it again, picks it up once more and shakes it like a dog worrying an old glove.

As a general rule, most bass that signal on the rod top in a determined manner have the bait well down inside their mouth and should be struck immediately. That is why a rod-rest is out of place on a bass reef. The rod should be held all the time. Bass have large mouths, but a crab bait larger than a standard match-box is less easy for them to inhale. A suspicious fish may be spooked while trying to cram an outsize bait into its mouth. Provided a reasonable bait is oozing juices, it is big enough. Beyond this point the law of diminishing returns takes effect. Big baits may just be carried off between bass lips, away from competing fish, in the same way as a sea-gull flies off with a whole mackerel in order to choke it back at the edge of the flock.

I never use nets and gaffs from rocks. Tackle is carried in pockets and a bucket holds the bait. In summer, a can or two of drink replaces moisture sweated out while turning rocks for bait. Work out where you intend to land a hooked fish. A small, shallow gully will enable you to lead a beaten fish into it on a wave so that you can jump down behind it and deal with it. Kill or return the fish swiftly and get the bait back out again before the shoal moves on. The fight of a reef bass is rarely exciting unless the water is clear. They don't run for snags, although some may accidentally take the line round a rock, often while kiting away from the pressure of the rod.

On a favourite mark, which is deeply fissured, the standard bite there is a tap followed by yards of slack line, especially when they feel the hook. Obviously it is impossible to run backwards either to keep in contact or to set the hook. The ratio of bites to fish landed there can be very slim. Interestingly, the bass feed right on top of the reef, in 2 ft of water, and not in the deeper water to either side.

Eels, rockling and small wrasse are adept at impersonating bass bites. These can be infuriating until 'just another bloody eel' turns out to be a lusty 10 lb momma. In March and April, some south-eastern bass reefs fish well for spring cod using identical tackle and tactics. In October and November big cod may run with the bass. A friend once had a 23-lb cod and an 11-lb bass in the same hour. One June morning some friends and I landed a 7-lb bass, a 12-lb conger and a 14-lb cod all within ten minutes.

Weed-bedraggled reefs are natural larders, full of prawns, small fish and crabs. They also have clouded water and shading weeds that make even spooky predators at ease on hot bright days. Even so, dull conditions, dawn and dusk are the best times. Curiously, some reefs fish best when there's a moderate surf running (force 4–6 winds), others in flat calms. Why? I don't know.

Years ago, many anglers used to float-fish for bass using crabs or prawns. Prawns are good if pouting and so on aren't around and there are plenty of bass. However, they don't have the scent, or therefore the results, of peeler crabs. The trouble with weeds and rocks is that they often reach to the surface and grab at tackle. As the float drifts with wind and tide it frequently snags. Anyway, the running paternoster with a short hook-link and long lead-link anchor the bait where the fish expect to find it, even though the technique isn't as visually appealing as float fishing, a technique that requires an even bottom and fairly slack water for success.

Live baiting

In July, bass are to be found in increasing numbers along open beaches, up estuaries and around piers and jetties. As arch opportunists, they are drawn away from the crab reefs by numbers of small pouting, whiting, scad, mackerel, sand-eels and smelt that appear inshore at this time of year. Piers are best fished very early or late in the day when boat and tourist activity is light. From piers – and some steep-to rocks and beaches – a small fish, fished close to the bottom, will score well. Bass that can be seen cruising close to the surface around pier piles are rarely hunting. Feeding bass prefer the lower layers of water. Use a single hook and nick it through the live-bait's lower jaw. Don't manhandle it, as it must be lively. Some anglers fish two rods – one to catch the bait, the other the bass. Takes are generally savage. However, when fishing piers, the best place is right in among the ironwork. Big fish must be winched smartly up to the surface, where a drop-net will be required to land them.

From solid piers, a float can be used, though many prefer to leger a live bait. The current around the end of a solid pier often produces well. A legering technique that works from places that allow a steep angle between rod-top and water goes thus: thread line through a swivel (A), and tie on another (B). Tie 4 ft of line to the other eye of swivel B, then a suitable sinker. Tie 1 ft of line to swivel A, then a 4/0 hook. Catch the hook round one of the rod-rings and cast out. The line will flow through the eye of swivel A on the cast. Tighten up when the sinker hits bottom and put the rod to rest. Now hook on a live fish and let go of the swivel. The bait will then slide gracefully along the line and down into the water where, if all goes to plan, a big bass (sometimes a conger, cod or pollack) will snaffle it.

A friend uses this trick, as well as float-fishing, from a harbour wall, starting before sun-up. His success is due to the fact that large shoals of mackerel swarm where the wall meets the shoreline, trapping fry in the bay thus formed. Big bass follow under the mackerel, picking off stragglers, and he is often home by breakfast time with three or four good fish.

As in all forms of sea fishing, everything has a reason for its success. Bass eat plenty of small mackerel each year so it pays to take note of those little corners which mackerel frequently habituate. Other places are where other small fish gang together. Small whiting and pouting haunt the bases of piers and gantries and shoal around boulder-built causeways. Sand-eels gather with the tide in small pockets. Bass profit from their knowledge of these events.

One trick that works along some stretches of coast is to free-line dead whiting and pouting at the edge of the water. Ideal conditions are darkness, clear water and calm seas. On many beaches small whiting and pouting are caught by tourists during the day. Those that are put back rarely survive the experience. Bass come in under cover of darkness to mop up the cripples and any sun-dried corpses the gulls failed to find. Two friends learnt that the bass work along the beach, ending up where most of the corpses drift to – a corner between the shoreline and a jetty. Working in total darkness, they merely drop small dead pouting 2–3 yd out from the edge and wait; some float, others sink. Bites are signalled by line tearing off the spool before the bass slow down to turn and swallow the bait. Floating baits are attacked in a manner similar to a brown trout hitting a surface lure – a heavy swirl followed by a run.

This trick of using floating dead baits works around many harbours where locals often use a hypodermic syringe to inflate the fish's swim-bladder. Bait can usually be had for the asking and a supply kept in the freezer. These bass must be feeding by both sight and smell.

When the pouting are in – and in some places the July rock pools are full of them – bass can be taken from shingle beaches on pouting – or half sides of mackerel and other fish baits. Or small live pouting hooked and left out there in the manner used for cod. Night-time is best, along with clear water conditions and calm seas. These beaches are heavily touristed by day, peaceful by night.

By late July and into early September, most of the bass are offshore, chasing small fish like sand-eels and sprats. A boat is required to reach them. But some fish linger around the shoreline. They'll take live-baits, or pieces of mackerel, mullet, squid, crab, whiting, pouting, herring, and so on. These are most effective if legered in a spot that experience tells you will be visited by bass. Or you can float-fish prawns under piers or down estuaries for school fish – and the occasional bigger one. Or, in some select areas, fish live peelers and prawns along the edges of estuary channels where bass are known to hunt.

The fascinating thing about bass is that they're so at home wherever they are. The shoreline is their kingdom. The ardent bass angler has to learn not only the major methods of catching them, but how to winkle them out from a host of mini-environments. For example, a man who fishes near Brighton's Palace Pier has perfected a method of catching bass on cheese paste – an effective bait where bass frequent sewer mouths and food-waste outlets. Many bass experts live to a ripe age and admit there is still much they have yet to learn about this most worthy adversary.

Bass on spinners and flies

Bass, especially big ones, are notoriously hard to catch on spinners and red-gill sand-eels – even dead sand-eels mounted for spinning. Most of the time they just follow out of curiosity. But these lures do work and sometimes produce vast catches.

One place a spinner can be fished is under a mackerel shoal or in an area of fry activity. By 'spinner' I'm referring to all the lures that catch bass, be they artificial eels, shiny metal spinners, plugs or whatever. One of two conditions has to be fulfilled before bass will hit lures. Firstly, the fish need to be actively feeding on small fish, or better still, be in a feeding frenzy. If they're not excited, neither will you be. Otherwise, the lure should be fished in fast water where the bass have only a brief chance to snatch at it before it is gone, carried away on the current. Such conditions exist in deepish water off rocky headlands, though light beach-casters and large lures may be required to get through the layers of mackerel close to the surface. The bass are most likely to be feeding close to the sea-bed, in ambush for small fish carried out of control with the tide. Other places are sunken rocky causeways, clear-water reefs and piers with an open structure. The bass are likely to be hunting along such grounds, so the lure should be cast out and along, brought back as though it is slipping from boulder to boulder, pile to pile. Successful spinning is normally had only after a great deal of observation.

A favourite activity of mine is to catch bass on flies. By flies, I mean the mylar/goat-hair/marabou-herl creations used by reservoir trout men as imitations of fry, 2–3 in long. Bass like munching these, especially in fast water. The reason, I believe, is that the flies move in a more whimsical manner than spinners. The fibres breathe life, making them look more realistic. Bass that often ignore spinners will take flies. In shallow water they are more effective than spinners, which keep clinking over the bottom or skipping over the surface. They're excellent for small bass that shoal up where a warm-water outfall or an estuary hits the sea. In the fast current these fish strike with total conviction.

I use a reservoir trout outfit, number nine shooting-heads and 9 ft leaders of 8-lb test nylon. Just belt out the lure across the current and let the water do the rest, retrieving slowly to keep in touch. A stripping basket is necessary to keep the fly line and backing out of the water where it frequently tangles around seaweed. Chest-high waders enable you to approach shoals feeding outside casting range. In very shallow water a floating line is adequate, while a sinking line is more effective in deeper water. In very deep water, a lead-core head may be necessary, though I have found such lines are no use at all over snaggy ground where the line drapes itself round rocks and snags up. If all this terminology is baffling you, ask a trout-fishing tackle-dealer to explain.

School bass prove to be amazingly naive when confronted by a fly, a trait that has given me hours of fun. After careful unhooking I put them all back. When a big fish takes a fly it puts up a superb fight, with more fireworks than a rock or surf bass will provide when taken on standard tackle.

If a complete fly outfit is beyond you, try a trout spinning rod. Load a small fixed-spool reel with 4-lb line, tie on a lure, then crimp on one or two swan-shot just in front of the fly and toss it about like an American bass bug. Stronger line may be required where big bass are found, though only if the ground out there is snaggy or the current very strong. This trick is less effective than a full fly outfit because the lead near the fly's head detracts from much of its inherent whimsy. Provided the fly is 2–3 in long, colour isn't very important. But light size 2 long-shank hooks are necessary because heavy irons spoil the fly's motion. In deep water, a large fly can be rigged in paternoster style above a suitably small sinker. Much larger flies can be fished like this, ones that would defeat even a powerful fly outfit casting a bug-taper line.

With all forms of lure fishing, it is vital that the spinner fishes in the same plane that the fish are swimming. They're not going to come up 60 ft off the bottom if your lure is fishing just under the surface. Count the lure down after it hits water at the end of a cast. If you feel it hit bottom at say sixteen, then mid-water is at the count of eight.

When casting to surface feeders, snap the reel into gear when the spinner is still some feet from hitting the water. Thus you can start to retrieve it before it has time to sink. Retrieve carefully, moving the rod to impart

extra action to the lure. But don't do so violently, as you risk whipping the lure away from a fish that has lined itself up to intercept. Steady retrieves catch more fish than violent ones.

Flat, planing spinners should be fished fairly slowly. They are less likely to sink during the retrieve, though too fast a rate of retrieve will cause them to fish progressively nearer to the surface. The right rate comes with experience and observation. Compact spinners plane less, so can be retrieved much faster. Bass in some locations won't take a slow spinner, but will clout a fast-moved one. Even so, it is frustrating to have one's hand whizzing round, the reel's bale arm a blur as one retrieves as fast as one can, only to see a bass glide up behind the lure, then slowly slide away when it decides that this meal is a fraud.

Of all shore fish, bass repay the intelligent approach most handsomely. While the water tables of the high surf are the altar at which the high priests of the sport pay homage, the same mental approach is required by them as it is by the school-boy who trots a live prawn down an estuary channel for schoolies. Good bass can be caught by every angling method known to man. This variety of method and environment makes bass our most rewarding inshore species.

Fly-fishing for estuary bass is hectic when schoolies shoal up at dusk during high summer.

6
Cod and related species

On a hot summer night I lie asleep, and dream of a leaden sky and rolling breakers exploding on a steep shingle beach. Two matching rod tips, starkly illuminated by a lamp against the gathering night, bend in affirmation of the flooding tide. I'm desperately sucking life into a small cigar when suddenly one rod begins to pogo out of the rod-rest. Whoopee! I grab the rod and immediately I feel life out there under the waves. Far out to sea, a mighty cod accelerates into third gear and the 6-oz grapnel loses contact with the sea bed, quickly allowing a belly of line to form. I swiftly dance backwards, furiously cranking the small casting multiplier until the rod assumes a graceful arc. I grunt enthusiastically. . . . a fish, and a big one at that. Then begins the slow, laborious task of pumping the plump one towards the shore. Many minutes later, I glimpse two broad fins as the fish wallows in the shallows, then glides with the surf towards my feet. Reaching down, I insert my hand into the cavernous gill-cover and struggle to lift the handsome brute off the pebbles. The prize, a perfectly-conditioned, broad-shouldered twenty-pounder, is mine.

Then my idyllic slumber is shattered by the staccato burst of alarm-clock fire. . . . A dream, but what a dream. But then, big shore-caught cod really are the stuff that dreams are made of.

The species

It is hard to pin-point one single factor contributing to the popularity codding now enjoys. In these dark inflationary times when a man has to take out a second mortgage to finance an off-shore wrecking trip, cod stand out as a worthwhile target for the shrewd angler. What with rocketing fuel prices, exorbitant tackle costs and black lugworm costing more than small cigars, only a fool could fail to realize that cod fishing still represents good value for money. The species grows big, is reasonably easy to catch, and best of all you don't have to leave good old terra firma to catch a freezer-full.

It is the head of a large family of fish that includes pollack, coalfish, rockling, haddock, whiting and pouting – to name its best-known relations. It is so well known that a description would be redundant. A specimen fresh from the pounding sea is a handsome creature, far removed from the glassy-eyed corpses displayed on the fishmonger's slab.

Primarily a cold-water fish, cod are widely distributed throughout the North Atlantic, the North Sea and up into the Arctic Circle. The largest concentrations around British coasts are situated in the North Atlantic, the North Sea, the Dover Straits and the Bristol Channel.

Cod reach sexual maturity at the age of four years. Spawning takes place in mid-water, well offshore, in the New Year. When one considers that a big female laden to bursting point with eggs, may carry up to ten million prospective twenty-pounders, it is disappointing to remember how the world's trawler fleets can make such a dent in the stocks.

Naturally there is a massively high mortality rate among both eggs and hatchlings, but many little critters do survive. The fry are rarely evident in their first year, but by the end of their second spring the shallow east coast beaches are transformed into giant nursery playgrounds for the tiny codlets.

Spawning completed, the adult fish shrug off their post-natal depression by making a bee-line for the shallow offshore banks and reaping the glittering harvest of sand-eels, sprats and other small fish that swarm around them. By early summer the larger cod, twelve-pounders and upwards, having gorged themselves back to physical fitness, assume a more solitary lifestyle. In twos and threes they begin to leave the shallow banks and disappear out into deeper water. Many of them seek sanctuary among the countless wrecks scattered beyond the horizon. However, some of the smaller fish hardly leave the shoreline all year round in the North of England and around the Scottish shores, feeding hard on the rich crustacean life among the kelp and boulders.

Above: Night tide on a top cod beach — typical action at Dungeness.

Left: Terry Carroll casts with his reel low down the butt, even though this increases leverage against him from big fish.

As for the little fellows, they enjoy a phenomenal growth rate encouraged by the wealth of food organisms found in the shallow waters off the British Isles. Within three years, for example, junior weighs about 4 lb. Two years later the same fish will have reached double-figure proportions. All fish under 7 lb are generally referred to as codling. Once they reach this size they have few natural enemies apart from man and sharks.

A big eater like a cod is rarely finicky about its food. It therefore consumes an incredible variety of marine life – anything, in fact, that it can swallow and manage to keep down. Offshore fish feed primarily on herrings, sprats, sand-eels, pouting and so on, while those inshore become pre-occupied with crabs, shellfish, and any small fish they can find – pouting, whiting, sprats and so on. The stomach of a freshly-beached ten-pounder is likely to reveal a close-packed assortment of molluscs, small fish and crustaceans, together with a host of other grisly unidentifiables, including assorted scrap plastic and metal.

Not surprisingly then, the British shore-caught record stands at $44\frac{1}{2}$ lb, taken from South Wales in 1966. Wreck fishermen regularly take forty-pounders and if the commercial fleet wasn't so efficient, a 75-lb cod would not be beyond the realms of probability.

Every October, stimulated by the gradual drop in sea temperature, and possibly by developing gonads, a massive inshore invasion begins. First billions of whiting joined by a phalanx of codling, spearhead a move into casting range. By early November they are joined by a lesser number of large specimens, some up to 30 lb. The shoreline comes alive. Beaches which a few weeks earlier were host only to immature pouting and the occasional bass suddenly become of great interest to the shore angler, with the night skies illuminated by thousands of Tilley lamps. For the shore angler, Christmas has arrived two months early.

In some areas, this exciting period lasts only a few brief weeks, in others, many months. In January, most of the bigger specimens swim beyond casting range, inspired by the need to reproduce. Thus the cycle repeats itself. The immature fish linger on, however, depending on suitable climatic conditions, until around Easter time. They may stay longer along the East Anglian shoreline, while further north in Yorkshire, Scotland and similar areas, the season peaks at Easter with fish present all year.

For reasons best known to cod themselves, certain areas of coastline are favoured by the fish to the detriment of others. Identifying these hot-spots presents no problems because they return to the same haunts year after year – although in recent years some areas are experiencing a cod recession.

Cod beaches vary tremendously from steep-to-shingle platforms like those in Kent and along the Chesil Beach, and Orfordness, to the shallow shoreline of East Anglia and similar flatlands to the North, and on up to the rocky stations of Yorkshire and Scotland. If there are any common denominators that characterize cod country, they are fast tides and abundant natural food.

Tackle
Shore fishing for cod requires a positive no-nonsense approach and tackle to match. At many venues, the ability to present an appealing bait at long range is all important. Therefore there is no substitute for efficient and technically superior equipment. Fortunately, the high initial cost of such tackle can be offset, over a successful season, by a wall-to-wall carpet of fillets in the freezer.

Tackle has already been discussed in an earlier chapter, but briefly a good cod rod must be powerful enough to project a 6-oz weight complete with bait to distances of 150 yd if required. It must have sufficient tip flexibility to receive bites from that distance and be pokey enough to deal effectively with a large, powerful fish in heavy seas. Sensitivity must be sacrificed when removing cod from their natural habitat and a potent weapon is required to overcome both fish and environment.

On the subject of reels, the majority of competent shore casters choose from the excellent Ambassadeur range of multipliers. Personal preference and location of the venue dictate whether a 6500C, 7000, 8000 or 9000 is suitable. I use them myself and consider that their reliability, durability and performance justify the initial outlay.

Monofilament nylon is both durable and reasonably cheap. Again, it is worth the extra cost to purchase top quality line, because the investment is repaid in terms of longevity and reliability. However, whether exposing your line to the tender mercy of barnacle-covered rocks, or having this slender lifeline continually covered by tons of shifting shingle, you can appreciate just how quickly line deteriorates.

Lines must be checked after each outing for signs of abrasion, dryness and weakness. At the first indication of fatigue the offending length must be stripped from the reel and, if necessary, a completely new line wound on. This might seem extravagant, but when compared to the costs of bait, petrol and other items, it works out very cheap. Many are the punters who have travelled 150 miles to a first-class cod beach and waited two hours for the first fish, only to lose it in the surf due to worn line. Be warned. It is pitiful to see a grown man repeatedly banging his skull against the frozen shingle and crying real tears.

As a brief guide, 15–20 lb monofil will suffice on most sand and shingle beaches, but once over rock 30–40-lb line may be necessary just to have a fighting chance against the terrain. Some Yorkshire anglers go as high as 70-lb test.

To combat the tremendous strain imposed by long-distance casting, a shock leader is required. Because cod eagerly scoff any tempting mouthful, the terminal rig is required to anchor the bait down where they can find it. When complete with bait, it must be sufficiently streamlined to permit long casting and allow the bait to stay firmly in one spot. On many occasions, the sea will be full of loose weed and simplicity of tackle helps keep the angler's sanity on an even keel. It is for these reasons that the ubiquitous paternoster comes up trumps.

Once baited, the hook length is held close to the main leader by means of a bait clip. These can be made easily at home. When codding with lugworm, it is wise to fix a coarse angler's leger stop a few inches away from the hook to prevent the worms sliding up the trace. If this happens, you get superb bites but no contact.

In early autumn, when the sea is swarming with whiting, pouting, dabs and small codling a two- or three-hook paternoster will produce a good mixed bag. Tie the snoods as suggested by Alan Yates in his chapter on match fishing. Because the hooks are smaller than those used when the bigger fish are about, and the baits correspondingly smaller, bait clips aren't required. When the big mommas hit the shoreline, a single hook paternoster will produce the goods. When they are about, it is much wiser to load one hook with plenty of bait than to divide it between three smaller hooks.

Early in the season, Mustad Aberdeens and Break-away Spearpoints will suffice for the general mixed fishing. Both makes are lethal and ensure that any mischievous codling attempting to play kiss-chase with the bait gets its just deserts. By November, when the plump ladies are around, use a medium-gauge 4/0 or 5/0 carefully sharpened to give it a better chance of snagging into that fleshy mineshaft of a mouth. Don't be shy of using a decent size hook. Take one look into the maw of a twenty-pounder and you might reflect that a 20-lb anchor might stand a better chance of touching the sides. Patterns to use are the Sundridge Specimen Longshank, the Mustad O'Shaughnessy or the Mustad 79510. All are fairly fine in the wire, capable of being sharpened to a lethal point and, provided elementary care is exercised, powerful enough to cope with large fish.

Every winter fortunate souls land big fish on small hooks. I prefer to make my own luck and use the most sensible size that prevailing conditions require. When big fish are around avoid the Mustad Aberdeen. This hook is sufficiently springy to open out and release a fish in the surf – or even on the take. If, while using this pattern, you get superb bites as big fish clobber the bait, then nothing, it is because the fish hooks itself then tears itself free on the take. Use a forged hook and this won't happen.

Another ace up the sleeve of the successful shore cod fisherman is the two-hook tandem live-bait rig. Sometimes conventional baits just don't score either because they aren't large enough or because the big specimens become preoccupied with chomping pouting and whiting. Double-figure cod are lazy fish and require a lot of food. Faced with the prospect of spending hours foraging for lugworm or alternatively eating two small whiting, they invariably plump for the latter.

The rig is made by tying a length of 30-lb line to the bottom of the shank of a well-honed 5/0 with a spade-end knot. A size 1–1/0 is fixed 3–4 in away from this.

It is very frustrating, after unhooking your ump-teenth whiting, when you know the big cod are out there. That's the time to swap over to this rig. Bait the small hook with a whiting delicacy like frozen sand-eel, herring or mackerel strip and, of course, blow lug. Leave the large hook bare. Cast far out and wait for the persistent rattling of the rod tip that proclaims a well-hooked bait fish. Now sit back and wait for the action. This may take seconds, maybe hours.

Cod locate their prey by several methods, as outlined in Chapter 1, and can sense a small fish in trouble from a considerable distance. Believe me, a whiting or pouting transfixed to a live-bait rig in the heart of cod country is in deep trouble. If ever you reel in a whiting – possibly after a superb bite and a heavy tussle with a big fish – and find it almost completely de-scaled, with gashes along each side and the skin shredded between the fin rays, then you will realize what those boney plates are for at the entrance to the gullet. Sometimes an angler is

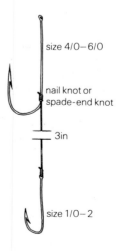

size 4/0–6/0

nail knot or
spade-end knot

3in

size 1/0–2

2-hook livebait rig

lucky and the whiting hasn't swallowed the hook. If it does, the cod will let go a few yards out. That is why the two-hook rig is essential.

The cod looms up, swallows the tethered baitfish and gets hooked in the process by the large upper hook. The angler's rod also ends up in the sea if left unattended. So it may be wise to bang a peg into the shingle behind the rods and, using string and dog-lead clips to the reel cross-bars, ensure that £100 plus of rod and reel isn't dragged out to sea.

An irritating problem when using long, juicy worm baits threaded up the trace is that cod will sometimes attack from the wrong end and miss the hook. This problem is overcome by using a two-hook tandem rig with a pair of 3/0 or 4/0 hooks 4 in apart. Try this rig on nights when you are getting plenty of bites but no fish. It will greatly improve your chances.

Because the best cod fishing so often takes place at night, save yourself needless fumbling in the dark by spending a couple of evenings preparing terminal rigs, complete with leader, bait clip and so on. Pack each individually in a small polythene bag. Cod tend to move along the shore in shoals and if you hook one you are very likely to catch another within ten minutes. On occasions I have caught two fish while a hapless companion has been furiously preparing a fresh trace after a crack-off. Always aim to have one bait in the water at all times. When you catch a fish, quickly re-bait and re-cast. On those rare nights when the score has mounted to, say, 50 lb of fish on the beach with the best part of the tide still to come, it pays to lay out snoods with a loop at one end and a hook at the other so that they can be baited up ready in-between bites. On these magic evenings bites come as soon as the tackle settles on the bottom, so the faster your turn-around, the more fish you will land. Clomp the fish on the head, cut off the trace and loop on another. The top cod anglers who make hundredweight-plus catches don't do so by fumbling about, tugging at bird's-nests, and taking ages to unhook fish and re-bait.

The current trend of employing a matched pair of outfits is not, as some people think, a status symbol.

Above: *Big cod demand generous helpings of bait.*

Right: *Casting skill is a basic essential for the cod fisherman.*

Instead it is merely another method of improving the catch rate. This occurs in two ways. Firstly, bite detection is improved by virtue of the fact that both rods should be behaving in a similar manner. It becomes obvious when something is occurring at the business end. This is especially important when very big fish hit live baits. They sometimes just sit there and the line slackens off very slowly. So while one is still bowed to the tide, the other slowly unfurls. Secondly, codding tends to be made up of long periods of inactivity interspersed with flurries of action. When the cod do come along the beach there is no harm in having two separate baits lying provocatively in their path. Moreover, two baits allow you to cover both close-in and far-out feeding zones. The use of two rods rarely means twice as many fish, but over a season your catches will improve considerably. They also permit the angler to fish a conventional worm or mollusc bait on one rod and a live-bait rig on the second. This is a useful tactic when the fish can't make up their mind, or when a few large fish are interspersed among plenty of middle-weights.

Let us assume you have selected the finest tackle hire-purchase can buy, and have spent the entire summer on a local field honing your casting skills to tournament standard. You have learnt how to extricate black lugworms from their deep-delved burrows (or have cultivated a close relationship with someone who can). Your uncle in Devon has agreed to remit a bucketful of peelers each week throughout the winter. Next stop is the beach.

A check on the coastal reports in the angling press soon reveals where all the cod are being caught. It is far better to travel sixty miles to an accepted hot spot than waste an evening feeding the pouting on a marine desert close to home.

Steep shingle beaches

The desolate steep-to shingle platforms such as Dungeness in Kent, Orfordness in Suffolk and Chesil Beach in Dorset are, to my mind, the archetypal cod beaches. Cod are lured here each winter by the fast tides and rich feeding. Each season many big fish – some over 30 lb – are taken.

Anyone faced with the prospect of fishing such a place for the first time is instantly struck by both the vastness and the lack of obvious clues as to the location of the fish. In reality, there is no need to worry. In season, weather permitting, the fish are always nearabouts. When they are running, the positions within easy walking distance from the car parks soon become crowded. Men carrying a mountain of tackle, lamps, food, shelters and bait are physically unable to walk far. It is wiser to streamline gear and walk for an extra twenty minutes to secure an isolated spot where nobody can cast over your line and where a big cod that is homing in on your bait won't tactlessly pause to scoop up an hors d'oeuvre offered by someone nearby.

I fish Dungeness often. One night, unbeknown to me, I fished half a mile away from an acquaintance. During a conversation later we realized this coincidence and swapped notes. He had caught a dab and I had caught five beautiful cod weighing nearly 50 lb. Apparently it had been a good dab, though! He was fishing the accepted hot-spot, The Point. The trouble is that on many of these beaches the cod don't realize where the hot-spots are.

Long casting with fresh black lug is a deadly combination for cod from such beaches. When a winter's gale has been raging from the south-west for a few days and suddenly the barometer rises with the wind turning to the north-east and then dropping, ideal conditions occur. Drop your knitting and jump into the car as cod are almost guaranteed. Shellfish, lugworm and every conceivable marine knick-knack will have been wrenched from the sea-bed and will be washing ashore. The cod go crazy, and so do some anglers, arriving bleary-eyed at dawn's first light, falling out of their cars, impatiently pulling on waterproofs over their pyjamas and setting out across the shingle to where the cod are queuing to snatch their baits.

When these excellent fishing conditions prevail it matters not one jot whether you fish the day or night tides. The sea is a murky brown colour and the fish are just too pre-occupied with food to care. Upon arrival at the chosen mark, first jamb a monopod rod rest into the shingle as a symbol of your territorial rights. Remember to keep the rest of your gear above the high water mark, away from the ever-present huge storm swell cascading up the beach.

The tide has just begun to flood so there is no hurry. Tackle up and clip on a 6-oz grapnel weight – the breakaway design isn't man enough for these conditions, the water being too deep and powerful. Limber up with a few practice casts. Some people rush to the water's edge and attempt an almighty heave, which is almost certainly followed by a sharp crack as the reel backlashes and the line parts. It is far better to spend a few minutes warming up with progressively longer casts. Besides, dry line is very prone to tangling. Once confidence has built up, put some real power into those casts.

Now bait the hook with two glistening black lug and maybe a razorfish washed up at your feet – shellfish cocktails are murderously effective after storms. Before casting, walk 30–60 yd up-tide from your rest, depending on the strength of tide, and then let fly. Once the tackle hits water, thumb the spool to a halt, then let the tide take enough slack line to form a belly as you walk back to your peg. After a few minutes it will tighten up and half a dozen turns of the handle will pull the rod tip hard over to the line running straight out in front of you. When a strong sea is running with a big tide – and maybe wind behind both – merely casting out and tightening the line immediately will not allow the essential bow to form up-tide from your stance, so the grip-wires won't have a chance to bite into the sea-bed. This is why many anglers can't hold bottom.

Bites from small fish are signified by a gentle nodded greeting. Pouting and whiting rattle at the rod-tip. Big fish tap once or twice, then accelerate away. This can be a frightening awakening as the complete tip section of the rod keels over as if the line has been hit by a low-flying condor. The rod rest, unless well dug in, is likely to collapse on to the shingle and the rod will accelerate into the sea, providing the unlucky owner with a sad tale to tell later in the pub. Pay attention.

Other times the cod will charge the bait and the tip will spring straight as the fish pulls the wires clear of the sea-bed and carries on shorewards. Sometimes it is wise to strike these bites. Most often the jolt of the fish coming up hard against the anchored weight will snub the hook home. Only strike once, either by running back up the beach or by winding down before belting the hook home. Repeated savage striking will tear a hole in the fish's mouth. Quite often hooks will just drop out once the fish is landed.

Slowly pump the fish ashore, using the waves. Take your time and don't panic. Once the cod is in the surf, back off the reel clutch a little because if a swell takes it at this stage the hook could tear free or the line snap. They may not fight, but that gaping mouth is an efficient sea anchor. Medium-sized fish sometimes slip into overdrive and bore away down-tide at this stage. Many anglers panic then and clamp down on the reel with obvious results. Have patience. Walk down the beach with a fish caught in the surf, following it down the tide. Either beach the fish with a surging wave or wait for one to roll it ashore. Keep that rod-tip up to absorb excess pressure. It helps to have a companion to run in and collect the fish or, if conditions are dangerous, just kick it up the beach with a well-aimed boot. If a fish does break free and is seen floating tantalizingly behind the surf, leave it there. Big seas on steep-to beaches are dangerous and no fish is worth drowning for.

Shallow-water beaches

The cod caught along these beaches are generally of a lower average size, but present in larger numbers. Double-figure fish are rarer. Aim to place the bait into the slightly deeper water in front of or behind the sandbanks that characterize these beaches because the fish invariably feed along the troughs. Look also for fish-attracting gullies and cross-tide obstructions behind which fish may shelter. Tackle and techniques are similar to those used for deep-water codding except that 5-oz breakaway leads are normally adequate with reel lines of 12–15 lb.

It is not accidental that 90 per cent of the country's top tournament casters come from the east coast. They are well aware that distance means fish. In this shallow water, especially during daylight, the fish stay well out and casts over 140 yd may be required just to reach them. Not everybody can belt a sinker these super distances and luckily the cod move closer at night.

Pier fishing

Many cod anglers shy away from piers, preferring to fish the less crowded beaches. Piers are generally associated with beginners. However, they provide excellent sport, especially when rough weather wipes out the beach. Tackle and tactics remain the same as before, but take along a large drop-net and learn how to control it in fast tides and high winds by putting a heavy weight into the mesh bag. Often pier club officials refuse the use of their drop-net, so take your own. Drop-netting is a skill so the netsman whose dexterity clinches your success should be rewarded with a pint.

Every pier seems to have its special cod corners and these positions are eagerly contested. I prefer to avoid such potential war zones and fish the pier stem, casting up-tide. Don't employ potentially lethal casting styles. Distance is unimportant. A 90-yd lob is usually adequate.

Rods should never be left unattended. When a big tide is running a cod merely has to exert a few pounds of extra pressure to catapult your outfit over the side. So tie an unattended rod to the pier rail with a rod bag.

By increasing the length of your shock leader to 15 yd you can lift codling up to 5 lb slowly by hand up the side of the pier.

Support your local piers. You may be surprised at the results.

Rock fishing, Yorkshire style

The red-brown rock cod which seek their food among the barnacle-encrusted boulders and kelp tangles of the Yorkshire coast present the angler with the formidable problem of mastering the environment rather than the fish. The traditional method is to employ a stout glass rod with a large Scarborough centre-pin winch, loaded with 55–70-lb line. The terminal rig is a simple paternoster with a 4-ft lead link and 1-ft hook link, both of weaker line, coming off a large swivel. Expendable weights of about 6 oz are used. Even with tackle of this calibre more than half the fish hooked never emerge from the kelp.

Many anglers now prefer to travel to less daunting venues where lighter, more enjoyable tackle can be used, even though the cod are present all year round along this inhospitable coast-line.

Peeler crab and lugworm/mussel cocktails prove effective. Invest in a good pair of studded boots – not waders. Fish with a companion. Always pay attention to both tidal and weather conditions – the sea is neither kind nor cruel, merely indifferent. The North Sea in particular has a notorious reputation for claiming people's lives.

When rock fishing in other areas, sinkers can be lost thus: form the end of the leader into a loop and tie a few inches of 6-lb line from the loop to the eye of the lead or whatever. Take a panel pin $1\frac{1}{2}$ in long and impale on it a wee piece of expanded polystyrene. Poke the leader loop through the sinker eye, insert the pin and cast. When the tackle hits the sea-bed, the pin will float free and allow the angler to retain tension to his weight through very light line.

Pouting

This small, pop-eyed plague of British coastal waters is invariably caught by anglers legering on sand or amongst rocks for more worthwhile species. Pouting ravenously attack any bait but show a slight preference for blow lug, squid, fish strips and peeler crab. A good shore-caught specimen weighs $2\frac{1}{2}$ lb but very few over $1\frac{1}{2}$ lb are caught inshore, because the grand-daddies live out to sea around wrecks and reefs.

They are of little culinary value as their gastric juices quickly spoil the flesh after death. Anyone nurturing a compulsive desire to eat pout should therefore gut the fish promptly after capture.

Give them their due, though; pouting do give a tremendous rod-rattling bite, out of all proportion to their size. Unfortunately, once hooked they assume the fighting potential of a short length of tissue twirling in the tide.

September and October brings a glut of them inshore and many evening beach competitions are won with large bags of these persistent nocturnal feeders. The larger ones are caught all too often by bass anglers legering peeler crab over rocks. These rock pouting are deep bronze in colour, and are quite fierce-looking beasts.

It can be a traumatic experience for a dedicated bassman, having struck a terrific rod-shuddering bite, to witness a 2-lb pouting spiralling apologetically through the water towards him.

Whiting

This species enjoys a wide distribution around our coasts – over sandy, shell-grit, and muddy inshore marks. Those huge spring tides that coincide with the autumn equinox encourage the first shoals to head inshore in pursuit of small fish, crabs, shrimps and so on. These fish are generally larger than the tiddlers that linger close to the beach all through the year.

This species is primarily a nocturnal feeder. Best sport can be enjoyed on beautiful flat-calm starry nights when there is just a hint of frost in the air. By using two- or three-hook paternosters with long-shanked fine-wire hooks (2–2/0), large bags can be taken from pier heads, shelving shores and harbour breakwaters. The premier bait is strips of mackerel or herring (as fresh as possible) but blow lug, squid strips and frozen sand eels also do the trick.

Most shore-caught fish average less than 1 lb. A specimen weighs $2\frac{1}{2}$ lb. They provide consistent sport provided the tackle is not hopelessly heavy. If ultra-light tackle is used you may acquire a new respect for this plucky little fighter. It is equipped with small, outward-pointing, needle-sharp teeth. Since it has a tendency to swallow the hook, a good pair of artery forceps or long-nosed pliars is needed. It tastes good provided it is eaten very fresh and is never deep-frozen, as this ruins the subtle flavour, making the flesh dry and unpleasant. Just keep a few of the better fish, returning the rest.

Haddock

The haddock is a silver-grey member of the cod family, easily identified by its outsize eyes and the prominent St Peter's thumbprint next to the caudal fins. A handsome, spirited fighter, and prized as a table fish, its range is sadly restricted (for the shore fisherman) to the upper North and Irish seas, Scotland and Ireland.

Shore-caught specimens are usually babies of a couple of pounds. The senior citizens prefer deep water – hence the big eyes. Generally speaking, it is the angler who is prepared to travel to the sea lochs of Scotland and Ireland who will capture the odd haddie amongst the resident shoals of codling and billet. It prefers sandy and muddy sheltered venues and readily accepts lugworm, mussel, clam, worm and crab baits, showing preference only for soft foods.

Paternoster tackle suffices. Never try to horse a haddock or strike too fiercely. This species has a soft mouth.

Conclusion

All of these species are mainly winter fish. Through perseverance and learning from mistakes, you will

Three good cod are the prize for a successful night's fishing.

experience a wealth of fine sport. Big cod will hit the bait and your heart will pound with excitement as you struggle to lift them off the beach – long, broad-shouldered specimens with flanks of speckled gold. Arranged around the Tilley, they advertise your good fortune. Admire them and count your blessings for you have triumphed over the sea, maybe with a coveted twenty-pounder. I have yet to hook one from the beach. But it will come – maybe this winter, maybe next, and the alarm clock won't spoil the magic – it will be real.

7
Major predators

At first glance, it may seem odd to group together tope, rays, the dogfish tribe and conger eels. The list could also include angler fish and monkfish, but these are pretty rare from the shore. These species are aggregated because they share similar methods of feeding.

With the exception of that most cunning of seducers, the angler fish, which twitches its lure (on a rod formed from a highly-developed dorsal spine) in order to entice small fish close to its man-trap jaws, the species considered here are generally caught from the shore on pieces of fish anchored to the sea-bed. They will, of course, attack live fish and will occasionally take live baits should they be presented properly, in the manner advocated for cod.

Tope

Under the right circumstances, tope are undoubtedly the most glamorous and exciting fish for the shore angler to latch into. Hook one in very shallow water and it will streak away at a sizzling pace, with line pouring from the reel, sometimes to the bitter end. This is a deliciously alarming moment for the angler as he isn't sure whether to watch the reel with mounting anxiety or to gaze wonderingly as the fish leaps clear of the water in great greyhounding jumps. In deeper water the fight is less spectacular, the tope's reaction to being hooked is soggy by comparison. This species is the blood brother of the equally sleek and graceful blue shark.

Sadly, good shore tope fishing is less widespread than it used to be when a handful of diehards discovered the when, where and how-to and practised their art while others with less spirit in their souls concentrated on lesser game. This species is thinner on the sea-bed than of yore. Marks have changed and the pressures of modern life — and the costs — frequently preclude much chance of research.

Tope are found all round the British Isles, though the best shore fishing is undoubtedly along the Western fringe, with south-west Ireland offering excellent opportunities. Most consistent sport is to be had from male fish — the ones with claspers amid-ships — that grow to around 30 lb, travel in packs on occasions, and fight like demons. Their ladyfolk are more sedate, though grow to a better size. Tope to 60 lb are caught each year around our coastline. They are sharks, of course, and much of the information about catching them can be applied by the adventurer who fishes for sharks from tropical shores, though it needs to be up-graded where large hammerheads and similar battlers abound.

Tope are great wanderers. Tagged fish have turned up virtually all over the North Atlantic. They arrive off British coasts in April and depart in November. The best time to fish is from May to October, depending on the weather and local movements. Sometimes shore tope can be taken during a warm spell in April. When mackerel are dense offshore, inshore toping suffers. During the early summer months, females visit favoured bays and estuaries to deposit their young, tope being viviparous.

This species has a bulbous snout that is packed with sensory cells. Not only can tope pick up the scent of a mackerel strip from afar, but they also have the requisite eyesight to snatch at small fish and spinners being retrieved by anglers intent on lesser game. They are happy to hunt for flatfish and similar species over open, sandy ground and, if pickings there are sparse, to chase wrasse, bream, pollack, bass, pouting and so on around reefs. However, most anglers prefer to fish for them over clean bottoms. Such locations are to be found around surf beaches during calm spells, deep channels around headlands and estuaries, and from select rock ledges. Wherever they are found, tope keep to fairly rigid timetables, arriving and departing at about the same stages of the tide.

Tope move fast while hunting, their keen eyesight, scent organs and lateral line system enabling them to form a picture of a bay without pedantic snuffling into every corner. Groundbait pays enormous dividends. A suitable mixture can be made from minced fish mixed with pilchard oil, dried blood, dry sand and bran, hurled out in paper or polythene bags with the ends folded over, not sealed tight. You can use a throwing stick for this purpose. It should be introduced to the water on a regular basis so that there is always at least one bag oozing scent all the time. Baits, which should be suitably bloody, should be changed frequently. But don't let time pass without a bait in the water – that is when the fish may pass through. So have a spare trace baited and ready to go.

Tackle need be no more powerful than is necessary to hurl a bait out there. If you can achieve this objective with a bass rod casting 2–3-oz sinkers, then the ensuing battle will be great fun. Plenty of line is needed, at least 250 yd in most places and maybe 400 yd on very shallow beaches. Load up an Ambassadeur 7000 or 9000 with 0.40-mm line and that will be ample even for a record-buster.

At the business end a special running paternoster is employed. A 4/0–6/0 hook, honed to a needle-sharp point, is crimped to one end of 2 ft of braided trace wire. I use 200-lb wire only because mine is so supple. Thickish wire doesn't deter tope, and it takes the crimps better than fine wire, which tope have been known to bite through. At the other end is a reasonably large swivel. The other end of the swivel is knotted to a rubbing leader of around 80-lb test. This not only takes the shock of the cast, but also the rubbing of the rough skin of a hooked tope which would otherwise cut the line. Immediately above this swivel should be slid a large bead to prevent a split-ring jambing over the swivel. This ring needs to be large enough to slide over the leader-knot unchecked when a fish makes off with the bait. About 3 ft of standard leader line connect this ring to a sinker, above which a bait clip will facilitate casting. This clip should be larger than usual to prevent the bulky bait from flying free in mid-cast.

When a tope takes, it sets the reel screeching. No! Don't panic! With the reel in free spool and the check on, a bite is signified by a couple of bobs at the rod tip before it bends down as the fish sets off on a ridiculously unnecessary sprint. Then the check screeches. Too many anglers grab their rod at this point and hang on, both thumbs hard on the spool, until the line snaps; a classic case of panic, with all logic and sense abandoned for a primitive, terrified response.

What should happen is this. Let the fish take line – as much as it wants – without feeling any drag at all. It will eventually slow down, turn the bait and start gulping it back as it moves off again more slowly. Wind down hard and run backwards, bumping the hook home as you go. Keep the drag at a safe setting, applying additional pressure with a thumb, for when a fish takes

off in panic, too tight a drag will pop the line. Normally the fish will run up and down the shoreline, not out to sea. If it is held too hard it will try to roll up the leader and may touch the line with its rough body.

Play the fish out, get the leader back onto the reel and walk the fish out through the surf and tail it. Tope tails offer a superb grip. There is absolutely no reason why any tope should be killed. They are marvellous fish, great sports and highly-tuned hunters. A dead tope testifies to only one thing: that the angler has an ego so swollen that it overshadows all concepts of fairness, good taste and conservation. Tope are virtually inedible. Don't murder the poor fish for providing you with good fun. Take a few pictures, then release them.

I advise that you hold them by the tail and dorsal or pectoral fin to prevent rupture of internal organs. Slosh the head back and forth in the water so as to pass water over the gills of an exhausted fish to revive it. Rock anglers should take an efficient pair of snips rather than a gaff with them. Make the wire trace into a loop, passed once through the eye of the hook and held closed right there with a few turns of thread. To release the fish, snip through one side and the fish will be released as the wire slides out through the eye of the hook.

The manhandling of tope up onto rocks and subsequent wrestling with hooks are likely to cause fatal internal damage. The survival rate is higher if the fish is allowed to get rid of the hook in its own time. Where possible, don't land the tope but grip the hook with pliers. The tope will thrash about and snap itself free. If necessary kneel astride the fish, hold open its mouth with a leather industrial glove and, if the hook is hard to remove, make a neat incision with a very sharp knife along the barb. It is advisable to use carbon steel hooks which will rust away without harming the fish.

Many anglers don't allow the fish to run when it takes the bait. They hit it there and then. This can result in fewer gut-hooked fish if they are feeding wolfishly, but some will be missed. If they are gulping baits with excessive enthusiasm, mount a whole fish hooked through the root of the tail. Thus more will be lip-hooked. This voracious feeding is frequent where tope are hunting in packs and competition for food is high. Lone fish can be remarkably shy. When this happens, the bait comes back with razor-like slashes from the tope's teeth along each side. Then is the time to use finer wire, smaller hooks and less bait. Even so, some may be lost or missed.

Tope baits should be as fresh and bloody as possible. Mackerel, herring and other oily fish are ideal. Squid also works, as do chunks of silver eel and small mullet – conservation permitting. Tope will eat soft crab, and they'll occcasionally take baits intended for lesser fry. Greater sand eels catch well in some places, and frozen

Above: Nothing to get nervous about. Tope tails provide a firm grip which prevents the fish from biting your legs.

Left: A mouthful of razors – the teeth of tope, and all sharks, are constantly being replaced.

trout are increasing in popularity. Whatever bait you use, it must be well mounted and changed as soon as the scent washes out.

A useful trick where mackerel strip is used is to thread the strip onto the hook so that its eye is just inside one end, thus allowing the rest to wave about unimpeded. A sliver of matchstick poked through the eye will support the bait and prevent it sliding down into an unappetizing bundle that chokes the hook. This trick is superior to those awful baitholder hooks with little slices up the shank, and less fiddly than elastic thread.

A formula for weighing tope with a tape-measure goes thus. Measure the girth in inches, then square it. Multiply this total by the length and divide the sum by 800. Therefore a tope with a girth of 25 in, and 54 in long will work out at $25 \times 25 = 625 \times 54 = 33750 \div 800 = 42.19\,lb$ — easy.

Finally, tope dislike cold weather and unsettled conditions. They revel in hot, bright days and warm nights with calm seas. They move out to moderately deep water during cold spells and storms — beyond shore fishing range.

Dogfish

Among this gang of little sharks are the lesser-spotted dogfish, the greater-spotted dog (also called bull huss), the black-mouthed dogfish (a deep-water species from the north), the spurdog, and the two smooth-hounds. Some anglers have difficulty differentiating between the species. The black-mouthed species has a black mouth. The lesser-spotted dog has little spots and, sometimes, a pouting-like banded appearance. The greater-spotted dog has more blotchy spots and its nasal flaps are separate while those of the lesser-spotted are joined. Big bull huss are reckoned by some to be worth catching. Small ones are insigificant enough to make it of little importance whether or not you can tell them apart from lesser-spotteds.

The starry smooth-hound has light-coloured spots along its upper half and a fairly smooth skin while the other one has a rough skin and no spots. Their teeth are flat grinders like those of most rays. This is where they differ from tope, which have fearful dentition. Spurdogs have disconcerting green eyes and wickedly sharp spurs ahead of each dorsal fin.

This motley collection arouses mixed emotions in the angling world. Spurdogs don't fight but taste good (as huss or rock salmon), greater- and lesser-spotted dogs don't fight but taste fair – they try to climb up the line backwards rather than run away. The smooth-hounds are virtually inedible, although they are sold commercially as huss, but even when small they fight with a

turn of speed and manoeuvrability that frequently dumbfound the uninitiated, who approach them as 'just another dogfish'.

The misfortune of the lesser-spotted doggie is that it is such a highly-tuned hunter, with a snout packed with sensory organs of the most refined type, that it tends to get to a bait before any more interesting species. It prefers fairly clean ground, where it can sometimes be caught by the sackful on baits fished hard on the bottom. It is sad that such a highly-tuned fish should be despised for its acute efficiency at hunting, but there it is.

Lesser-spotteds eat just about anything. They'll even attack mackerel live-baits if hungry enough. It seems that no bait is too large. The trouble is that when one has engulfed a tope-size offering, it rarely gives much indication of its presence and will sit there, deterring a lately-arrived tope from attacking the bait, which still protrudes from its gaping jaws. The major concern of many anglers is how to avoid these pests. Both they and bull huss have a habit of wrapping their tails around the wrist of the hand that holds them for unhooking. Their rough hides can leave the human skin very sore, so take precautions.

Bull huss lost my affection when I learned of their tendency to throw up all over my trousers while trying to rescue the hook from their thuggish face. They reach a good size, and prefer rocky ground. Any standard bottom tackle will catch them, with fish baits being most effective. They are quite catholic in their tastes. A 40-lb nylon trace defeats the teeth of large specimens. Bull huss annoy some people by coming to the surface, apparently well hooked, then dropping the bait. Fear not. Cast out a fresh, new bait and the same fish is likely to come back. Night fishing produces best results. Their stronghold is along the western edges of the British Isles where deepish water comes close to rocky ground, piers and so on. Large specimens struggle a bit. They taste good if you can stomach the brutal and messy process of skinning them. Small specimens of both these species are regarded as a delicacy by large skate – who don't skin them first.

Spurdogs are sometimes caught from rocky western and Scottish beaches, from some surf beaches, and from deep-water shores like Chesil beach. Most of the time they display a calm disregard to being hooked, refusing to offer even token resistance to being dragged ashore. But they grow to a fair size, with a ten-pounder possible from the beach. They, too, eat just about anything. Some fun could be had if the vast shoals that sweep up the coasts of the British Isles in April and May were to come closer to the shore, but while catches are measured in hundredweights from boats, odd individuals are the lot of the shore angler. Perhaps this is a good thing as spurdog spines can inflict an ugly wound on the unwary, so be careful.

Fish legered baits on the sea-bed for best results. A 40-lb nylon hook link defeats their teeth. Apart from their eating qualities, there's not much good to be said for them.

The smooth-hounds, however, are a different kettle of dogfish. Indeed, it is unfortunate that they are not found in greater numbers. These two species are very fond of crustaceans, which may explain why they're uncommon outside estuarine waters like the Thames, the Solent and the Bristol Channel. Where they can be caught from the shore they offer great sport. Boat anglers using light tackle obtain fast fights even from small fish.

For a species that spends its normal day chugging about the sea-bed in search of crabs, whelks and similar fare, these species have an amazing turn of speed and frequently leap when hooked. This makes them the odd-balls of the dogfish camp.

The wise angler arms himself with the lightest outfit possible, terminating in a standard running leger or whatever he fancies, and baits with peeler crab for preference, baby squid, squid strip or ragworm. A rubbing leader is advised – 40-lb nylon – when using light line for hounds.

High summer is their season, going into autumn when the bigger fish show up. Runs of these species vary in strength from year to year, but as little is known about their biology and seasonal movements, no explanation can be offered for this phenomenon. Both prefer the warm, settled conditions that favour tope fishing.

While the greater- and lesser-spotted dogs lay eggs in 'mermaids' purses' – an attribute shared by rays – the spurdog, tope and smooth-hounds are viviparous. Curiously, while baby tope often reach plague proportions in some sheltered areas, baby spurdogs and smooth-hounds are rarely caught in such quantities, if at all. While the rough-skinned variety of hound is truly viviparous, the starry version is ovoviviparous.

Rays

The advent of power trawling was bad news for the ray tribe. Being somewhat sedentary beasts, their main centres of population were swiftly ransacked and their numbers drastically thinned. Rays are slow-growing fish and not prolific spawners, and mature late – male thornbacks at seven years, females at nine–ten years – so today they are less easy to find than in the past. Only the thornback (also called roker) and small-eyed (also called painted) rays are caught in any numbers from our shores. Occasional spotted (also called homelyn), undulate, blonde and cuckoo rays are taken from time to

time. As this book is largely concerned with how to catch fish – and all the above respond to similar tactics – the keen student is advised to check out the distinguishing marks of each species in one of the many books devoted to fish identification.

Likewise the skates, which differ from rays in that a line imagined between wing tip and snout does not cut through the leading edge of a wing. 100 lb-plus common skate used to be taken from western piers and rocks, but today such captures are exceedingly infrequent and are likely to come only to the dedicated specialist who searches deep water with very strong tackle (up-rated conger gear), outsize baits and patience.

The ray's disc is formed from the evolution of the fish's pectoral fins – they have taken over the whole body. With this it flaps silt over its back for camouflage as it lies on the sea-bed. Close to each eye is a spiracle through which it breathes.

Rays vary widely in colour according to age, sex, and the type of sea-bed they call home. Males have claspers at the base of their tail, and a patch of small spines at the tip of each wing; males of some species have pointed teeth. However, ray dentition is designed mainly for crushing, so generally the teeth are flattened and slab-like.

Females lay eggs on hard rock surfaces. When the empty hulls are washed ashore after storms they are called 'mermaids' purses'. A female thornback can lay up to 150 eggs. Each species has its own shape of purse, and eggs are laid in March through to July. Often a group of rays is found to consist of one or two females with several attendant males. When fishing, it often happens that the female has first chew at a bait, with the males following after. While boat fishing, it is not uncommon to hook a female who has decided that the fresh herring lying on the sea-bed holds more appeal than the male with which she is copulating. But then lady rays are able to store male sperm for several months. They also travel in unisex shoals.

As with most species of fish, the first of the season's thornbacks are contacted by boat anglers. This is in February – sometimes earlier – especially when the fish have grouped together where herrings are spawning to prey on spent fish. While the boats have good sport in March with fish to 25 lb or so, the shore angler has to wait until late April when the first of the peeler crabs appear. Even so, this species is the first worthwhile game after the departure of the winter cod.

May through to July are the best months for shore rays, though odd ones – especially small-eyeds – are taken right through to November if the weather holds. The average shore thornback is 5–8 lb, or better where commercial pressure is light enough to allow a degree of longevity. Their maximum weight is 40 lb. In winter they move off to more equable temperatures offshore. No long migrations are made – rays swim slowly but with a graceful undulating movement. They are largely localized in distribution, and ray marks can be surprisingly small.

Preferred habitat for thornbacks is shallow depressions among sand, mud, gravel, shell grit and similar out of the current. They are more widely dispersed when there is little strength in the tide. Estuaries and sea lochs are favourite places, and sandy patches among reefs. They are also fond of the shallow gulleys that run along some sandy beaches.

Rays prefer a moderate depth of water. They appear to realize that they are not too agile, and they don't take the risk of being stranded by the tide through coming too close to the edge. Long casting is often vital for success. They dislike rough seas, moving in closest during periods of calm – and they often feed well in water clearing after a storm. Warm, settled conditions are best of all for rays. In areas of strong tide, best sport is to be had at high and low water slacks and when the new current is starting to move. In other places, a gentle current helps distribute the scent of a bait, thus improving results. Hot, bright conditions are not ideal for shore thornbacks but small-eyeds quite like such weather. Thornbacks bite best under cloudy skies or at dawn and dusk. A warm sultry night offers perfect conditions in most localities, with the fish moving close to shore.

Thornbacks tend to move down the tide. If after a succession of bites there comes a quiet spell, a move along the beach could put you back among the flock. However, today's pattern of shore ray fishing is of just the occasional fish – and quite a few blank trips.

A standard 5–6-oz rod is perfect for rays. Heavy leads carry big baits out to the ravening hordes more effectively than lighter sinkers. A bass rod is sufficiently potent to play most rays. However, the ability to place a bait well out from the shore is frequently the one factor that produces fish. Adequate end tackle is a running paternoster, with a casting leader and a 40-lb hook link to cope not only with the ray's crushing teeth but with sharp spines that frequently tangle and chafe the tackle. Rays often tail-tangle the leader and are brought ashore stern first. Offshore, attractors like spoons produce good results, even when legered, and rays frequently contain small fish – though these may have been picked up dead. Best results inshore come to baits with scent appeal anchored to the sea-bed. These should be mounted on strong 4/0–6/0 hooks like the O'Shaughnessy or the Sundridge Specimen Longshank which will withstand a good chew.

There are two schools of thought relating to ray baits. Some people like their baits to smell because they are high, while others prefer the scent to be strong because the baits are very fresh. I opt for the latter approach. Baits include peeler crab, hermit crabs, fresh-minted herrings, sprats and mackerel – or chunks thereof with the hook passed around the backbone for firm anchorage – king ragworm, bunches of lugworm, baby squids, squid strips, sand-eels, fresh pouting and sometimes razorfish. Different items work better than others around the country – some need to be seasonally adjusted. All should ooze juices and scent. Rays have good noses but poor vision, so baits should be changed when the attractiveness washes out. A groundbait trail will bring rays from afar. An old trick used to be to anchor a sackful of sun-ripened mussels uptide from a favoured area.

The attack of a ray is entirely logical. Because it is not agile and expects its food to dart away, it flops onto the bait and smothers it with its wings. It then shuffles about until the bait is near its mouth, when it devours it. On shore, the rod tip bounces, trembles and bucks a few times. The line may even slacken off. Do nothing until the fish moves off. Then you can assume that the fish has successfully manoeuvred your offering into its mouth. Too great a hurry foul-hooks the fish or pulls the bait away. The hook needs to be well inside the mouth in order to obtain a good hold. Point the rod along the line, wind up the slack, then belt the point home. Rays fight by deflecting water off their backs so that they can adhere to the sea-bed. Some rays – especially small-eyeds – make short runs. In deep water a ray will kite in the current.

Gaff in a wing, if necessary, though a net is a more refined piece of equipment. To remove the hook, flip the fish on to its back. It is kindest to make an incision along the barb to remove the hook; this is preferable to a wrestling match, which would damage fish intended for return. But take care – jaws that crush crabs can do the same to fingers.

A heavy blow between the eyes kills rays intended for eating. Now, rays must be bled for the table. Either cut off the wings or cut open the blood vessels at the gills. This ensures white meat. It is best to wing skate when fresh caught so that they may bleed freely, there is less weight to carry home, the spare parts can be left behind for scavengers to recycle (provided the beach isn't heavily used by tourists by day), and the ray can be dealt with before the slime appears, which happens within an hour of death.

When handling rays, wrap a cloth either around its tail or your hands – those spines cut like pike teeth. Rays should be skinned before eating: remove excessive slime, trim off the leading edges of the wings and cut out the thorns. Lift a flap of skin from the leading edge, slam the body onto a nail board (a board with nail points

Thornback rays – just one of several ray species available from British beaches.

protruding $\frac{1}{4}$ in all over it), grab the skin with pincers or pliars and commence battle. Good luck go with you. I enlist the aid of a friendly fish-monger.

Small-eyed rays are caught mainly from deep-water beaches and sand patches at the base of rocky outcrops from the Isle of Wight westwards to Wales and the south and west of Ireland. Their season corresponds with that of the thornback, with an average size of 5 lb. Similar habitat and habits obtain for both species, except that small-eyeds don't move as far up estuaries. The killer bait for this species is sand-eel, especially fast-frozen ones, which often outfish fresh. Its distinguishing pattern is of white lines that run parallel with the edges of the wings, a white fringe to the disc, and light-coloured (and some dark-coloured) spots on a greyish background.

Sting-rays

The stinger behaves so differently from the general run of skates and rays that it has to be dealt with separately. Several species are found throughout the world – with some inhabiting fresh water. The tribe is represented around the British Isles by the rare eagle ray and by the more common *Dasyatis pastinaca*. On tropical bonefish flats, it is not uncommon to see big stingers sun-bathing in just a few inches of water, black shapes on the dazzling white coral sand. This tribal custom is observed by the British species, where possible, in sun-warmed shallows from the Solent round to Felixstowe, in the Bristol Channel, Ireland's Tralee Bay and, no doubt, in other undiscovered locations.

Typical colouration is black or dark olive-brown. A stinger's colour can be changed by scraping off the thick coloured mucous that covers its baby-smooth skin. This species is more dumpy than other rays and at least twice as thick in the body with a rat-like apology for a tail armed with a long, evil dagger-like spine. Its fight is characterized by fast runs with rapid changes of direction and not infrequent leaps.

Although the species is believed to grow to 100 lb in British waters – and some scientists believe it is a summer migrant – 50 lb is the general upper limit. Stingers like soft bottoms of mud, perhaps with a little sand or gravel mixed in with it. They spend much time in one spot. As they flap their wings to distribute camouflaging silt over their backs, they make depressions over a period of days. Such nests have been discovered on low spring tides. From these depressions they observe the world like dug-in Centurion tanks. While small stingers move about in groups, the larger fish are generally loners.

Late April, if the inshore shallows have been dosed with sunshine, is the earliest one can take sting-rays from the shore, with the summer months offering best sport. Hot, calm weather is preferred. The trouble with such weather is that the shore crabs hold a ceaseless fiesta and ravenously guzzle baits as fast as the angler can get them out there. Tony Gittins of Norwich, who fished the St Osyth shoreline very intensely one year used three rods, reeling in and rebaiting them in rota. The three large stingers that he caught cost 500 rod hours per fish and a fortune in ragworm.

Standard shore-casting rods are adequate. The reel's drag must be smooth enough to cope with a battling stinger. Line of around 0.40 mm is ideal. Hook links of 30-lb nylon will withstand their grinding teeth. Any bottom-fishing end-tackle will suffice. Baits should be king rag, peeler crab or lugworm for preference – depending on locality – and sometimes mollusc, fish or squid baits appeal.

In shallow water, the usual reaction to the angler setting the hook into a big stinger is a small eruption on the surface as though a Polaris missile is about to burst forth. Land the fish either by towing it ashore with the leader, or using a net. A small gaff can be slipped into the leading edge of a wing, but as stingers are inedible, a gaff should not really be used because an infection may set into the wound. A landing net not only restrains a lashing tail but also allows the angler to tip the fish back into the water with minimal distress.

Watch out for that sting! It is a brittle, horny dagger dipped in venom. Medical treatment is essential if it does manage to stab you, as the wound is likely to turn septic with blood poisoning and paralysis as possible complications. The breaking off of stinger spines is an unnecessary and barbaric practice. After giving good sport, its reward should be careful treatment and a return to the water. There is no valid reason for killing one. Yet another feature that sets these rays apart is that their eggs hatch internally, making them ovoviviparous. However, not a great deal is known about the biology of this shallow-water swordsman.

Conger eels

Compared to the conger eel, every other British fish has missed out in the folklore stakes. This sea serpent of the Middle Ages still commands the right mix of curiosity and fear to keep the popular imagination fired by tales of its antics. Such legends are highly colourful distortions of reality. Congers don't rear up and strike like snakes: out of water, big fish haven't the strength nor the purchase to raise their heads more than a few inches clear of the ground. Neither do they bark like dogs. The burping, coughing sounds a fish may emit are caused by air venting to the throat from the swim bladder. Neither do they attack people, even though they do transfix their captors with a malignant, baleful stare and slither about in their efforts to regain open sea. Nor is there adequate power in their jaws to bite lumps out of boats or to chop the toes off heavy sea boots. But they can do damage by thrashing their tails about in a confined space, and their small, serrated teeth and powerful jaws are capable of inflicting a painful bite.

Conger fishing is pleasant enough from the shore. The fish grow big – up to 50 lb in some areas – and the catching of a big conger appeals to the machismo of many shore anglers. Some people find little appeal in the somewhat brutal tactics required when conger fishing, while a wider group of anglers simply dislikes the slime.

The silver eel – the freshwater eel – is also caught in large numbers in the sea. They give fair impersonations of bass bites, for which they are not popular. The way to tell the difference between the two is to compare dorsal fins. That of the conger begins at the tip of the pectoral fins, while that of the silver eel begins a good way down the body. In addition, the lower jaw of the silver juts out while the reverse is true with conger.

Although the female grows to a maximum 200 lb, the male rarely exceeds 4 lb. Because all congers migrate beyond the one thousand fathom line to spawn, at which time they degenerate and die, the ones we catch are maidens. The conger is a fast-growing fish and as prolific at spawning time as cod – a 30-lb female laying around 7,000,000 eggs. Males mature at about 2 ft long, females at 4 ft.

Fish over 100 lb are regularly taken from off-shore wrecks and some inexperienced anglers may think that a 30-lb conger is small. Such a fish from a rock mark, shore, or a pier is a real handful and on the right tackle, every bit as fun to catch as a 60-lb fish hooked over a wreck and swept up in the water by the tide so that it comes in like a drowned sack. 50 lb is near the upper limit for shore conger and such a fish, if angry, would be very hard to cope with.

Deep Scottish sea lochs, some steep rock marks like Portland Bill, old West Country piers and harbours are all places that have yielded big conger. This species lurks down the dark back streets and unlit alley-ways of the sea bed. Cover is their watch-word. Most frequently they are found in the jumble of rocks that form the base of a harbour wall, in the cracks and fissures where a pier joins a rocky sea-bed, and in heavy rock country. For some reason, bottom-fishing for conger from pollack country seems to produce small fish. Perhaps it is just that the straps reach the bait before a senior matron.

Summer and autumn is the best time to fish inshore. For most of the summer they hole up in lairs, but as autumn approaches many migrate along the coast, often tracking the shoals of midget pouting and whiting, well away from dense cover. In shallow littoral waters they migrate out deeper as the year cools down, but in a mild winter plenty stay close to shore in moderately deep water and may be caught out – sometimes fatally – by a sudden cold spell. In the West Country, and where the North Atlantic Drift provides a warming influence, congers can be caught from the shore throughout a warm winter.

Congers are, of course, active hunters – wreck anglers catch them on pirks. A favourite mark of mine is at the mouth of a small river at low tide, fishing 100 yd out into no more than 8 ft of water. I assume the congers come together there to prey on the shoals of school bass, mullet and pouting that group up waiting to run the estuary with the tide.

A conger will fight only if the tackle and circumstances make it panic. For this reason I have caught several up to 20 lb on light bass rods and 10-lb line. The gentle pull from the rod baffles them and they swim docilely to the edge of the jetty (where I caught most) in preparation for landing. This was in calm weather. Rock conger, taken from bass reefs, often come to the surface and allow themselves to be towed ashore. The best fights are to be had from rocks or piers where the fish have to be lifted in the water. On strong tackle, they resist powerfully.

While standard beach-casting tackle is adequate where congers can be taken in snagless areas, a 30-lb class boat rod, Ambassadeur 8000 (or 9000) and 30-lb line will prove most useful from piers and harbour walls – the best fishing area there is close in to the structure, so casting isn't necessary. The fighting of a conger involves levering it up in the water, so too long a rod permits the conger to apply excessive leverage against the angler. When fishing from rocks, a 9–10-ft weapon is advisable. Casting distance should be minimal because the further the fish is away from the angler, the greater its chances of hanging onto a rock with its tail as it is being brought ashore. Under such circumstances, it is best to lob out a short way so that much of the fight involves lifting the conger away from the rough stuff rather than pulling it over the top. So the shortish rod should have plenty of meat in its middle to allow the angler to use it as a lever.

Fixed-spool reels are virtually useless. The gearing is too high, and their bale arms aren't strong enough to cope with the tug-of-war type of fight. From the open shore, some congers will make runs when hooked, but most of the time this species fights by backing off.

Braided wire isn't necessary for conger traces. A 2-ft length of 100–150-lb commercial nylon, carefully crimped to a hook and a good swivel, will defeat their teeth. Traces of stiff stainless steel wire are sold in some shops.

I have always considered the stiffness likely to deter a shy taker. Big baits are used for conger, so hooks of 6/0 to 10/0 are ideal. They should be strong — O'Shaughnessy type are perfect — and of carbon steel rather than stainless as nylon traces can be cut close to the hook for returning unwanted fish (and who wants to keep 100 lb of conger in his freezer?). The hook will rust out without harming the fish. Hooks with built-in swivels, intended for commercial long-lines, are too narrow in the gape for proper congering. And the swivel is crude and inefficient. Some shops stock ball-bearing big-game swivels and these are the ones to use. End the trace with a clip so that congers can be dealt with at leisure — sometimes the feeding spell may be very brief. Retrieve the hooks from keepers later on, not while alive and thrashing. So take plenty of spare traces — and test each one after making it, to check for flaws in the crimping of the heavy nylon. If it is crimped too hard, the nylon may be damaged. It is best to use two crimps, as in the method shown for crimping wire traces.

Never be tempted to retrieve a trace from a conger until it is well dead. I once put a knife into the jaws of the severed head of a fish that promptly chewed at the blade. Their nervous reflexes continue for some time.

Congers feed best during dull conditions by day, except when out and about in the autumn after small whiting. In harbours where fish are gutted or lobster pots baited, they'll feed by day if there hasn't been any activity for several days and therefore no free food. From rocks, which offer low light values, congering can be good by day, and where there is a fair depth of water. But night-time is best of all. They aren't too fond of rough seas and strong currents, though they'll feed when surf is rushing over shallow reef. Flat calms, with a hint of sea fog or thunder have always given me best sport, especially during a slow, ebb tide. After dark, congers leave their lairs to feed. They can be caught in deep gullies like the ones bass anglers leap over to reach other parts of a reef. As a general rule, flying-ant weather is ideal.

Baits should be fresh. Only ravenous fish will take stale baits. Groundbait, as used for tope, will bring the fish around. Baits include live and dead fish like pouting, whiting, herrings, mackerel, small pollack, wrasse and so on. Squid and cuttlefish are excellent, if very fresh. Congers are most partial to a large edible peeler crab. They'll take lugworm at times — and even fillets of conger if hungry enough. Harbour congers may become accustomed to scavenging, though there are few harbours nowadays where fish waste is dumped overboard. Hook all fish baits through the head, using a large hook and passing it through the eye sockets. Congers always take baits from the head.

This species doesn't eat baits, it subverts them. The first signs are a wavering of the rod-tip, or a clickety-click. Hold the rod and you may feel the sinker being dragged over the sea-bed. Don't be in a hurry to strike. Wait until the fish has moved off with the bait, then thump home the hook. Strike too soon and the conger will hang on to the bait for a while, then spit it out. When fishing into rocks and other snags, wind the conger up off the bottom for as far as possible before banging home the hook. It often surprises people how willingly they will allow themselves to be led. The idea is to get the fish away from its refuge before it panics. Many anglers use the ratchet on the reel to signal bites. There are few sounds that are more heart-stopping when fishing for big conger than the initial clicking of a ratchet as the fish backs off with the bait, tugging at it gently, before taking it properly. The strike is generally met with a series of shoulder-wrenching jolts. For this reason, many anglers use a boat angler's belly pad to cushion the stomach from bruising.

You can't often catch and gaff a conger on your own. Most times a friend is required to wield the gaff — or a knife lashed to a pole to cut the trace and release the fish. When fishing from rocks and piers, make a daylight trip to clear slippery weed from steps, rocks and so on from which the gaff man will be working. He should have a powerful headlight (which he doesn't use until the fish is close in, to avoid panicking it more than necessary). The secret of landing a conger in the dark is to be totally prepared and not to hurry. Most fish are lost through the angler wanting to take a look at them too soon in the fight. And the gaff-man won't be thankful if he has to land a fish that is still full of fight. Once you can hold it away from danger, fight it out, if possible, in open water. Don't use brute force, but skill, and retain the initiative!

A strong gaff is vital. One with an unscrewable head should have this locked in the handle with a split pin. Or use a pukka gaff. Congers writhe and try to twist off, so only a strong gaff will do. Little ones will end up bent and useless. An alternative is to use a flying gaff with a removable handle, the head fixed to a rope.

Off beaches, congers will occasionally try to run. One of the strangest experiences I have had with a conger was when fishing from the end of a sewer pipe — the fish swam up inside it, chafing my line on the edge of the pipe. But it was a small one, and I won in the end.

Once a conger's head is turned for home, keep her coming. If she wants to dive, let her go at the last second so she doesn't break the line. Expert judgement is needed here and the ability to feel how much pressure the fish is putting on to the line. Some are lost when they regain a sanctuary and get their tails round a rock. Sometimes they'll be bluffed into letting go if you

Conger (Conger conger).

slacken off and leave them in peace for a couple of minutes. Most times, however, this allows them to reach an even better sanctuary.

When the man comes to gaff it, keep the line tight else the spinning eel will wind line round its body. The gaff is best lodged either just behind the head or near the vent, with the former position best.

Don't stab at a live conger's head with a knife. If the eel twists while you're doing this you stand a good chance of having your hand severely gashed by the knife. Instead, drag the fish on the gaff – and the bigger the gaff, the less able it will be to writhe off it – to a safe place, then thwack her across the back close to the vent with a lump of wood. This is where the lymph heart is, and the fish will then be quietened. Now a knife can be

banged through the spine just behind the head, if you feel the need.

Either way, place the fish in a sack (polypropylene material won't absorb slime and will stink for weeks after) so it cannot regain the water should your last rites have been less effective than hoped for.

Well, I warned that congering is a somewhat brutal game.

I can recall four occasions when I have been bassing or have struck too soon at conger bites and have been able to rebait – and on one occasion, retackle with a bite-proof trace – and cast out and up-tide so that the bait's scent was wafted down to where the conger was. On all four occasions the trick has produced the fish at the second attempt. All eels have highly-tuned nostrils.

8
Minor predators

Mackerel, garfish and scad are the sole British representatives of three large groups of fish that offer superlative sport in tropical seas. Mackerel are of the tuna family, garfish have a warm-water counterpart called the houndfish (other members of this tribe, the half-beaks, make superb trolling baits for marlin), and the scad belongs to the *Carangidae* family, the jacks, a group that fights with uncommon verve and tenacity. Compared to other members of these tribes, our UK species are puny. But we make up for this by using the lightest possible tackle in order to obtain worthwhile sport.

Mackerel

Built for speed in a medium that is 800 times denser than air, mackerel have jaws that fit precisely together to form a friction-free nose-cone. Its eyes are set in streamlining pads, and its fins fold flat into grooves in its body. It has no swim-bladder, so is not affected by sudden changes in depth. Its gill-rakers are set with comb-like bristles which it uses for feeding.

In winter these fish cease to feed and hibernate in dense shoals on the Continental Shelf where they are slaughtered by commercial boats. Spawning takes place at the end of the second year, such early maturity befitting a species which most predators regard as lunch on the fin, when the fish weighs 6–7 oz and measures 12–13 in. Growth rate slows down after this – a 1-lb fish is about seven years old and a 1½-lb fish twelve years old. This ranks mackerel among the slowest-growing fish in our waters.

Mackerel start moving early in the year, spreading out along the coasts, spawning as they go. This is mainly ended by mid-July. May sees reasonable shore catches in western areas. Other parts of England and Ireland must wait until mid-June (or later on the east coast) before the fish hit the beaches. In Indian summers they can be caught right up to November, when herrings and mackerel are often taken on the same strings of feathers in favoured locations. Autumn storms drive the fish out and they make their way back to over-wintering grounds. At this time of year they sometimes take baits legered for other species.

Early in the year, inshore mackerel feed extensively on plankton, which they sieve through their gill rakers. The resultant sludge, varying from orange to dark green, depending on the plankton species, may account for the old wife's tale that this species eats sewage. Or it may be because mackerel often herd fry into a current that flows around the end of a sewer. From rock marks it is common to see mackerel swimming slowly along with their nose clear of the water, their mouth open as they strain out the food.

They largely ignore spinners while doing this and will dive in unison when one lands too close. These fish will sometimes take very small lures, but foul-hooking is more likely. When feeding on small fry, mackerel rush through them, again with their mouths open, straining fish from the water. Small fish – and angler's lures – are attacked individually.

Fry swim close to the surface, feeding on plankton, moving against wind-induced surface drift. So a northerly wind brings them close in to south coast beaches. Estuaries suck fry into them when the tide is making. The mackerel follow. Other feeding areas are rocky headlands, tide races and overfalls, and corners between the beach and a harbour wall. They feed by herding the fry into the current or trapping them against the surface or in a tight corner. Mackerel attacks are less haphazard than many would imagine.

Mackerel are mainly sight feeders – as are all the species in this chapter – and are caught most easily when the water is clear. They dislike heavy seas and chilly weather, when they move out from the shoreline to deeper water. Early morning and late evening are the best times to catch them. Rarely do they move into very shallow water or work along the beach at low tide, but come closest at high water. This is less critical when fishing from rocks and piers.

Flying-ant evenings are best, when the sea-gulls are trying to behave like swallows. Shoal after shoal move along the beach, dashing through the fry then vanishing, leaving only an area of rippled water, before resurfacing many yards away.

When after mackerel for bait, use a string of three or four feathers tied on size 1 stainless steel O'Shaughnessy hooks. Instead of a lead weight at the end, use a small pirk which will cause the feathers to move more erratically through the water and send out come-hither flashes. For this reason, when one fish strikes, leave it out there. Its flashing gyrations make the others believe it has found a large shoal of fry and they'll come looking. Use a bass rod, reel and light line for this. If the fish are well out, heavier casting tackle will be necessary.

Most times the fish will be close to the surface, so the lighter the end tackle, the more slowly and seductively it can be retrieved. A heavy sinker often causes the feathers to fish below the feeding zone. Watch other anglers, noting the weights they use and the speed of retrieval. Results that come to a heavy sinker fished slowly should be interpreted as a sign that the fish are feeding close to the sea-bed.

When they're right on top, thumb the spool and start to wind when the tackle is some 10 ft from hitting water. Thus the gear will fish at the surface. Don't cast into the middle of travelling mackerel shoals, but a few yards ahead, giving them a shot-gunner's lead, else the tackle may land astern of the shoal and be ignored. Many anglers use a violent sink-and-draw motion when feathering. This is counter-productive. A steady retrieve catches more fish while a jerky motion snatches the lures away from attacking fish.

It is unwise – and often bad manners – to charge up and down the beach in pursuit of the shoals. Stay in one place, unless they appear to have settled into one area, and wait for them as they move back and forth in front of you. This will give you time for a cast or two before the idiot horde comes trampling by. On long, featureless beaches, it often happens that the only way to build up a score is to keep spare tackle on your person and be mobile, following the shoal down the beach.

Self-weighted spinners weighing $\frac{5}{8}$–1 oz, feathered lures fished paternoster style, a single feather with a couple of swan-shots crimped close to the hook – all of these provide excellent sport when fished on a light spinning outfit. Under some circumstances, a trout fly outfit can be employed, but is less easy to use when fish are changing direction fast. Mackerel fight hard and should be given every opportunity to do so. There is no logical reason why feathered lures should be dressed on long-shank hooks. Mackerel hit at the head of a lure, so short-shank hooks are more efficient.

A float-fished strip of mackerel belly skin, using a match angler's freshwater rod and reel, will provide excellent sport, especially from Western rock ledges later in the year with large 'harvest' mackerel up to 2 lb. Piers and rock ledges offer best opportunities for this technique.

The bait should be cut 3–4 in long, $\frac{1}{2}$ in wide, with a scalpel or razor blade. Thread it up the hook and on to the line, leaving most hanging free. Hook sizes 4–6 are ideal. The bait must not slip down around the bend of the hook as this blob will not interest the fish – they're hunting for fry-like shapes.

Results can be improved by groundbaiting with the mixture used to attract tope. Don't strike at the first bobs of the float, but when it dives away – or sideways. The float should be a slider in deep water. Under usual conditions, depending on the weather, floats supporting one to three swan-shots are ideal.

Mackerel flesh is very oily and rich in vitamins. Some people prefer to bleed them for the table. Cut the tail off a live fish and the heart will pump out the blood. The fish will die peacefully as it doesn't have the human emotional response to such blood loss. Don't store mackerel in polythene bags in hot weather – they'll cook. Either take a portable cooler loaded with ice packs, or a matting bass and soak it in water, keeping it in the shade or buried under wet shingle. Mackerel flesh deteriorates rapidly.

Garfish

Gars arrive a little before mackerel, between April and May, depending on locality. Weather is less of a problem with them. They don't move far away should a summer storm blow up. They spawn soon after arriving inshore, from May to July in shallow water. Their eggs have fine filaments which tangle among weeds. The juveniles reach 7 in by the end of their first year and 14 in by the end of the fourth year. Small gars are preyed upon by bass, pollack and other predators.

This species is famed for jumping over flotsam. On a calm summer's morning they can be seen hopping about on the surface for a long way out to sea. A curious habit.

A species similar to the gar is the saury pike, an unusual visitor that is deeper in the body, with dorsal and anal fins separated from the tail by mackerel-like finlets.

The gar's beak shows that it feeds mainly by seizing fry. It is more astute than mackerel. Sometimes it is caught on spinners, but these must be small or slender and fitted with small hooks. Rarely do gars take feathers. The best method is float-fished mackerel skin. Tiny jigs can be made from size six hooks dressed with white chicken feathers. One or two swan-shots are crimped to the line just ahead of the eye. A very light rod, fine line and a baby fixed-spool reel are best for casting these out to where the shoals of garfish can be seen swirling at the surface. Sometimes they leap while feeding.

Because of the beak, gars have problems hitting spinners. They use it as a truncheon, sometimes tapping a lure several times before the hook bites them. Float-fished skin baits are easier for them to take. Even so, the float is likely to bob several times before the fish moves off. They, too, respond to groundbaiting.

Scad

This representative of the mighty jack family is pathetic in comparison to the superb fighters that carry the family banner in tropical waters. It is characterized by bony plates along the lateral line towards the tail. These have backward-pointing spurs, like lateral keels. The species has a hard feel to it generally.

Although named horse-mackerel, it doesn't have half the verve of true mackerel, to which it isn't related anyway. The species sometimes takes feathers, spinners and other lures. Best method for catching scad is the float and mackerel belly skin outlined above. It doesn't fight, nor is it edible. Immature scad are preyed on by major predators when large shoals of the little fish are about, and its flesh makes passable baits when mackerel can't be obtained.

In full daylight this species goes out deep, coming to the surface inshore at dusk. It is attracted to lights after dark and can be seen darting about in fair numbers where a pool of light hits the sea. When float fishing, scad will shy away from baits suspended in dead water. Indeed, all three of these mini-predators bite best when the float is being jigged about in a choppy sea, causing the bait to dance about down there.

Apart from its notable relatives, the scad's only claim to fame is that first-year juveniles shelter harmlessly among the tentacles of pelagic jellyfish. Altogether, the scad is a rather useless species.

Pollack

Some beginners have trouble distinguishing between pollack and coalfish, especially in the smaller sizes. However, there are plenty of points of differentiation. Colour is one, even though deep-water pollack have dark greenish backs while shallow-water fish have golden, russet-brown backs with red-speckled flanks — ideal camouflage when living among kelp. The lateral line is the give-away. With pollack, this is curved and dark on a light background, while that of coalfish is straight and light on a dark-green flank.

The pollack tail is less deeply forked than that of the coalie, and its pelvic fins are smaller. Coalfish are more rounded — pollack are slim across the back, which is why they weigh less than they would appear to. Pollack have no barbel, while that of the coalfish is vestigial. The pollack's lower jaw under-juts, while the jaws of coalies are uniform in length. Confusion can also arise when one reads American sport-fishing magazines, as they call coalfish 'pollock'.

Clear Atlantic water is the best place to hunt for decent-size pollack. They prefer deepish water. Schools of immature fish abound around piers along the south-eastern shores of England, while the West Country, South Wales, south and west Ireland, the west of Scotland and the outer isles that benefit from the North Atlantic Drift current all produce good specimens. Pollack thin out in colder northern waters where coalfish take over (as in Yorkshire, North Wales, and the eastern coast of Scotland; both species are fairly abundant on the west coast).

Inshore, a double figure pollack is a hefty fish. The average Atlantic specimen weighs 4–8 lb. Some marks yield pollack of above average size. This is normally due to exceptional feeding in those parts.

Think of the pollack as the hit man of the sea and you will understand why this predator rarely takes a lifeless bait. The angler should fish live baits, such as sand-eels, pouting, whiting, baby mackerel, small flatfish, prawns, king rag, rock-pool fish, live peeler crabs and elvers, preferably under a float so they swim within 5 ft of the kelp beds that make up the pollack's lair. Or he can fish a dead bait with life imparted by a float on a choppy sea. Most of the above plus squid strip, mackerel and other fish strips, sprats and so on will work. Or he can work similar baits through the water to impart the illusion of life. Small pollack sometimes take baits legered for other fish, but this species is less indulgent in this respect than coalfish.

But pollack free the angler from the necessity of collecting bait. Feathered lures, spinners and red-gill sand-eels all work well. Red eels are a proven killer bait for pollack. Weighted lures can be tied direct to the reel line while those without weight (often more effective because of this) should be fished on a long-trace paternoster. I have frequently caught pollack on feathered lures when they have refused a spinner. The feathers, hair, or mylar tinsel move in a more whimsical and, apparently, seductive manner. The fibres vibrate with life.

No matter what bait or method is used, the objective is to fool the fish into attacking a 'live' creature. Pollack have huge eyes — ample evidence that they are almost exclusively sight-feeders although, of course, vibration also plays its part.

Opposite page: *Captain Beaky in person — garfish.*

Right: *Eighty-three and still fishing, but fish stocks have declined a great deal in his lifetime.*

Below: *Mid-summer madness — a mackerel shoal hammering fry.*

Depending on locality and the size of the fish present, tackle need be no more powerful than a flimsy spinning rod and a small fixed-spool loaded with fine line, on up to a light beach-caster and a multiplier loaded with heavier string. Such an outfit would be used where heavy fish are found among tangled weeds and giant boulders. In this respect, it is worth tying on a 1–2-oz sinker and using it as a long-range plummet to explore a strange, deep-water mark. Count it down between the time it hits surface and reaches the sea-bed. Retrieve it slowly along the sea-bed. Thus a picture can be constructed of the underwater topography before any expensive spinners become snagged up.

Reflect that where rock falls steeply to the sea-bed more fish are likely to be found along the slopes. By casting along the rock face rather than out from it, more fish will be hooked. In some places, groups of big pollack herd together shoals of sprats and trap them in bays and rocky coves where they set about them with murderous ferocity. In other places they will lie in ambush on the down-tide edge of a reef, picking off small fish swept along out of control with the tide. Or they will hang among the wavering fronds of kelp growing over a submerged reef, ready to sweep up and sieze small fish.

Early in the year, pollack will travel into estuaries and pick off salmon and seatrout smolts migrating down to the sea. Big fish that turn up unexpectedly in autumn and winter are believed to be from those groups that tag along behind migrating shoals of herrings and sprats like U-boats dogging a World War II Atlantic convoy. A favourite tactic of pollack is to sweep upwards through a shoal of fish, taking as many as possible, before diving hard back to the bottom. When paternostering a lure it is not unusual to land pollack that have swallowed both lure and sinker.

If a bait is fished too high above their ambush, pollack will ignore it. This is why best results come to those who live dangerously, fishing close to the kelp. As dusk approaches, the fish move close to the surface, sometimes even jumping out as they hit a surface-fished lure. This time of day – and at dawn – often provides exciting fishing. When a big pollack hits close to the surface, it dives for the bottom again with the throttle wide. Such powerful dives typify the fight of this species, which makes shore fishing for this species more fun than the capture of monsters from deep-water wrecks where they suffer from decompression while being brought to the surface. In shallow water they fight all the way up – and back down again.

So the reel's drag must be set at around half the breaking strain of the line in order to control the dive. Extra pressure can be applied with a thumb or finger to the spool. Pollack are good at popping lines, so don't tighten the drag too far and never try to stop a pollack dead in its tracks when diving at full power.

Under bright daylight conditions, catches are often only of small fish. Some days it is possible to see the golden flashes as pollack come to a lure, refuse it, then dive back to the sea-bed. Evening and early morning are the best times of day. When they are close to the surface, excellent sport can be had even with small specimens on fly tackle designed for reservoir trout fishing. A slow-sinking shooting-head and streamer lures are ideal.

Pollack reach puberty at the end of their third year when 12–15 in long. They spawn in deep water between late February and early May. A ten-year-old fish is 1 yd long. The spent fish move inshore to reef country in April, with heaviest populations in May and June. While juveniles hang about inshore all summer, eagerly committing mass suicide on the strings of feathers jigged by kids on summer holidays, bigger fish tend to disperse from the reefs and become nomadic after the end of June, although an adequate nucleus is to be found over inshore reefs for most of the summer. Thus a good bag may be caught from a rock ledge one day in July, with little on the next visit. Or the size will vary as the fish move about.

By autumn, pollack shoals have become markedly nomadic. Very big fish track the concentrations of herrings and sprats. Some of these specimens roam close inshore and provide a pleasant surprise in autumn and early winter. The equinoctial gales generally disperse pollack from the inshore reefs, although Indian summers are known to produce superb sport, even up to November, with small–medium specimens. As the year draws to its close, the fish move off to deep-water reefs and wrecks in preparation for spring spawning.

One of the best attributes of a pollack angler is the energy – and the will – to move from one rock ledge to another until he finds fish. For much of the time, inshore pollack are in the ambush business and don't move about much while feeding.

When float fishing, a balance must be sought between the amount of lead needed to keep a bait close to the pollack's feeding zone and the size of the float required to support that weight among whatever wave conditions there are. All too often, vast floats are sold by tackle dealers. Pollack repay thoughtful, light-tackle fishing and should never be demeaned by over-heavy gear.

Coalfish

Coalies grow to around 50 lb and fight twice as hard as pollack. The problem is that such fishing is to be found the other side of the twenty fathoms line and requires

Decca navigation equipment and a sensitive echo-sounder. A six-pounder from the shore is a good fish. Most of the time the beach angler catches tiddlers of around 1 lb, such nippers frequently reaching plague proportions. Inshore coalfish are the northern and western anglers' equivalent to the pouting of southern and eastern shores. The juveniles are called billet – a suitably dismissive name.

So big fish are an offshore proposition, which is a shame because a big coalie is a handsome, thick-set and powerful fish. Reasonable specimens are caught from deep-water rocks and piers off Northern Ireland and Western Scotland. Their feeding habits are very similar to those of pollack. However, they move about more than pollack, not just covering a lot of ground, but being found virtually anywhere between the sea-bed and the surface depending on the movements of the bait fish. Like pollack, they are not true shoal fish with the facility to act in unison. They group together for the purposes of hunting and spawning, and then disband.

Coalfish mature during their fifth summer and spawn in deep water between January and May. A 20-lb female lays around 3,500,000 eggs. The juvenile fish have a complex migratory pattern between inshore shallows and offshore deeps, but move away from land for good once they reach maturity. Some of the best shore specimens are taken in winter when big fish roam close in.

Billet can often be caught in great numbers from the beach. Even at such a tiny size they struggle a bit when hooked, which is more than can be claimed for pouting. They take a wide range of legered baits. In surf they give bangs at the rod tip that fool the unwary into believing bass are about.

On calm evenings when fry are amassed inshore, billet swirl at the surface, sometimes leaping clear like trout – and that is the best way to catch them. Use either a tooth-pick spinning rod and miniature fixed-spool reel, or the fly tackle and wet flies – or small lures – as suggested for school bass. Fly fishing, light spinning, and float-fished strips of mackerel belly skin are the best ways of catching billet. Such methods have to be superior to towing them ashore behind 6-oz sinkers.

Seatrout

The seatrout is a sea-going version of the brown trout. However, it does not spawn with brown trout. Just to confuse the picture, some brown trout take to living in estuaries, where they are termed slob trout, having the silvery dress of the mature seatrout. A licence is required from the local Water Authority to catch any of them, even when fishing from the shore or out to sea. This species is more common inshore than many people realize. I have often seen them attacking shoals of fry or sprats.

The adult fish run up rivers throughout the summer, with autumn through to Christmas being a peak period in some rivers. They spawn on river gravel beds in autumn. Young fish ('smolts') run to sea during their second or third year at a size of $\frac{1}{4}$–$\frac{3}{4}$ lb, depending on the richness of the river that started them off. Large seatrout are often caught in the sea in areas where rivers are populated only by small fish. It appears that seatrout migrate over large areas of coastline. They are very nomadic and irregular in their activities, but feed over inshore reefs and banks, round rocky headlands, along sandy beaches and in tide-ways. Their main food is small fish like brit and sand-eels, though some crustaceans are taken. At sea they are voracious hunters, but rarely feed in fresh water.

The best method of catching these fish is with representations of small, live prey, even though the odd one is caught on a bottom bait from time to time. Generally, smallish lures are best – spinners, bar-spoons, fry-like streamer flies and surface lures that throw out a vee wake.

Seatrout at sea have mouths that are extremely tough and boney. Hooks need to be very sharp, preferably with a cutting edge along the front of the barb, and should be banged home hard. Curiously, their mouth softens in fresh water.

Although this species feeds at all depths, many successful anglers prefer to spin a small lure just under the surface in water no more than 15 ft deep. Fishing is possible in daylight, but early morning, late evening and full darkness are most profitable even at sea.

Like most predators, they have preferred ambush points which are used at different states of the tide. Around many rivers, the fish will group up in the estuary during drought conditions while waiting for a flood of freshwater to enable them to run up. Although most of the sea-shore provides free fishing, such estuary fishing may be owned and the riparian owner is likely to object to freelance activities. Some estuaries fish better than others. In many, a spinner worked during the aftermath of flood conditions will score. But as the water drops and clears, more subtle fly-fishing techniques will be required. One of the best times to fish for estuary seatrout is at the turn of the tide when the fish move about looking for fresh lies as the direction of the current changes. They sometimes take baits intended for mullet – and those of coarse anglers further up-river.

In Scotland, this species is taken on surface lures fished into light surf. A side-wind pulls at the belly in the fly line, making the lure slither up the waves and into the troughs. Careful control is required so that the lure moves over the waves and doesn't plough through

Pollack country.

When bottom fishing among rugged territory, you have to accept high losses of hooks and sinkers.

them. Sometimes the fish will follow and take at the very edge, so each cast should be completely fished out before lifting off for the next throw. On the take, and this applies to all fly-fishing tactics, give a little slack line so that the fish can turn away without feeling the rod. Then tighten to it and the hook should sink home in the scissors of its jaw, which is the most secure hold available.

Finally, although seatrout are voracious, they require more subtle presentation of tackle and more stealth than are required by other inshore predators. At sea they can be just as spooky as they are when in fresh water.

9
Flatfish and small bottom-feeders

Flatfish are unique among all species of fish for several reasons. The most obvious is their shape. They live on the sea-bed and have developed a form and a method of movement to suit this. In effect they swim on their sides, unlike skates and rays, which assists their breathing as water can pass unhindered into their mouths and out through their gills.

One eye migrates during the fish's infancy so that both are on the upper side when juvenile. The lower surface of flatfish is pale in colour, but the top-side varies in tone to provide extremely effective camouflage. The immature fish lives in the middle and upper levels of the sea and only moves to the sea-bed when its body shape has made the change that suits it for a life on the sea-bed. Some species have both eyes on the right side, the others on the left. The majority of flounders lie on their left side, and their eyes are on the right. A few examples, however, are the opposite way round. Likewise, some specimens are partially pigmented on their underside.

Most shore anglers experience a certain satisfaction when landing a flatfish, especially a plaice or sole. This is probably due to the fact that they make excellent eating. But none of the general run of flatfish offers much resistance when hooked and could never be described as sporting, even though large plaice and sole taken from piers on ultra-light tackle will make purposeful dives. Another reason for satisfaction is that flatties are nowadays rarely caught in large numbers and a couple of plaice or sole in a bag is a great bonus. Flounders and dabs can, at certain times, be caught in good numbers, but, as with all flatfish, their numbers are decreasing because they are so vulnerable to the trawl.

There are three families of flatfish, of which some eighteen different species are found in waters around the British Isles. Some of these, however, are rarely caught from the shore, so I will deal with the five most commonly caught: flounder, plaice, dab, turbot and sole.

Flounders

The flounder is the most common of all the flatfish in British waters, and is also one of the most common sea-fish. One reason for its abundance is its ability to thrive in all types of water, including brackish and very shallow water where it is safe from trawlers and trammel nets. It is an ideal beginner's fish because not only is it so frequently caught, but it is also very obliging and will take almost any sea bait which is offered.

Identification of the flounder can be difficult. The way to be sure is to run a finger over the area behind its eyes. It will be rough and scaly. Other means of identification are the square-edged tail and cream underside, which is not opaque like that of the plaice and dab. Often the underside may be brown or brown-blotched, and this is especially true of estuary-caught fish.

Flounders spawn in the sea during the late winter months and congregate in large shoals for this purpose. The infant fish spend their early life in fresh water but, once mature, return to the sea and then only occasionally venture back to brackish water. It is unusual to find a fully mature fish in water where the salinity is much reduced.

Flounders can be caught all the year round but the winter months bring the largest catches especially from the English Channel coast. After a gale, the flounders invade the storm beaches in this area in search of the many shellfish which have been gouged from their shells. At this time baits such as razorfish, cockles and butterfish can be used with great effectiveness. At other times, the best general baits are peeler crab and white or red ragworm. Flounders are very inquisitive and are attracted by movement. For this reason, ragworms are effective when fished in clear water. They should be mounted on the hook so that the tails wriggle.

The flounder spoon is a highly favoured method among dinghy anglers who fish in estuaries and along

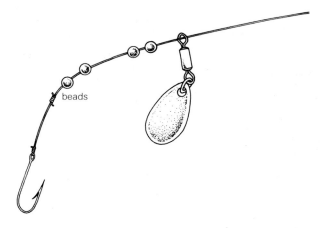

beads

Flounder spoon

sheltered beaches. It is less effective from the shore and its success is very localized. In general, a flounder spoon is of white plastic or chromed brass/steel about the size of a tablespoon – locally larger on occasions. This is mounted at the end of a short trace via a swivel with the hook tied 4–6 in behind the spoon. This is baited with ragworm, and so on. As the tackle is retrieved slowly across the bottom, the spoon flutters and kicks up the sand, which arouses the fish's interest. I suspect that when the spoon does work its vibrations are also an attraction. That is the theory, but in reality few shore anglers will give the baited spoon any thought because it is rarely as deadly as normal legering techniques.

The most effective method of flounder fishing is with a large piece of peeler crab that is oozing juices, mounted on a size 1/0 Mustad 79510 or size 2 Spear-spade. This is cast out and retrieved by inches at intervals, and I mean inches! When worm baits are used, a size 6–2 Aberdeen or Kirby longshank is ideal. It is surprising how big a bait a flounder can engulf in its mouth. A 1-lb fish can take a golf-ball-size bait, but it can't spit the hook out so easily, so once the hook is inside, he is invariably caught.

Flounder bites vary between short plucks and rod-bending runs. They should never be struck and as is the case with all flatfish, time is the key to success. Left to their own devices, flounders will hook themselves.

This species has a poor reputation on the table so is not sought commercially on a large scale. Sea-going flounders are, however, excellent – greatly superior to their muddy, estuary-dwelling brothers.

Plaice

The plaice is the largest flatfish encountered by the majority of shore anglers, with the exception of the turbot and, even more rarely, the halibut. Its numbers

have been drastically reduced by commercial fishing and, although it is still fairly common during the summer months, the largest specimens are rare indeed. The average-sized fish caught by the shore angler is in the region of 1 lb with the occasional specimen up to 4 lb. Bigger fish are more common in the waters off the south-west of England with a few stragglers reaching the northern end of the English Channel and the North Sea. Plaice are found all around Great Britain, but are very localized in some northern areas.

Plaice are relatively easy to identify by their large red spots. A further aid, especially useful for avoiding confusion with flounders and dabs, is that the area on top of the head has a series of horny knobs and the topside of the plaice is smooth, not scaly like the other two. The underside is opaque and white, with the subcutaneous muscle forming chevron stripes throughout the fish's length.

This species is best sought by legering on the sea-bed – either a flowing trace or a mono paternoster can be employed. Hook size depends on bait being used. Long shank size 1 or 2 hooks are best for worm baits and short shank 2/0 for peeler crab. This bait is especially useful for the bigger fish, and other baits worth using include lugworm, king ragworm, harbour ragworm, mussel and other molluscs. Plaice are often found in large numbers over mussel beds – where they are quickly caught by trawlers.

Plaice are the one flatfish which rarely feed at night. Some of the best catches come at dusk, but as soon as darkness falls they stop feeding. They can be caught all through the summer, but during the early months of the season they are in very poor condition, having just spawned. Unfortunately this is the time when they are easiest to catch as they feed ravenously. During July and August, however, plaice are fat and in prime condition. As they are reeled in, they hug the bottom and then appear in the surf at the last minute, deflecting the water to force themselves down.

Turbot

Small turbot are often confused with brill, which can be identified by the scales on its upper side. Turbot have boney tubercles. The brill is also more rounded than the turbot, which has a slight diamond shape. The turbot always lies on its left side, its eyes on the right.

Commercial fishermen seek the turbot in large numbers as it is highly prized for its excellent flavour. Consequently its numbers have declined so that good specimens are but rarely caught by shore anglers, although small and immature fish are sometimes caught from some southern and western beaches, and especially in Ireland. The turbot grows to about 30 lb, with a

Above: *Once hooked,
plaice are almost
impossible to lose –
thankfully. They are too
tasty for their own good.*

Left: *With strong teeth,
a large mouth, and
efficient camouflage, the
turbot is an effective
predator.*

Right: Soles are bearded with tiny barbels called 'villi', with which they locate prey.

Below: Gurnard – a sea-bed curiosity.

15-lb fish being an excellent shore-caught specimen. Turbot are predominantly fish-eaters and can be caught on mackerel strip, sand-eels and herring. Large fish occasionally take small fish that have hooked themselves (i.e., pouting and whiting) without the angler being aware. Leger tackle should be used with a simple, one-hook, running paternoster most successful. For fish baits, hooks up to size 3/0 are ideal. The turbot, in common with all fish-eaters, has a large mouth and a 5-lb fish can easily engulf half a fillet of mackerel.

The summer months produce most turbot with September and November giving the southern-based angler the chance of a rare large specimen. This fish is a master of camouflage and is almost impossible to see when stationary on the sea-bed. It favours sandy or gravelly bottoms, where it can use its ability to hide in ambush for passing food.

Dabs

The dab is one of the smallest of the flatfish tribe. A 1-lb shore-caught fish is an excellent specimen. It is widely available and can be caught from most steep shingle beaches that have a sandy bottom. It also frequents piers and estuaries – in fact most locations around the British Isles will yield dabs all through the year. The larger fish tend to be caught in the spring and autumn, when the sprat shoals are around.

Identification of the dab is relatively easy as it is a sandy brown colour and much lighter in tone than the other species of flatfish. It also has a pronounced curve in the lateral line near the pectoral fin, while this curve is less remarkable on the plaice and flounder. The dab is sometimes confused with small plaice as it, too, has small flecks of orange. These, however, are orange, yellow and tiny. The plaice has definite red spots.

Dabs feed on the many minute creatures found on the sea-bed and are rarely caught with lugworm in their stomachs. Anglers, however, find that lugworm is by far the most successful bait for dabs. Many swear by stale black lugworm as the killer bait. The best tackle is either a flowing trace or a paternoster. When this species is dense inshore, some anglers use a three-hook paternoster and take them three at a time, arguing that best sport is had from dabs not with a fishing rod but with a knife and fork in their hands. Hooks should be small – size 2 is ideal for use with lugworm. An excellent summer bait is the peeled legs of a peeler crab. This is particularly successful when crabs are removing lugworm quickly as it will stay on the hook longer because crabs, although cannibalistic, do not eat their own kind all of the time. During the spring and autumn when dabs are following the sprat shoals, a cocktail of lugworm and strip of sprat can prove deadly.

Sole

The sole family is divided into four species, all of which have the characteristic tongue shape and are very difficult to tell apart. But one member is regularly caught by shore anglers, the Dover sole. It is the biggest of the soles and can be identified by both pectoral fins being of identical size, the dorsal and anal fins are joined, and the nostril on the under side is very small.

Soles are common along many of the English Channel beaches and are also found further north in both the Irish and North seas. They are very localized and, for some reason, can be caught in good numbers from one place while another, two miles away, will never yield one, even though nets catch plenty. Summer and early autumn are best for sole fishing and the best months are July and August, though this can vary with locality.

The sole feeds ravenously in the dark and often swims very close to the shoreline. Shoals are often of fish of an average size with the bigger specimens loners. If you catch one, there is a good chance of others. The most successful bait is black lugworm. Leger tackle should be used and the best rig is a flowing trace. Hooks should be small – size 4–6 is ideal for worm baits. Sole fishing is a waiting game, and sport can be either non-existant or hectic. Often they are present in large numbers but aren't feeding. When one feeds they all feed. Their favourite time for feeding is the two hours before dawn or during those times when the direction of the tide is changing. Soles bury themselves in the sand when the tide is flowing strongly, but swim out to turn around and face the other way when the new current starts to flow. It is at this time that they will often feed for a brief period.

Soles make good eating, but should be skinned first. They taste best if kept in the fridge for a day or two.

The breams

The sea breams are tropical and sub-tropical fish. Only two members of this family are commonly caught in British waters, and these mainly in the English Channel and around some southern areas of Ireland. Several other members of the family are caught on occasion by shore anglers, and these include the bogue, pandora, gilthead, Spanish bream and dentex. The Ray's bream is not a member of the bream family but turns up from time to time along the northern coastline of England, arriving there with the currents rather than through any voluntary planned migration.

Of the two species regularly caught in British waters, the red bream is the most common but is a deep-water fish. The shore angler is likely to encounter only small specimens, weighing up to 1 lb. Its cousin, the black bream is rarely caught in large numbers from the shore except in a few areas of the south and west of Britain and from the Channel Isles. In other areas, the occasional specimen turns up during the summer months and this will often be a respectable fish of 2–3 lb. Both types of bream grow to around 6 lb, and a 3-lb specimen is a good one. Preferred habitat is rocky ground, although shoals will roam widely over many types of sea-bed except open sand.

Identification of the bream is easy as it is a deep, flattened fish with large scales, mainly silver in colour. The dorsal fin is spikey, and the teeth flat and suited to breaking food away from rocks and so on. There is often confusion between the two species as small red bream are very similar to adult black bream. In general, the red bream is a pronounced orangey-red all over the body, while the black bream is dark, shading to purple over the back. The black spot on adults of both species at the front of the lateral line is absent on small red bream.

Favourite baits for bream are king rag, lugworm, slim strips of squid, sand eels, mackerel strip and peeler crab. They are caught over rough ground and from piers, usually down the side of the wall or piles. Bream feed on the bottom and in mid-water so both leger and float tackle can be used. Fishing from rocks with a sliding float will reveal the excellent qualities of this species. Their shape affords them both power and manoeuvrability and they put up a good scrap. Bream have small mouths so bait and hooks should be small.

Gurnard

The family of gurnards contains four fish which can be caught in British waters. As one species they are immediately recognizable by their bright colouration and peculiar shape. They have a rather blunt head tapering rapidly to the tail, with spiney plates around the gill covers. Unique to the gurnards are pelvic fins that have evolved until rays are free from connecting membranes, giving them the appearance of claws. The fish use these fins to feel for food as they move along the sea-bed. This gives them the appearance of crawling, and they can very quickly dig themselves into the sea-bed with these fins. Almost as if to compensate for the loss of these fins for swimming and buoyancy, the pectorals are enlarged. These are brightly-coloured and appear like huge fans behind each gill.

Gurnards feed mainly on the bottom and are mostly found over soft sea-beds. However, a swarm of fry will induce them to rise up and give chase, sometimes even breaking the surface like mackerel. But this is rare.

Of the four species, the grey gurnard is most commonly encountered by the sea angler. It is the smallest of the four and reaches a weight of only 2 lb.

The tub gurnard is occasionally caught inshore and is a larger fish. Small tub gurnards are often confused with grey gurnards. The difference is that the latter is grey or dark brown with white spots along its flanks, while the tub does not have spikes on the plate-like scales along its lateral line. Its pectoral fins are bright blue on top and orange underneath. The red gurnard is occasionally caught from the shore. Its lateral-line scales lack spikes and it is a pronounced red colour. It is frequently caught on cod pirks almost as large as itself, over offshore sandbanks.

Gurnards are rarely sought on purpose by the shore angler. Because they are bottom-feeders and inhabit open ground they are very susceptible to the trawl and are comparatively rare. They are highly prized as eating fish. The grey is found mainly in the south but does venture all round the British coastline, whereas the tub is rarely caught in northern seas. The red gurnard is a fish of the south and west.

These species are usually caught on baits and leger tackle intended for flatfish or whiting.

The weevers

This family contains two species that are the only poisonous British fish. The lesser weever is the commonest – and the smallest – and the one most likely to be caught by the shore angler. Its poison can cause considerable pain. There have been several cases of death among trawlermen through weever stings, but in general a healthy person without unusual allergies can treat it as little more than a wasp sting. The poison glands are situated on the gill covers and at the base of the dorsal fin. Weevers are caught mainly from sandy beaches and are most prolific during the warmer summer months.

They are not unlike small bass or whiting at first glance, which is why anglers are very often stung. The lesser weever averages 4 in in length. It is silvery with a dark brown back, a stumpy head and long anal fin which reaches its tail. The front dorsal fin, which consists of a row of venomous hypodermic needles, is black and often has a yellow spot on it.

Obviously anglers do not set out to catch weevers and even matches bar them from being weighed in. Yet they are often caught by accident. Many other mini-species of sea fish are mistakenly identified as weevers and suffer mutilation as a result. These include blennies, rockling, dragonets and the shanny: all are harmless.

The greater weever is a deep-water species and is rarely caught from the shore. It grows to about 2 lb and is as deadly as its smaller brother. For all that, the greater weever is said to taste good, once carefully prepared. Cooking destroys the venom.

10
Wrasse

Seven species of wrasse are found round our shores. It was once thought there were more. For instance, the male and female cuckoo wrasse differ so greatly in colouring that they once were counted as separate species. Five species are very small and are generally found in rock pools. Sometimes these are caught in prawn nets and crab pots. They make attractive additions to a saltwater aquarium. They also make useful baits for bass, conger and pollack.

Cuckoo wrasse grow to around 2 lb, but are found in deeper water where boat anglers classify them as a nuisance. So ballan wrasse are the ones that command the attention of the British angler. Not only do they grow quite large (they've been caught commercially to 20 lb, if such reports are accurate), but they are also readily available close inshore.

Wrasse fill a slot in the marine ecosystem where competition from other species is virtually nil. Their flesh is barely worth preparing for the table, and their habitat defies all means of commercial exploitation. They are our most colourful species, though it is hard to explain why. Do their dappled colours blend with the interplay of light and wavering weeds in their preferred habitat? Generally, their flanks are a reddish or greenish brown, darker on the back and shading to lighter on the lower flanks. The throat is orangish, speckled with different shades of orange and red. But that is just the start! They vary in colour independent of sex and location. One rock mark will produce a whole range of shades. Many of the beautifully-coloured fish that throng around tropical coral reefs are members of the wrasse tribe.

Precise identification can never be determined by colour. Fin-ray counts and examination of the lay-out of teeth are the most reliable means. These details can be found in better books on marine biology.

Although it is often surprising where ballans turn up, they are most common on the Atlantic shores of the British Isles. Devon, Cornwall, Wales, Scotland and Ireland all have populations on their west-facing coasts.

The further south and west one travels, the larger the fish become, the reason being the stable temperature of the North Atlantic Drift.

Wrasse are very sensitive to cold. In Arctic winters, several thousand may perish. They do not migrate any distance in winter, going only as far as offshore reefs, away from the influence of winds chilling the tidal zone. Naturally they wait until the water has warmed up a little before spawning – high summer is their time. The fishing season extends from May to October, with a shorter span in colder areas and seasons.

I have never heard of wrasse being caught from open ground. They prefer dense cover. Small ones are taken from shallow-water reefs and harbour walls all the way up the English Channel. They're fun on light tackle when nothing else is around. Specimens of better quality are to be found among jagged, precipitous, submarine rock faces. They colonize the fissures in the face. As a general maxim, the deeper the fissures, the better they like it. A favourite mark of mine, on Ireland's Clogher Head in Co. Kerry, is comprised of massive boulders of conglommerate smothered in thick kelp, dropping away to deep water. It is not unusual to catch six-pounders there. One day we had seven over that weight between five of us, along with a gross of lesser ones.

Deep water is another important consideration. Wrasse don't move in and out with the tide as do many other species. They prefer to dwell in one place. At least, it is in such areas that they grow biggest. Instead they move up or down the rock faces as the tide rises and falls. Tide does affect their feeding habits in some localities, with high tide producing most activity in areas of relatively shallow water and scant cover.

It has been suggested that their large scales are armour plating against the buffeting of waves in such a rough environment when heavy seas are up. The age of larger ballans is hard to determine from scale readings owing to the large number of damaged and replacement scales. Of course, wrasse will move out to more

Right: Rough and ragged wrasse country. Keith Roberts primes his hook.

Below: With rabbit-like front teeth for eating barnacles and mussels, and a coat of tough scales, wrasse are well equipped to live in rock tangles.

comfortable quarters when heavy swells are pounding the rocks, but gentle surfs that colour the clear blue Atlantic water a greeny-white produce the most consistent results.

A wrasse hole is generally quite a small area, sometimes no more than a cleft in the rocks or boulders where the waves are funnelled somewhat to produce that tickle of surf that is frequently so essential to success. A word of warning: several of the best wrasse marks require stiff climbs down cliffs before fishing can be had. Many anglers guarantee their safety by taking proper ropes, boots and other climbing equipment. It is unwise to fish such ground alone. A sprained ankle is less serious if somebody is around to help out.

There are two biological facts that are curious about wrasse. Firstly, they are among the few species of fish to build nests at spawning time. The males do this before finding a mate. The second, which means that after-dark fishing is a waste of time, is that they sleep at night, propped on their sides.

Wrasse, then, are the inhabitants of deep water and undercut ledges out of the light. In this sheltered world they feed no matter how hot and bright the weather, a facet of their nature that makes them ideal holiday fish, and a species to pursue when more spooky predators are inactive, pending twilight. Tackle doesn't need to be chosen for casting but to match the fish's fighting ability and the ruggedness of its environment. A powerful carp rod or light bass rod can be used where the fish grow to around 4 lb. Larger specimens may be lost, but the philosophy behind this approach is that the standard run of fish can show their mettle and put up a good scrap. Where fish of 5 lb and over are to be found a stronger rod, which will cast up to 4 oz, is needed.

10-lb line is ideal for the first outfit, 18 lb for the second. It should be a hard grade of nylon to withstand the abrasive environment. The only reel worth using is a multiplier, as a fixed-spool reel makes a poor winch.

Terminal rigs need to be easily made and cheap to replace. Wrasse jungle claims plenty of tackle because the only place to fish is right in the thick of it. If you cast out into clearer water you'll catch few fish, and they'll be juveniles. A leader is a waste of time, for the obvious reasons. Tie hooks to a length of 20-lb line to take abrasion from teeth. Other tackle should be tied direct to the main line.

There is one rig that suffices for wrasse, with two variations – a paternoster, or one supported by a float. Tie 4 ft of weak line to a swivel fixed to the end of the main line. Tie on an old sparking plug – or whatever – as a weight. Tie 2 ft or less of 20-lb line to the top eye of the swivel and end this with a strong, forged hook around 1/0 size. Only one at a time here – two or more hooks is courting disaster.

If the rock falls away sheer beneath your feet, tap bottom then wind up a few turns. Bites come faster if the bait is allowed to waft about. Or use the float. Take a chunk of expanded polystyrene and clove-hitch it to the line. A more sophisticated version entails tying line around the foam, with a swivel tied to a loose end. This makes a sliding float that can be stopped at the requisite depth with a bead and stop-knot. Use pukka floats if you wish, but the cost of such losses would put many people off wrasse fishing for life.

Some days the wrasse will be a long way down the rock face, at other times they'll be higher in the water. It pays to fish at different depths until the fish are found, though groundbait can influence matters considerably.

The main food of wrasse is crustaceans, molluscs and fry. All British wrasse species have a hinged upper lip that exposes their chopping front teeth for action. They eat a lot of barnacles, seed mussels, prawns, crabs and other fare. Baits vary in effectiveness from place to place. Something that runs contrary to all logic is that wrasse are very fond of float-fished lugworms – or lug in any style. Some people extol the use of common limpets. Well, I would hate to use limpet where anglers nearby are fishing with fresh lug, crab or live prawns. Although one can catch prawns in a baited drop-net in many places while fishing, it strikes me as an awful waste of good prawns and an unnecessary encumbrance. Crabs are very effective. Indeed, bass anglers fishing soft crab over shallow reefs often have their baits shredded by juvenile wrasse. Half a large hardback, with the legs removed and the hook threaded through two leg sockets is a good bait for specimen wrasse as its size and hardness deters also-rans.

Wrasse can be caught on spinners, flies and red-gills. But the frustration of continuously breaking free from snags, and the cost, make this a better way of losing red-gills than of catching wrasse. A better system is to float-fish small strips of mackerel, sand-eels, squid or small rock fish, though a bait with smell appeal works best.

Groundbait is a great help at times. Whether you throw in spoonfuls of tinned cat food, handfuls of crunched crabs or loose-feed with stale lug, the effect can be spectacular. In hotspots, groundbait is not necessary as the fish are so populous. The smell of the bait alone is enough to bring them around. It seems that for the first half-hour sport will be slow, but the scent of the bait is gradually filtering through the crevices and caves where the fish hole up. Gradually they make their way towards the source, then the fishing takes off. You get take after take, fish after fish until sport simply stops. Perhaps all the takers have been hooked. Perhaps they go off the feed. In any event, it is time to find another hole. In some places a group of anglers can catch over a hundred good fish from the same hole.

Although wrasse use their front teeth for chopping barnacles and seed mussels from rock faces, they have grinders embedded in the pharyngeal bones at the entrance to the throat. They chew their food with these. You will discover how effective they are if you use light hook-links and dither over setting the hook. The trace will come back with the hook bitten off. That is why long traces should be avoided; they are too insensitive. A shorter one gives the angler more definite indications that a fish has the bait, so he can set the hook before the fish swims back into cover.

Bites normally consist of a couple of tugs and a solid pull. If the fish keeps plucking, slowly draw the bait away to provoke a positive take. Ideally, the clutch of the reel should have been adjusted prior to fishing so that it slips at a firm, but safe pressure. The first dive of a hooked wrasse is impressively powerful. Hold on tight, and yield line only if it is likely to pop if you don't – you must prevent the fish getting back to its hole. With very big ones, however, line has to be given. If a fish regains cover, slacken off completely for a couple of minutes and try to con the fish into believing it has escaped, and into coming back out again. However, that is not much good if the fish has already wound the line twice round a thick kelp stem. The more vertically you can fish over a wrasse hole, the better will be your success rate. By pointing the rod down the line, you can strike and lift in one movement, thereby taking it by surprise before it starts fighting.

Once the first dive has been controlled, the fish is virtually beaten. When it hits the surface, success is guaranteed. Wrasse are susceptible to changes in water pressure, which is why they often come in with the anus protruding. The change in pressure causes the swim-bladder to distend and press against other organs. However, there is no evidence to suggest that this condition causes lasting damage to fish once they have been returned to the water.

When rock fishing, a landing net is not really practical, neither is a drop-net. Both get swirled about by the surf. The best way to land a wrasse is to wind down to the fish, then smoothly swing it ashore. If it drops off, well, it would have been put back anyway.

It is possible to fish close in to rocks from a boat, using lighter tackle, where fish can be pulled into clear water, away from their jungle, and a more prolonged fight can be expected. There is, however, the chance that a big swell may come and pick up the boat, dropping it with an expensive crash onto the rocks. The landlubber should also beware of the odd growlers that creep up; swells from distant ships that are stalking the unwary even on days of flat, calm, glittering seas.

When handling ballans, beware of the sharp spines at the front end of the dorsal and anal fins, which can cause uncomfortable pricks. Long-nose pliars or artery forceps are best for removing hooks from their leathery mouths. Watch out for a nip from those rabbit-like incisors. In bad cases, cut a small slit alongside the hook rather than wrestle with the fish and risk damaging it.

Once unhooked, pop wrasse back into the sea. From a height, drop them back head-first rather than allow them to slap their flanks on the water, which could stun them. Obviously, the closer you can fish to water level, the kinder you can be – and the greater the risk of being drenched by a growler.

About the only use for wrasse flesh is for lobster potting. Their tough scales make them ideal for this as they resist the attacks of crabs. But a punctured tin of cat food is an even better pot bait, so it's best to return all fish. Virtually all other sea fish are more edible than wrasse, and it is better by far to let these slow-growing fish live to fight another day.

11
The mullets

The species

To the practised eye, the three British species are easy to tell apart. Most of the mullet caught around the British Isles are of the thick-lipped variety ('thick'), so-named after its gristly rubber-tyre of an upper lip. It differs from the thin-lipped ('thin') in that the jugular inter-space (the area where the gill covers meet under the chin) is narrow and parallel. That of the thin is wide and oval, and its upper lip is less large. Other differences become noticeable with experience. The golden-grey ('goldie') looks similar to the thin, but prefers open sea, while thins are normally caught well upstream in estuaries. It has a large golden spot on the gill cover and a thick coat of mucous over its body, neither of which are found on the thin.

Thicks are caught in both open sea and brackish water all round the British Isles. Thins are to be had from several slow-flowing lowland rivers in the south-east of England, while goldies are caught around the south-east coast, Worthing's sandy beaches being their strong-hold. Because many of the general observations about mullet apply exclusively to thicks and thins, I shall dismiss goldies thus: light tackle fishing with harbour or white ragworm during fine summer weather produces best results, using the leger tactics advocated for flounders. Average weight is around 1 lb.

Incidentally, the so-called red mullet is not a mullet, shares none of their characteristics, and behaves in a manner similar to gurnard.

General observations

The habits of the three British mullet, and the tackle and techniques used to catch them, differ markedly from those of other fish. The mullet angler is required to blend some tricks of the coarse angler with some techniques of the shore fisherman and add a good number that are unique to mullet angling. The central problem is that mullet do not feed like any other fish.

They occasionally eat conventional food like plankton, fry, small molluscs and crustaceans, worms, food waste and sewage. However, most of their diet consists of algae and diatoms, which they digest in a gizzard-like stomach.

You can sometimes see thicks and thins doing this. They sweep in to a bank of clay, skim the surface with their lower lip, and swim away with silt streaming from their gills as they filter out the food particles. These scrape marks, which look as though somebody has rubbed two finger-tips over the mud, can be seen all over such banks at low tide, along the hulls of boats in marinas, and in the fine film of algae covering inter-tidal rocks. Not only do they reveal where mullet are feeding, but how big the fish are (the marks indicate the size of the lower lip) and how far up an estuary the fish can be found.

The angler's task is to wean the fish off this diet so that they will accept a food item that can be mounted on to the hook. This involves ground baiting, and also allows him to choose a bait that is convenient to use. Finely-minced fish, mashed bread (remove air bubbles or it will float) and, for thins, surface mud, all produce the required effect. A thin cloud in the water is not enough, though. They have to be educated into accepting particles of the right size. So bait-sized pieces of bread, fish and so on, have to be included. The intention is to re-programme the fish, not to feed them. One idea for thicks is to pulverize several canfuls of sweetcorn in a liquidizer, then add a tin of whole grains, the mixture being introduced to the fishing area on the little-and-often basis that is so vital to success.

There are places where thicks have already suc-cumbed to revisionist propaganda — marinas where tourists dump food scraps, dumping areas for fish and shell-fish waste, overfalls from food-processing plants, and sewers. In such places the angler is playing to a receptive audience.

When fishing to less domesticated thicks, success depends on their mood. If they feel like it, they will wax

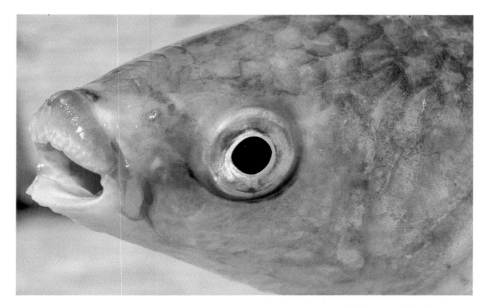

Thick-lipped mullet.

Thin-lipped mullet.

Golden-grey mullet.

101

enthusiastic over the groundbait and become easy to hook. But if their mood isn't right, failure is certain. Anglers who fish for open-sea thicks in Cornwall groundbait for days with a putrid fish soup called browse. Good catches are made when, after a long while, the mullet decide to feed. It was once believed that the continuous pre-baiting paid dividends. When one considers the dilution factor of a gallon of browse among several million gallons of sea water, together with the prolonged indifference of the fish, it seems likely that a distant shoal did not even notice it. But the stimulant proves right when their mood changes and they move close to feed.

In smaller environments, like rock coves, harbours and estuaries, the fish can more easily be made aware of the groundbait, and are thus more easily educated. This can take time – maybe minutes, maybe hours. Mulleteers prefer water with minimal current and wave action, lest the groundbait be washed away taking the fish with it.

Most successful fishing occurs in quiet places. Thins and thicks in estuaries become excited when the new tide pours inland and swim with it, scooping at clay banks as they go. However, the angler is unlikely to find success while they are travelling, though thicks can sometimes be persuaded to linger awhile with a groundbaiting trick described later. When the fish settle down in one area in a moderate current, confidence should be rewarded. In open water, the more sheltered the fishing area, the better the fish like it, even though mullet are often to be seen lying close to the surface just behind breaking waves and in the wash on some western surf beaches. Because groundbaiting requires fairly static water, the angler's first consideration must be for an area where he can fish with ease, even if fewer fish are there.

Mullet are famous for their spookiness. They take fright at any shadow, having excellent eye-sight. Even a shooting-head fly line whistling out high overhead will startle them. They will swirl and bow-wave away when a gull swoops low over the water or an angler walks along the sky-line, but they soon recover their composure. They will become agitated if there is a lot of disturbance and may retire from sight. This is why early-morning and late-evening sessions are more productive from piers and marinas. Thins, however, are more resilient. I once had ten canooists in my swim. One capsized and another two ran aground while trying to help him. People were wading round my float. But the thins were biting again within half an hour of their departure. Maybe the stirring up of the river bottom stimulated them to feed.

On two occasions I have known thins to take general fright and fly off downstream in a wild stampede.

However, once they had forgotten their fear, they began to feed again. During each stampede every thin in that section of the river joined in, so I ended up fishing to one large group of mullet with excellent results. Don't terrify the fish while groundbaiting. It should be introduced surreptitiously to the water, not pounded in like hand-grenades.

Generally, a fish that is pricked and lost will take the rest of the shoal with it, although when thicks are feeding hard this is not always the case. When thins get their heads down it sometimes seems that the angler can do little to frighten them. When thicks start feeding hard they are less abandoned. It is vital that the angler keeps off the sky-line and blends into his surroundings as much as possible. On exposed estuary muds this involves laying out a sheet of polythene and sitting on it. A mullet fighting in the swim will scare off the others. Cup a hand over the reel spool and point the rod at the fish. It will allow itself to be towed clear of the fishing area and can then be fought to the net. On your return the shoal will still be eager to take the bait.

Thins normally drop down-river when disturbed, so the angler is likely to find them again 10–50 yd further down. While thins tend to feed whether there is groundbait or not thicks are less responsive in the absence of groundbait·and have to be persuaded patiently back into the swim. A trick which can work is heavy baiting of three swims that thicks are known to frequent. So when a shoal spooks in one, there is a good chance of finding a group in another.

In marinas where human traffic is commonplace, thicks frequently show total indifference to this activity. Once, while filming for a TV series, a thick appeared from under the walkways and began to take floating bread within feet of five anglers, a camera crew, a sound crew and various other unit personnel.

Mullet tackle owes more to coarse fishing than to sea angling. An 11–13-ft match rod (matted down with Scotchbrite or scouring powder), a small fixed-spool reel, 3–6-lb line, sizes 8–12 hooks, freshwater-type floats, landing net and ancilliary gear are suitable for fishing from piers and in harbours, marinas and estuaries. Much of the time, freshwater float-fishing and paternostering tactics produce best results.

Mullet tend to suck at baits rather than inhale them in conventional manner, so many mullet experts often under-shot their floats, allowing 2–3 in to protrude above the surface. The logic here is that a sucking bite will make the float bob while one that suggests the fish has the bait inside its mouth causes the float to disappear. When you have experienced fifty bites within two hours, each of which has dragged the float from sight and you still haven't hooked a fish, you will realize that mulleting isn't that simple.

Thins bite very fast as a rule and it is vital to hit them as the float flashes under water. Thicks give all manner of bites. Sometimes the float lies flat. At other times it slowly slides away. Experience is required before correct interpretation of these movements is possible. A float that is locked on to the line with a split shot each side of the wire loop at the base of the stem makes less surface disturbance on the strike than one clamped to the line with rubber rings. Such disturbance often spooks shy fish just starting to take an interest in the groundbait. As will have been gathered from earlier comments, thicks have to be induced to have confidence in strange hook-type food and it may take a long while before they recognize that the unusual substance is good grub. Sometimes mulleteers don't strike at inquisitive bites early on, feeding in more groundbait instead in order to boost confidence.

One thing is important: stick to floats and shotting patterns that produce results. Thorough familiarity with the behaviour of your end tackle enables you to recognize and interpret its characteristic movements.

It is essential that you learn to interpret mullet behaviour. All too often, anglers find shoals of them cavorting about the river, harbour or wherever, and become more and more frustrated as these blatantly visible fish refuse so much as to nibble at the bait. This is often because the fish aren't interested in food. Although they are built with an inefficient digestive system that has to cope with a food source lacking in nutrients, mullet are never as hungry as logic suggests they should be. Feeding mullet are often out of sight – their natural food lies on the sea bed. Those meandering about aimlessly near the surface are rarely interested in food. Many tyros fish for these with baits suspended between mid-water and the surface, and catch nothing. But down there, out of sight, a group of fish is busy tucking into the carpet of groundbait.

In harbours where thicks rest under boats and pontoons, it is sometimes possible to tempt a few to venture out. Obviously when thicks are seduced by floating bread they can be seen to feed. Now, because of the thick's habit of sucking at baits and because all three species take only soft foods, it often happens that a floating piece of bread is gummed at until it disintegrates away from the hook. A method that can produce well is to fish a piece of soft bread just under the surface. Dampen it a little before casting out so that it doesn't float. This must be nicely judged, so that the bait sinks very slowly. Bites are much more positive and it is often possible to strike when the mullet is seen to inhale the hook. This trick also works when mullet eagerly mop up every piece of bread other than the one on the hook. This is because the bait isn't sinking at the same speed as the free offerings, and may be just

hanging there in the water – a totally unnatural phenomenon.

One method of casting out a floating bait is with a controller. This can be made from a length of balsa wood, shaped like a zoomer float, with lead wire wraps glued close to one end. These wraps are not to cock it, but to provide casting weight for a dart-like floating missile. The tackle can be controlled so that the bait drifts several inches ahead of the controller. When a float is used, the bait tends to float alongside it. Always angle the line when striking fish that take a floating bait when facing you, so that the hook is pulled into a corner of the mouth, not out of it.

Mullet have tough mouths and strikes must be positive. The freshwater matchman's flip doesn't set the hook. Mullet hooks have to be banged home quite firmly. Generally it is wise to grease the line for float fishing so that contact between rod and float is immediate. If the line has sunk, strike sideways rather than upwards so as not to frighten fish by ripping it through the surface.

May to October sees the peak of the mullet season in most areas, with June–August the most profitable months. These fish like warm, settled weather. Cold, rough water produces inferior results. A still, muggy, overcast day in July will produce excellent sport. Thicks and thins arrive inshore in April. In the West country, thicks are to be found all through the winter months, if mild. Warm water outfalls from power stations provide good fishing during the cold months. During cold weather or periods of heavy rain, mullet will drop down estuaries as far as the open sea. An Indian summer attracts the fish back up again.

Although both thicks and thins can be found as far up an estuary as the freshwater zone, thicks prefer more salt with their diatoms. In most rivers where both are present, the thick-lip legions will be encamped closer to the sea. It appears that once both groups have found a preferred strength of salinity they will keep with it. Thus they alter their position according to the amount of fresh water coming down after heavy rain. Spring tides, which push salt water further inland than neaps, will cause the two groups to move higher up. During the flood tide, as seawater pushes into the estuary, both groups will stay with their preferred salinity band as it is driven up the river. As the tide drops they will move back again with it. Of course, estuary water is usually much warmer than seawater, being shallower and more responsive to sunshine and air temperature. This could be the key to their movements rather than salinity. However, salinity is likely to be relevant because diurnal changes would require the fish's kidney to be changing at each tide to the amount of salt it must filter out of its body.

Thin-lips like to live high up estuaries, where fresh water meets salt.

Right: At low tide, when most estuaries have minimal flow, ground-baiting tactics pay off.

Below: Harbours are excellent places in which to hunt thick-lipped mullet.

With experience, it is possible to work out from a tide chart where the shoals will be, bearing in mind recent rainfall (and remembering that summer showers are absorbed by dry ground, with little run-off). I take my dog for walks along my local estuary. While he terrorizes (so he believes) the rabbits, I wear polaroid glasses and a long-peaked baseball cap for spotting the fish. Such equipment is essential as it is important that the angler fishes to the shoals rather than expecting them to come hunting his groundbait. This means that the well-equipped estuary mulleteer should travel light.

Thin-lips

For much of the time the angler has to search out shoals of thins that are interested in taking his ragworm. If they can't be seen, the water must be searched methodically. A group of mates helps here.

But thins have an endearing trait that produces exciting sport at times. Close-packed groups of them will stand on their heads and tear up the river bed. Clouds of mud drift downstream like smoke. Often 200 yd of river will be thick murky brown as they go about this method of feeding. Cast a ragworm just ahead of such a mêlée and bites will soon follow. Sometimes the shoals are of tiddlers up to herring size. Other times they are of good fish.

Once a shoal of feeding thins has been found, all hands fish to it, sometimes with the floats only inches apart. It seems that the more ragworm scent there is in the water, the more willing the fish are to bite.

When a smaller group of fish is found mudding close in to the bank, it pays to hold a float-fished bait as close as possible to the patch they are working – sometimes the coarse angler's trick of 'laying on' works best. Concealment is vital, with the rod pointing along the bank rather than out over the water. These groups are normally of good fish, and there can be no better sight in mullet angling than to see the float twitch sideways and sink as a 4-lb thin (a specimen) swims into view.

Groundbait is less effective for thins than it is for thicks. It often attracts bream, roach and dace to the swim, none of which are worth catching – mullet fight ten times harder than coarse fish of similar size. But mashed bread will excite a shoal and make it more interested in taking the ragworm, even though bread is virtually useless as a bait for thins. Mud sometimes gets them feeding. Use the sloppy, algae-rich surface mud, not the dark stuff underneath.

On a few occasions, a very slow retrieval of the ragworm through a shoal of nibblers will provoke more positive takes. As the line is tight to the float, fast striking is comparatively easy. Because thins tend to

bite at supersonic speeds, it is important to hold back the float when trotting it down a swim, so that the line is kept tight and ready to bang home the hook as soon as the float goes under.

A characteristic peculiar to thins is their habit of hopping. A warm, muggy afternoon is the best time to witness this. Every so often one will leap out and plop back in. Small fish are more fond of this game than bigger ones.

Because both thicks and thins have very loose scales, it is unwise to retain either species in a keep net. Slip them back with a minimum of handling some way away from the swim. Use a landing net made from knotless fabric and hold the fish inside this for unhooking, using the fabric folded over the fish both to restrain it and to provide a firm grip. Then put the net back onto the water and empty out the fish unharmed.

Thick-lips

This species is heretically unorthodox in behaviour. General fishing is with bread, pieces of fish, or whatever it happens to be scavenging in pre-baited zones. Float fishing and paternostering produce most results, fishing tight to a groundbait pattern. From piers, fill an onion sack with mashed bread and let the waves and water movement distribute it through the fishing area.

There are times when this species does strange things. Many are caught each year on lumps of squid and mackerel – and even lugworm. One trick is to fix a mackerel head to a large hook and have a small hook on lighter line hanging 1 in or so beneath the head. The fish take the little hook, baited with a morsel of fish flesh, as though it has broken free from the head.

Another trick is the carp angler's decoy crust method of fishing floating bread. A large crust is threaded on to the line and held in place by a couple of leger-stops 3 in away from a dime-size morsel on a size ten hook. Again the fish accepts it as though it has broken free from the main mass. The best bread for bait is the mass-produced variety.

Ragworm scores well in some estuaries, and exceptionally well around the mouth of sewers. In estuaries it tends to be a hit-or-miss bait, lacking the precise control that is possible when fishing bread flake to a carpet of mashed bread groundbait – or whatever you decide to inflict on the mullet.

When seaweed has been mounded up by a summer storm and has been allowed to rot for a few days before a spring tide comes lapping at it, sand flies will have used it as a nursery and maggots will be washed into the water. With the spring tide come thicks, bass and eels to feast on them. Excellent fun can be had under these special – and somewhat rare – circumstances. Once I watched such a marine compost heap each high tide for days during clear water conditions. I was on a low cliff immediately above. I saw only gulls pecking at the maggots – and a shoal of mackerel haring after a group of terrified fry – but nothing else.

A trick that stands better chances of success is to dig little pits in an estuary bank and fill each one with mashed bread – or whatever. The bank needs to be fairly steep so that there is adequate depth to fish in out of the current. A stick marking the end of the line ensures that the swim is not lost when the tide covers it. Thus the thicks can be held for several hours and the angler can fish close to his groundbait. A little mashed bread is also thrown in from time to time.

Some anglers experiment with condensed milk, custard powder and similar flavourings in their groundbait. No doubt somebody will make a break-through one day and find something that really makes the fish wild.

In Cornwall, when fishing at long range to open-sea mullet, a special float is used that looks like a cross between a torpedo and an antenna float. The reel line is tied to the base and the trace to the tip of the antenna. Bites are shown by the float toppling onto its side like a skittle. The design of these self-weighted floats is critical. The point of balance needs to be at the water line, so that it topples easily on the take. This design also scores with mid-water predators – when the trace doesn't tangle.

When fishing for thicks in harbours, it is vital to know where all the mooring ropes and similar hazards are and what effect they will have on your chances of landing a hooked fish. A specimen thick of 5 lb will run 50 yd with the unstopability of a run-away truck. Some anglers who are adept at this 'suicide' fishing use powerful rods and lines and try quickly to bully the fish

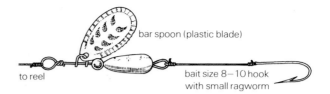

Baited mullet spinner

out of the water immediately after hooking. Once on the surface, a fish has lost most of its strength, being unable to get much purchase. Planning is essential when fishing harbour jungles, as many a disappointed mulleteer has had cause to reflect while checking his broken line for fraying.

Both thicks and thins sometimes hit baited spinners. Preference is for a $\frac{3}{4}$–$1\frac{1}{2}$-in bar spoon, lightly-built, with a size 8 hook hanging 1–2 in astern and baited with ragworm. Why does this work? Who knows! It just does. Places like Christchurch harbour in Hampshire are famous for it. The tackle needs to be retrieved with the rod high so that the lure fishes slowly close to the surface. Takes are generally pretty hard. The spinner fails to work when the ragworm are not there – and when the rag itself is spinning. Ball-bearing swivels and an up-trace anti-kink device ensure that the line doesn't snarl up.

With so many apparent contradictions in its make-up, it is worth remembering that mullet are related to barracuda. They belong to the same family. But while one is a sheepish, marsh-loving set of gums, the other is an ocean-going dental display. But then mullet are unorthodox. Patterns of behaviour cannot be categorized because the fish so frequently contradict themselves, which is why this chapter does little more than sketch a few outlines. The only way to learn mullet fishing is to get out there and do it.

12
Match fishing

The competitive side of sea angling has its roots in the hundreds of clubs throughout the United Kingdom. Since the foundation of these in the early part of this century, anglers have met together in the social atmosphere which usually accompanies a match. In the early years, matches took the form of a monthly get-together to fish for small prizes and trophies, the venues being as close to the local tavern as possible.

Gradually, as the number of clubs increased, matches grew in both size and numbers. The arrival of the car allowed anglers to fish matches away from home, and thus were born the large open matches. In the last twenty years, the open circuit has developed into the many national championships which are today fished by up to 3,000 anglers at a time. Such has been the rapid growth of match angling that clubs have joined forces to organize such giant events as the European and All England Championships, the Forward Chemicals Masters, and others. Today the match angler is a specialist, but he fishes at both club level and in the large open events. The lure of large prizes in both cash and goods has attracted a growing number to the match scene.

Linked with this is the decline in inshore fishing. This has resulted in more anglers attempting match fishing as a means of compensating for the lack of fish with the added thrill of competition. Match fishing could be described as a drug, and, as in other competitive sports, the desire to win has gradually introduced a degree of professionalism among the top competitors. Thus luck is gradually diminishing as the major factor in success. Of course it still figures in results and is one of the main reasons why match angling is so popular – a comparative beginner can occasionally win a large match or, for that matter, catch a big fish.

If a match angler is to be successful he must first realize that the situation in which he finds himself during a match is very different from that of a freelance trip. He is placed at a position on the beach at a time not always best for catching fish and his task is to catch the greatest number or heaviest weight during the given time. It is of utmost importance to use none other than the most efficient method of fishing, the best bait, and so on.

The match angler will often be fishing at a time when only a few fish are available and these must be shared between the many rods on the beach. So when a shoal of fish is passing by, the match angler must catch as many as possible as quickly as possible. The freelance angler has no need to do this and can plan his sessions to coincide – at least sometimes – with continuous sport.

Any factor which contributes to loss of time during a match will lead to fish being missed and at the end of the day when fish are weighed, it is those missed fish which will cost the angler a prize, or the satisfaction of winning.

The competition angler must also be prepared to catch the prevalent species at a given venue and this may encompass many fishes which the freelance may not bother with. For instance, the humble pouting can be a better bet for a match-winning bag than the stray cod that the beach might offer. An important factor in success is often the decision on which species will give the greatest chance of winning.

On the other hand, where one species is sought by the majority in a match, the expert angler should not ignore other stray species which could swim by. This involves a method of fishing, which I will deal with later, for two completely different species at the same time, such as the bottom-feeding flounder and the pelagic garfish.

In the main, matches are won by a small margin, especially where fishing skills are widespread among the entrants. So a bonus fish or extra species are always valuable. In the same respect, competitors are always looking for an edge over their rivals. This may only be small and could be supplied by several different factors. Thus the skills required of a match angler are multiple. He requires casting skills, for he may need to cast a great distance. He must have the best possible bait and tackle and the experience to judge its propriety to each venue he fishes.

Do not risk being disqualified through trying to weigh in undersized fish. Play safe and make a measuring board.

The degree of competition amongst match anglers is such that the individual cannot afford to be unprepared for any event or to lose any fish because of tackle failure as at the top level if you lose a fish, another competitor will not. Conditions, tactics and prizes have changed a great deal since those days when top priority was the location of the nearest pub.

Choice of contests

There are a great many differences between the types of angling competitions and the match angler's first consideration is to select a match which gives him, personally, the best opportunity of success. Certain matches are fished over barren ground. These offer the pot-luck, one-fish tombola situation and are generally avoided by the top matchmen. Others are fished in areas with plenty of fish and offer better chances to an angler skilled at speed fishing.

Another consideration may be that of knowledge of the venue. Such is the lure of the big prize that an angler may compete in a locality about which he knows little, whilst ignoring a smaller match closer to home on ground with which he is familiar. Match fishing is about winning, and winning breeds confidence. This in turn has the biggest single effect on an angler's results. By studying the match list early in the year, the angler can select the matches he is to fish during the season. In this way he has time before each event to become completely conversant with all aspects of that match, paying close attention to the shoreline and its fish, the match rules, and the organization.

The main difference between matches is that they are either rovers or pegged-down matches. Both have their own distinct advantages. A roving match offers the knowledgeable local angler the opportunity to fish any hot-spot and also the option of moving from place to place as the fish change position because of tidal movements, and so on. The pegged-down match gives the angler an equal opportunity at fishing such spots and success depends more on angling skill, as well as knowledge of how to fish the place, rather than on the ability to pick the right spot.

The pegged-down match is growing in popularity because it incorporates section prizes, rather as if a series of smaller matches is taking place under the umbrella of the main event. Thus the man fishing an indifferent stretch of beach has an equal opportunity with his neighbour in the same section of qualifying for a smaller prize. Under this system, prizes are allocated to the anglers who win each section, even though they may finish well down the aggregate weight list.

Some of the most attractive matches are those offering very large cash prizes. The main disadvantage,

so far as the matchman is concerned, is that the odds against winning are lengthened considerably. Luck figures strongly in this type of match with the large venue invariably yielding one big fish to a lucky rod. Other obvious disadvantages are crowded beaches, parking problems, and the inevitable long wait at the end for results. Such matches often turn into bun fights because of an over-large entry. An increasing trend is to organize such large events in a series of heats culminating in a final on a length of coastline offering plenty of fish.

Planning and preparation

Advance planning and preparation for a match will always pay dividends to the angler who is not content to make do. Even the smallest detail, if over-looked, can affect the final result. Obviously tackle and bait are the two most important areas in which the matchman can prepare himself. Tackle needs to be first class – so don't make-do-and-mend! If something lets you down, it could mean the loss of a fish. This doesn't mean that rods need be shiny with pretty-coloured whippings and polished rings, neither does it mean that reels should gleam in the sun. But it does mean that gear should be in perfect working order.

A tidy tackle box containing spares of everything from reel to traces will save valuable minutes when the untimely bird's-nest claims half your reel line, or a snag your terminal tackle. Take along different rigs to cope with a variety of weather conditions or fish species, together with different hook sizes to cope with different baits. The combinations may seem to be endless, but each venue can be prepared for with a number of sets of terminal tackle of the type likely to be required. Prepared end rigs can be wound around chunks of polyethylene foam to prevent them from tangling up – and this is the best way of storing mackerel feathers when out freelance fishing.

To prepare bait entails much hard work with a fork or spade, as a necessity of match angling is that you dig all your own bait. Many of the most successful bait forms used by the matchman cannot be purchased from tackle shops. Baits such as white ragworm, harbour ragworm and peeler crab all have to be collected by the angler. He also needs to take to the match enough of each type to allow him to fish throughout with only one kind, should the fish dictate it.

Keeping records

There is no substitute for experience of a particular venue. Knowing how to fish and what to fish for is an ace up the sleeve for the visiting matchman. Whether the particular match is pegged down or zoned makes little difference as the top priority in either case is to catch the maximum from the drawn or selected spot – and in each case other anglers are in the same situation.

Experience is all about memory and being able to think out each particular match condition and come up with the correct fishing method to cope with it. This can be assisted by the keeping of a detailed record of results on all venues. Note every minute detail of a match result, not just weather conditions, state of tide, season, fish present, best baits and so on. Thus venues once visited can be logged in a diary and then, when you fish there again, your memory will be jogged when planning tackle, bait and strategy.

There is no one method of match fishing which will cope with every situation, although the majority of match anglers may think there is.

'Reading the beach' is a phrase often used by anglers, yet in reality very few are able to do this. It is a fact that what looks like a fishy spot to the angler is nothing of the sort to the fish. Many anglers visit a venue on the day of the match at low tide and then, if the match is a rover, select the most likely-looking fishing spot. This is a totally foolish approach to match fishing. The angler is far better employed keeping records and gleaning knowledge from the local experts about how the venue is fishing at the time. A few telephone calls to locals during the week prior to the match will quickly reveal the best spots or species to look for. Also of importance are the weather conditions likely to be found there.

Alternatively, the angler can influence his chances by a pre-match trip to fish the match stretch. This will give him up-to-date information of the fishing, but there are several pitfalls to be avoided. Firstly, on a recce trip, do not fish at a time different from that of the match duration. A practice session at night at the site of a match to be fished by day will tell you nothing except, perhaps, that a lot of fish are there in darkness. Do not fish with two rods as this will increase your catch during practice and give a magnified view of the area's potential. Practice sessions should be kept short: once the fish have been found, move to another spot. After all, you do not want to catch the fish which may be there on the match day. Marathon all-day practice sessions give a false impression of the venue's potential, and there is nothing more frustrating in a match than to be continually nagged by the thought of the bumper catch you had in practice, while catching little during the match itself.

Bait and presentation

Bait is the biggest single influence on an angler's catch rate. Having the best of the required type of bait can give an enormous advantage over other competitors. The act of catching fish when all those around you are not is the most satisfying part of match angling.

The most successful match baits are always those which are eaten by a wide range of fish, such as peeler crab. Virtually every species of fish will take peeler, making it a very versatile bait. Alternatively, white ragworm is the ideal bait when fish are scarce or small, as it is readily seized by the juniors of most species. Many may think that lugworm is the number one sea bait. Yet it only catches plenty of fish because it is the bait most widely used. The match angler does use lug when it is the first choice of a few species of fish, but even then, by digging his own, he discovers that there are many more types of lugworm than the basic two bought from the shop. Soft lug and black lug both have their uses for different fish and fishing conditions. Black lug, for instance, is thick and tough, making it ideal for winter cod but too big for summer flatfish. Black lug will withstand the attacks of shore crabs longer than soft lug and may be used for this reason. These are all important considerations for the match angler. Of the many worm baits available, there are several which cope with the match situation particularly well.

Harbour ragworm is an ideal small and wriggly bait for estuary matches or for use from piers for pollack and mullet. Rockworm, another very active worm on the hook, is tougher than harbour ragworm and therefore more suited where distance casting is required. White or silver ragworm is ideal in clear water because it wriggles and doesn't blend in with its surroundings. For the same reasons it is also a good mid-water bait.

Peeler crab is ideal in cloudy water because of its strong scent and juices. A favourite match technique is to employ peeler as an attractor when using other, less smelly baits, by using one hook baited with a large juicy peeler and two more hooks baited with wriggly white ragworm. The former attracts flounders to the tackle, where they readily take the worm baits. Without the crab bait, they take longer to find the worms.

The match angler uses much more bait than the freelance because bait in a match must always be fresh and oozing juices and scent. So all baits are changed on every cast. Even the potential of lugworm as a bait is improved by bursting the worm before casting out – once the juices are washed out, the worm is changed. This need for a large amount of bait means that the angler may carry to the match rather more than he needs. In order to prevent waste, he should be adequately equipped back home with a bait aquarium. These are dealt with in detail in chapter 4. However, there are some aspects of tanking white ragworm which are especially connected to match fishing.

After all the preparation, is it enough to win a prize?

Firstly, whites must be kept at a steady temperature. The use of a fridge is important for this, the worms being kept in small plastic containers. They should not be over-crowded (twenty to a sandwich box), and injured or dead worms should not be included. The airflow from the air stone should be kept to a minimum as over-oxygenated water brings them out in sores very quickly. When transporting them to a distant venue in warm weather, place them in a bucket with a small quantity of coral sand. They can burrow into this and will not then be damaged during transportation.

For the matchman, the bait is a means of presenting the hook, rather than the other way around. So the hook should suit the size of the bait and not restrict its performance. Because the matchman mainly uses small hooks, this is more important than that a bait should look, to the angler's eye, completely natural. In fact, what is a natural-looking bait? Very rarely do fish come across a whole and complete worm on the sea-bed. Natural bait invariably means something which is dead or dying, mashed or mutilated. A bait should be placed on the hook so that it releases attractive juices and does not impair hooking. It need not look neat and tidy.

Tackle

Rods and reels are generally the same for both freelance fishing and match angling, the only difference in rod design being that match anglers like slim-tipped rods that show up bites well. The terminal rig has the biggest effect on the bait's underwater behaviour. Various patterns of end tackle either move the bait differently or make it react to tidal movement in ways that are particularly suited to catching certain species.

By far the most successful all-round rig is the mono paternoster. This simple, streamlined make-up, which aids casting and presents baits without hook snoods tangling, is the first choice in many situations. Other variations, with longer hook snoods or made from lighter line, offer the matchman a choice when fishing is difficult. Yet many of the standard patterns of terminal gear, including the mono paternoster, are used by the matchman and often they are tied up to look perfect, with little regard to their behaviour underwater.

The most common fault is that rigs have the longest snoods nearest to the weight. Yet the snoods furthest away need to be the longest if the bait is to be fished on the sea bed. Such considerations are of particular importance to the match angler when selecting different species to fish for. Whiting, for example, may prefer the bait above the sea-bed, whilst flounders like the bait hard on the bottom.

Few rigs in use today are exclusive to the match angler except, perhaps, a design of my own called 'the

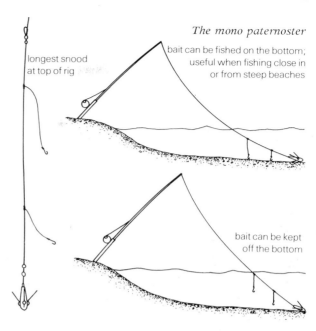

The mono paternoster
bait can be fished on the bottom; useful when fishing close in or from steep beaches

longest snood at top of rig

bait can be kept off the bottom

The flyer

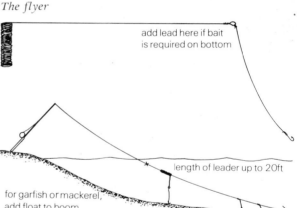

add lead here if bait is required on bottom

length of leader up to 20ft

for garfish or mackerel, add float to boom

flyer'. This entails using a trace or mono paternoster that contains two hooks. Above this rig, on a boom sliding on the main reel line, hangs a third hook. When cast, the boom travels back along the line as far as a stop-knot or the leader knot, whichever is chosen. Thus baited hooks can be fished either far apart or at different depths. This rig may include a small float fixed to the boom, allowing the angler to fish for garfish and mackerel while also fishing on the bottom for flatfish, and so on.

A growing trend among match organizers is to allow a method of fishing called 'two-patting' during competitions. This is simply the use of two baited rigs which are used on alternate casts, thus saving the time lost in rebaiting and removing hooked fish. The second rig is clipped on and cast out after the first is removed. The rig ashore is then rebaited for the next cast. This method is barred in some matches, but does increase the catch rate by about one third. It also makes it easier to change the terminal rig design or bait without loss of fishing time.

The one item of tackle which is of the utmost importance to the match angler is the hook. The most popular patterns include the Mustad Aberdeen Blue, Breakaway Spearspade, Sealey Flashpoint, and the Mustad Viking. All of these hooks have one thing in common – they are very sharp or can be sharpened to a perfect needle point with a small oilstone. They are all fine of wire but strong. This is important because match fishing always entails fishing for the smallest species, yet at the same time the tackle – especially the hook – must be able to cope with the unexpected large fish. These patterns offer perfect hooks on which to mount baits so that they do not crowd the point and blank out its efficiency.

One aspect of tackle in which the match angler specializes, is that of whipped hooks to nylon. There are two reasons for doing this. Firstly, some of the most efficient patterns of match fishing hooks, such as the Aberdeen Blue and the Spearspade, are without an eye, the former having a slightly ribbed shank and the latter a spade end. Both require whipping for a reliable fixture. Super-glue ensures this is done efficiently. It is then whipped with fly-tying silk and given a finishing coat of glue. The result is a hook to mono that is ideally suited for use with small worm baits, such as white or harbour ragworm. Without the usual knot attachment, worms can be threaded up the hook shank and onto the line without splitting them. This is particularly relevant to white ragworm which, when hooked this way and threaded up the line, still wriggle even when small worms are used to tempt the smaller fishes.

The second use for Super-glue whipping is the addition of a nylon bait-holding spur on the hook's shank. This is especially useful for razorfish and crab baits. It can also be used to glue small worms in bunches to a hook.

Whipped hooks are not suitable for all baits. Peeler crab is best used in conjunction with an eyed hook, with whipped-on spur, tied on with a half blood knot. A $\frac{1}{4}$ in of loose end can be left after forming the knot to aid the bait-holding power of this combination. A blob of Super-glue ensures a knot will not slip. A trick with spade-end knots is to glue the knot itself as near as possible to the spade to prevent the sharp end from damaging the line. Super-glue can also be used to hold snoods at right-angles to the paternoster. Form a blood loop, then twist it until only a small loop is left at the end. Coat the twists with glue and the loop will stand straight out from the rig.

Grip leads are very important to the matchman because they vary the behaviour of the baited hook. In common use is the breakaway lead. This is especially useful because the tension of the wires can be adjusted. In the main, anglers use grip leads to hold bottom

Nylon bait-holding spur whipped onto hook shank. Especially useful for razorfish bait.

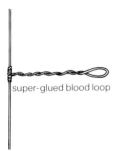

super-glued blood loop

Super-glued snood at a right-angle to the paternoster.

against the tide. Yet they are a most positive aid to hooking fish especially when used at slack water. Fish taking the bait soon meet the resistance of the grip lead and hook themselves, generally through trying to bolt. Codling and bass will tow a plain lead over the bottom, then drop the bait. The fact that the current moves the lead at all is due to tidal pressure on the length of mono between sinker and rod tip. Lighter lines require less lead to combat this pressure. This is useful to remember when fish are shy.

Scratching, and other business

The term 'scratching' must have been invented by a match angler, as it sums up completely the attitude and methods during a majority of matches when fish are in short supply. There is no magic formula for instant success, so on such days the task ahead is clear-cut. First you scratch your head to think of all the different methods and tackle you can try either to reach or find fish, or try to tempt the few that may be present to feed.

Changes in terminal rigs are the first choice as they alter the behaviour of the bait. Bait changes come next with the faithful peeler/worm combination a sure-fire success – occasionally. Distance is an important consideration. By decreasing the number of baited hooks, casting distance can be increased. Bait size, too, affects casting distance and very small baits may tempt a few fish. Sometimes it pays to fish even closer to the shore than the shortest average cast. Silver eels and flounders both frequently hug the sand line at the base of shingle beaches and can be caught as close as 10 yd! Obviously this is a routine consideration for the match angler because fish feeding close to the shore can be caught more quickly than those 150 yd out.

Another successful 'scratching' method is to move the bait. An occasional twitch or retrieve of line causes it to lift, drop, and flutter on the sea-bed in a manner which may tempt a not-so-hungry fish to bite. One such method goes thus. Once the tackle has settled, I release line from the reel at intervals, allowing the current to sweep it away from the fixed lead into a loop, thus moving the baited hooks very slightly each time. This is a deadly pouting tempter.

Groundbaiting is one area which is not exploited by the sea angler for several obvious reasons, yet it is possible and effective in certain conditions. When fishing close in for flounders or pouting, I employ a tin can, perforated with small holes, which I fill with dead crabs, stale lugworm, fish guts, and so on. I can throw this about 30 yd. When fishing against a groyne or in rocks it often holds fish for a considerable time. It is, of course, of no use when fish are well out or during strong tides. Other matchmen use cat or dog food to good effect. This may get a laugh from fellow competitors, but when I've walked up to accept first prize on more than one occasion, thanks to groundbait cans, I have been doing the laughing.

Finally, here is a selection of small (and, maybe to some, insignificant) points about match angling.

Having caught your fish, they need to be looked after prior to the weigh-in. Keep them alive, in the shade and in a bucket of water so that they do not lose any valuable ounces. Check on this point, however, for some match rules forbid it. It is important to remove the hook carefully as loss of blood means loss of weight, and could put you down the prize list. Keeping fish alive also means that they can be returned alive after the weigh-in. This is becoming the practice of many match anglers.

Be conversant with the size limits employed at every match. Some organizations will disqualify competitors who bring undersized fish to the scales. The needless killing of such minors also affects future fishing.

Do not throw undersized fish back into the sea from the top of the beach. Take them to the water's edge and release them gently – even if you are angry at that tiny pout which pulled your rod over. Disregard for fish welfare is extremely bad public relations, especially when non-angling spectators are about.

When fish need to be registered with a steward as they are caught, cast out rebaited tackle before going to see him. Don't leave your rod lying on the beach as you waltz along the shingle showing off your catch to your mates and stopping for a chat on the way back; this is fishing time lost.

Always remember that by using up to three hooks, three fish can be caught at once if they are feeding well. Don't strike at the first sign of movement on the rod-tip. Wait, and you may get two or three fish at once. Striking instantly will inevitably mean catching nothing.

At the weigh-in, watch your catch closely when it is being measured and weighed. Officials in a hurry are not infallible and their mistake could cost you a place in the prize list.

Index

Page numbers in italics refer to illustrations

THE AGE OF

EMPIRE

THE AGE OF
EMPIRE

BRITAIN'S IMPERIAL ARCHITECTURE
FROM 1880–1930

CLIVE ASLET

Aurum
Press

First published in Great Britain
2015 by Aurum Press Ltd
74–77 White Lion Street
Islington
London N1 9PF
www.aurumpress.co.uk

A catalogue record for this book is available from
the British Library.

ISBN 978 1 78131 225 4

2015 2017 2019 2018 2016

1 3 5 7 9 10 8 6 4 2

Printed in China

Staff Credits:
Publisher: Richard Green
Managing Editor: Vanessa Daubney
Designer: Sooky Choi
Picture Research: Daniela Rogers
Production Controller: Rachel Ng

CONTENTS

FOREWORD

*T*his book is the product of an abiding love for architecture at the turn of the twentieth century. I have had it since at least 1978 when, just down from Cambridge, I helped Gavin Stamp research an edition of *Architectural Design* on 'London 1900'; the binding of that magazine has long since disintegrated, but the pages remain wedged onto my shelves between other greats – Christopher Hussey's biography of Lutyens, Robert Grant Irving on New Delhi, Thomas Mecalf's *An Imperial Vision* to name but a few. In 1979, I helped to found the Twentieth Century Society, becoming the first Honorary Secretary. Then, the period fascinated me because of its remoteness. Now that London and the South of England have returned to conditions of plutocracy comparable to those of the Edwardian era, I am daily reminded of similarities, not all of them good.

The period that this book looks at is 1880–1930. It was an age of contrasts, when great artistic sensitivity co-existed with bombast, and earnest idealism walked the same pavements as opulence. I view it here through the prism of Empire. Before 1880, Britain had long possessed colonies, but did not consider them to be an essential part of her own DNA. That changed with the New Imperialism of the 1880s, a political movement that coincided with a surge of popular enthusiasm for Empire, which became nothing short of a rage. Nearly losing part of it in the close-run Boer War only stimulated a greater imperial consciousness. While the First World War ended the German, Hapsburg, Ottoman and Russian Empires, it left the British Empire bigger than ever. Its possessions now stretched in an unbroken line from the Suez Canal to Singapore and from Cairo to the Cape. For the public at home, the British Empire Exhibition at Wembley in 1924 showed what fun it was to run a quarter of the world's landmass; but the reluctance of some Indian states to participate sounded a warning note. The benefits of Empire were not always apparent to its subjects overseas. Palliation was wearisome, control expensive. Architects had their imperial self-confidence further dented by the awareness that a novel language of form was being developed on the Continent that advertised very different social ideas from those to which they were accustomed in Britain. The styles that had seemed so vigorous and exciting in the Edwardian decade – the High Game of Classicism, the zaniness of extreme Arts and Crafts, the anything-goes airiness of Free Style, the moral purpose of soundly-built LCC flats – failed to rejuvenate themselves and looked tired. But in the swagger years, Britain, having thrown off the mantel of free trade, wrapped itself in purple, a toga appropriate to its new sense of itself as the centre of a great empire – conscious that Paris, Vienna, Berlin and Brussels had beaten it to the dressing-up box. Imperial statesmen ordered new clothes for the Empire, too, including some very complete suitings for India and South Africa; local character infused with British purpose – or British purpose with a nod to native traditions – was the cut.

Domes multiplied, sculpture burgeoned, on buildings that had experienced a dramatic inflation of scale. Finance had developed in the late Victorian period to the point when the richest people in the country, judged by their wills, were bankers (*plus ça change* perhaps). This acted on architecture rather like a foot pump on one of the new pneumatic tyres; it swelled. Streets, monuments, offices, banks – all got bigger. Ultimately, under Baker's hand, the Bank of England itself rose like a soufflé above the austere, finely detailed pie-dish of Sir John Soane's curtain walls. Britain stood to attention and puffed out its chest – even if it did not always pull in its stomach.

The bugle of Empire did not sound everywhere. The rural aesthetic of the Arts and Crafts Movement did not lend itself to grand imperial gestures. But Empire was so big a fact, and the discrepancy in development between industrialised Britain and the tropical colonies so huge, that even the socialist William Morris did not attack it, while his mentor John Ruskin – radical in some ways, Tory in others – staunchly believed in it (which was odd, since Mahatma Gandhi, inspired by Ruskin's *Unto This Last*, turned post-colonial India, with its agrarian, village-based economy, into an Arts and Crafts state). Architects had every reason to support the Empire. It gave them superb opportunities to build.

In 1978, appreciation of the period was at a nadir. Most of Thomas Collcutt's Imperial Institute had been demolished in the 1960s; Sir Edwin Cooper's old Lloyds building would soon be reduced to a single façade. Now a different public response can be seen from the care with which both Admiralty Arch and the old Port of London Authority building are being turned into hotels and residences. Cathays Park in Cardiff, William Waldorf Astor's Two Temple Place on the Thames and even the Argyll Motor Works on Loch Lomond (now a factory outlet shopping centre) are beautifully maintained. People still dine beneath the mosaics of the Criterion Restaurant in Piccadilly, enjoy musical evenings beneath the globe balanced above Frank Matcham's Coliseum like a ball on the nose of a seal, or taste the saltiness of Britain's seafaring past in the sculptures on Deptford Town Hall (now part of Goldsmiths College). The City of London did not entirely expunge the old stateliness of blocked columns and sculptural pediments, gilded weathervanes and exuberant terracotta, now glimpsed between reflective glass walls. English Heritage displays the Durbar Wing at Osborne House, once derided, as an architectural entity of exceptional interest.

Empire is not a fashionable idea. Understandably many former colonies have distanced themslves from the past by changing their name or those of their cities. In this book, I have used the old names to avoid confusion when quoting original sources. The British Empire's great achievement was said to be Pax Britannia (enforced, admittedly, with the aid of the Gatling gun) but the legacy of Empire, with national boundaries drawn with a high and arbitrary hand, has not been universal peace. And it is no coincidence that loot is an Indian word. But architecture, of its nature, expresses another side of the endeavour, the lofty ideal of projecting order and immutability in stone.

The buildings persist, long after the Empire has gone.

INTRODUCTION

I am an Empress, Queen Victoria told her private secretary in January 1873, 'and in common conversation am sometimes called Empress of India. Why have I never officially assumed this title? I feel I ought to do so and wish to have preliminary enquiries made.' Four years later, Benjamin Disraeli had arranged to have her wish granted. It was a stroke of genius, which showed the understanding that the Queen, although retired from the public gaze, had of her people. They loved Empire, and so did she.

Attitudes had been otherwise in the mid nineteenth century. Such had been the indifference that in 1865 a parliamentary committee recommended that Britain should withdraw from her four bases in West Africa. The doctrine of *laissez-faire* was all conquering. During the 1870s, Disraeli not only made Queen Victoria Empress of India, but also allowed Britain to be dragged – by Lord Lytton, the Viceroy of India, and Bartle Frere, High Commissioner for Southern Africa for the British Empire – into war in Afghanistan and Zululand. The surprising thing was that his imperial warmth was matched after the 1880 election by the new Liberal cabinet; or perhaps less by them, than by the population at large. 'The British public just now is in a very aggressive and acquisitive mood,' the Colonial Secretary Lord Derby wrote to Gladstone in 1884. '… At least I find this is the opinion of every person I talk to, and it is certainly that of every newspaper.' When the Conservative Lord Salisbury returned to office in 1885, this time as Prime Minister, he was amazed by the change in the public mood. 'Nobody' had 'thought about Africa' in 1880; five years later, the whole of Europe was quarrelling about it. Lord Rosebery, the Liberal who succeeded Gladstone in 1894, was 'passionately attached to the Empire'. Even the Fabians Beatrice and Sidney Webb founded the Coefficients, a dining club to discuss 'the aims and methods of Imperial policy'. Populist newspapers such as the *Daily Mail* (founded 1896) and the *Daily Express* (1900) could be expected to blow the trumpet, but the Poet Laureate Alfred Austin as well as popular writers such as Rider Haggard and G. A. Henty produced almost as much noise. The Scramble for Africa saw that continent, only one tenth of which had been under European control in 1870, end the century almost completely (90 per cent) in European hands.

Britain's New Imperialism was not entirely a sign of strength. The rise of France and Germany as imperial powers – with indications that they would trade with their colonies on privileged terms – caused anxiety among British manufacturers. Fearing that previously profitable markets would disappear, some of them abandoned the principle of free trade, which had been such a powerful mantra only a few years earlier, in favour of an integration of Empire. This consolidated body need not worry about what harsh winds blew outside its borders. Naturally, the bigger the market the Empire provided, the better. And so more colonies were needed.

ABOVE An Imperial Federation League map
showing the extent of the British Empire in
1886. This map was published as a supplement
for *The Graphic*. Britain's imperial territories
are coloured pink. The elegant native maidens,
topee-wearing soldiers and exotic animals are
presented as a carnival celebration of Empire –
although the artist who drew it, Walter Crane,
was an anti-imperialist, who would resign from
the Fabian Society when it failed to condemn
the Boer War in 1900. The map was produced
in the year before the nation went Empire-
mad with Queen Victoria' Golden Jubilee. The
Imperial Federation League, founded in 1884,
promoted the development of the Empire as a
federal association, like Canada or the United
States.

Like the Queen's own girth, the Empire expanded ever outwards; and under
Joseph Chamberlain as Colonial Secretary from 1895 until 1906, the British
government took an increasingly direct interest in its affairs, promoting imperial
ventures or providing loans to those who did. Occupying 'great spaces of the
world's surface', Britain found itself in the position of a landlord, who had the
'duty' of developing 'his estate'. Chamberlain's policy of Imperial Preference hid
a malaise in the British economy, whose manufacturing efficiency had declined
in relation to that of the rising powers of Germany and the United States. But it
conformed to Britain's idea of its own identity. While the Scots, Welsh and Irish
may have been dismayed by ingrained habit by people saying England when they
meant Britain, the Empire was always British. It was the foundation stone of the
United Kingdom's collective identity.

By the end of the 1890s, Empire fever had become all but universal – certainly
among people who were commissioning buildings. The Empire was routinely used
as a justification of expense, at home no less than abroad. Indeed, particularly
at home. When London looked at itself, and compared what it saw with Paris,
sliced through with Haussmann's avenues and boulevards and glittering with

electric light, or Vienna, where old city walls had been replaced with the broad carriageways and Baroque edifices of the Ringstasse, it felt shabby. Black with soot, murky with smog, it was a testament to private property rights, *laissez-faire* economics and the Picturesque movement. Its best feature, the garden squares, were only accessible to keyholders; little effort had been made to make planning sense of the urban muddle since John Nash had built Regent Street for the Prince Regent; and grand Classical gestures – broad streets aligned on eye-catching monuments – were alien to its aesthetic nature. Dickens had given an adjective to the worst of the squalor – Dickensian; and the scars that the novelist described as the railways slashed their way into the heart of the city had not yet healed. The great town-planning achievement of the Embankments beside the Thames was almost an accident of the need to build Balzalgette's sewers. Indeed, the Metropolitan Board of Works, the body responsible for the development of London from 1855 to 1889, had little instinct for the texture of cities: Northumberland Avenue, ploughing through the remains of Northumberland House, one of the Tudor palaces on the Thames, makes nothing of its relationship either with Trafalgar Square or the river; while 'the mutilation of the ingenious and dignified arrangement of Piccadilly Circus' by Shaftesbury Avenue was, in the words of the Edwardian architect Beresford Pite, 'an irreparable outrage' (although Shaftesbury Avenue did have the merit of destroying a notorious slum). From the imperial point of view, London – the biggest city in the world, and the seat of Empire – hardly lived up to the role it so conspicuously occupied at the end of the nineteenth century. Architecturally, there had been few big statements since the Palace of Westminster had been rebuilt from 1840. Britain lacked an imperial manner. The New Imperialism needed a new architecture which would make the Mother Country look imperial and the Empire look to some degree as though it belonged to Britain. Architects were tasked with finding an image that encapsulated Britain's self-worth and purpose.

Queen Victoria intuitively realised that something was needed, and – as far as her own surroundings were concerned – set about providing it. She never visited India herself, but kept a keen eye on those who did – not least her eldest son, Bertie, the Prince of Wales, the future Edward VII, who in 1875–76, for once did something to please his mother by going East. 'The accounts of dear Bertie are good and satisfactory but he does too much!' she wrote to Crown Princess Frederick.

Calcutta put on a dazzling show for the first heir to the throne to visit India and Ceylon, as did every city on which he descended. Queen Victoria was a determined woman, whose adored, lamented husband, the Prince Consort, had mastered an almost Renaissance spectrum of subjects (including the early Renaissance painters, of which he was an early collector). She began to learn Hindustani and Urdu from her favoured Indian servant, Abdul Karim. He was soon known as the *Munshi*, or Teacher. The depth of her fascination with the subcontinent was boundless. Although she could not go to India, as Empress she could make parts of it come to her. And this she did at Osborne House.

Osborne was her favourite English residence, vying in her affections only with her Highland home, Balmoral. Both were hallowed by memories of Prince Albert. Osborne had been largely planned by him, in collaboration with Thomas Cubitt – hence the oddity of a palace, which would hardly have been regarded as an adequate country house by some of her more architecturally blessed subjects. Although strongly suggesting a corner of Belgravia that has become moored on a shore of the Isle of Wight, to the Queen, Osborne meant the romance of Italy. It was sacred in its association with her happy, early-married life, when she was still a vivacious, slim-waisted young mother. After the Prince Consort's death in 1861, most of the royal residences froze: no detail was to be moved, no change introduced, lest it should dispel the aura of the beloved dead. And yet, in 1890–91, a major alteration was perpetrated at Osborne. A Durbar wing was constructed.

In 1890, her third and favourite son, the dutiful Prince Arthur, Duke of Connaught, was still in India with his regiment, as well as his wife, and her grandson, Eddy, son of the Prince of Wales and soon to be Duke of Clarence, was making a seven-month tour. While there, the Connaughts took a lively interest in India. The Duke of Connaught had enjoyed strolling in the bazaars of Cairo, after fighting with his brigade – with distinction – at the battle of Tell al-Kebir. In 1883, he left for India and, at the Calcutta International Exhibition of 1883–84,

met Lockwood Kipling, father to the poet Rudyard. The elder Kipling was by then a sage-like figure with a white beard, who had been principal of the Mayo School of Art in Lahore since 1875. His approach was progressive. The son of a Methodist Minister, he had taken fire on seeing the Indian display at Great Exhibition of 1851, although he found the eroticism and capriciousness of aspects of the subcontinent's art too difficult for his Protestant sensibility.

Kipling was not the first man to interest himself in the subject. In the eighteenth century, the East India Company's nabobs, when in India, often lived surrounded by luxuries of the East, wearing Indian dress, smoking hookahs and keeping zenanas, a kind of harem. Such behaviour, even far from home, was unacceptable in the Victorian period, when the cultural influence was reversed: not only did the Raj perpetuate European habits of life, despite the incongruities of climate, but its example was apt to be imitated by the nascent Indian middle class. Furthermore, cheap imports from Britain were undermining local skills. In the two decades after the Great Exhibition, the quality of Indian craftwork fell off dramatically. The showing at the Paris Universal Exhibition of 1878 was not received with enthusiasm. Carpet-making was now practised by convicts under the supervision of prison jailers. The art of the East was 'fading away', observed William Morris, just as informed Europeans like him were beginning to idolise pre-industrial traditions. The answer, to the administrative mind, was to establish art schools in India; but the administrative mind being what it was, the people employed to run them were British teachers who did not understand local crafts. The results fell jarringly between the two stools. Such, however, was not Kipling's way. At Lahore, he revived the local crafts on their own terms. Native Indian techniques of jewellery, metalwork, pottery, printing and carpet-making were taught in workshops, operated by masters of their craft. Connaught was so taken by what he saw that he commissioned a billiard room to be made in India, and fitted into the dully conventional Bagshot Park in Surrey, given to him as a wedding present by his mother in the 1870s.

ABOVE In 1875, John Lockwood Kipling, father of the poet Rudyard Kipling, was appointed head of both the newly founded Mayo School of Art and the Lahore Museum. Such had been the volume of cheap, manufactured goods coming from Britain into India that indigenous craft industries were in decline. Kipling was one of a number of educationalists sent out to rectify the problem. Rather than teaching British methods, he established workshops in which students could learn native traditions. This photograph shows the metal-working department at the Mayo School of Art (named after the Viceroy Lord Mayo). A large lamp of hammered brass is being finished by the senior students at the back, while in the foreground small boys practise elementary repoussé.

The Duchess asked that the accompanying smoking room should be based on the Jain temples of Mount Abu in Rajasthan. When the Connaughts returned home in August 1890, they saw the work for the first time, and on the 22nd of that month, Queen Victoria visited them, in company with 'Mr Kipling (a gentleman Arthur knows well …)'; she liked what she saw. As she wrote in her journal that evening, 'I want Mr Kipling to design the decoration of the interior' of what was to become the Durbar Room. It would 'be Indian. We agreed upon what was to be done.'

The need for a new large room at Osborne – part of a new wing – had been felt particularly by her children. They were now adults, with children of their own, and Osborne had become cramped for gatherings that took place there, particularly at Christmas. Although unusual in style, the Durbar Room reflected the contemporary taste for living halls – multipurpose spaces that were more informal than the patriarchal medievalising great halls of the middle years of the nineteenth century: a place where house parties could congregate, linger or pass through, as they liked.

The Durbar wing was built by W. Cubitt and Company, the firm established

ABOVE Queen Victoria commissioned the Durbar Wing at Osborne, on the Isle of Wight, after seeing similar rooms at her son the Duke of Connaught's home Bagshot Park, in Surrey. Connaught had travelled in India, enjoyed its culture and met Lockwood Kipling in 1883–84. Kipling arranged for a team of Indian craftsmen to work at Osborne, installing pierced wooden panels that had been made in India. The room functions as a turn-of-the-century living hall, and is unlike any Mughal – let alone Hindu – room in India.

by Thomas Cubitt who had been responsible for the original Osborne; on the first floor were rooms for Princess Beatrice and her family. Externally, the style continued that of the existing Italianate house. Inside, it has the appearance of a Maharajah's palace, apparently marble but in fact a combination of fibrous plaster and carton pierre – a sort of papier mâché.

The style, as Kipling suggests, was not, strictly speaking, pure. To British eyes, the ceiling resembles a Jacobean one, smothered in a meringue of ornament. The peacock over the chimneypiece was suggested by Princess Louise who was herself an amateur sculptress; it neatly united the contemporary British Aesthetic Movement with a reference to the Mughal peacock throne. But the detail was authentically Indian, designed and supervised by Bhai Ram Singh, who trained as a woodcarver at Amritsar, became a student of Kipling's at Lahore and went on to become a successful architect in the Punjab. The progress of work can be followed through the letters that Ram Singh sent to report on the project, being sure to include compliments paid by the client: 'The Queen is very much pleased ... I have also designed perforated ventilators for the room and lamp stands for light and hanging lamp for Bay Window in centre of arch.'

The Durbar Room would not be the last or most complete tribute to India on British soil. In 1899–1903, it was surpassed by Duleep Singh's successor at Elveden, the Guinness brewing peer Lord Iveagh: his Indian Hall, on which Sir Caspar

15

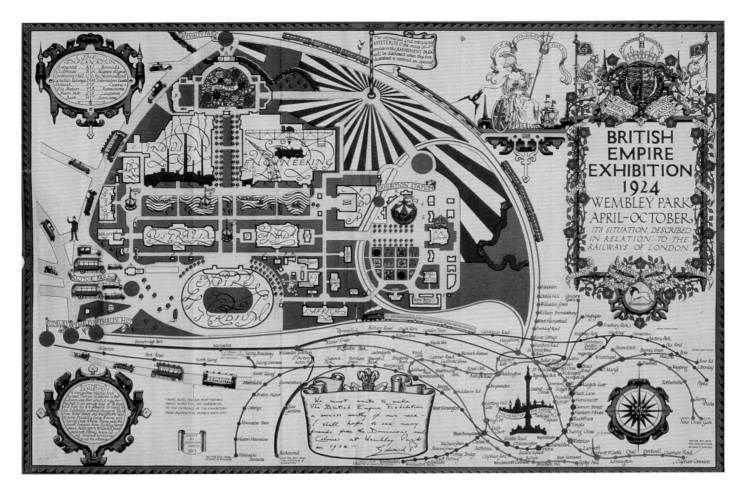

ABOVE A plan of the British Empire Exhibition, Wembley, 1924–25, in the exhibition's jaunty yet classical house style. The exhibition was intended to pick up the nation's spirits after the First World War, and championed the Empire in all its variety. From Ceylon came rubies and postage stamps; from South Africa diamonds and gladioli; from the Seychelles tortoiseshell combs; from India brocades, turbans, bedspreads, ivory inlays, tennis rackets, cricket bats, saucepans, gigantic gongs and shields … Salt cod from Newfoundland vied with chrome from Rhodesia. Canada's *pièce de résistance* was a statue of the Prince of Wales and his horse modelled in butter, that of Australia, a 1.5-ton cheese. Comparisons were inevitably made with the Great Exhibition: the British Empire Exhibition promoted trade, was not didactic and was eight and a half times the size.

Purdon Clark, Director of the Victoria and Albert Museum, advised, is all marble. Still, the Indian-loving monarch achieved a correlative to the subcontinent over which she ruled but could not visit. Could not visit in person, that is – for she was, in another form, omnipresent there. Her face was on the coinage. Statues of her stand, or, in overflowing robes, occupy plinths in Bangalore, Mathura, Madras and Visakhapatnam, as well as, with unforgettable solidity, before the Queen Victoria Memorial in Calcutta. From time to time, these images attract the attention of nationalists who demand they should be moved. Though, in contrast to the lesser imperial figures who have been herded into parks or zoos, she has held her ground, being an accepted fact, too inaccessible or cumbersome to move.

Osborne's Durbar wing shows what Queen Victoria felt about the Empire; but what did her British subjects make of it? Let us take another snapshot, this time from a different source from Queen Victoria's journal: the Tickhill Parish Magazine. Tickhill is a rural parish in South Yorkshire, and in August 1924 was getting ready for an outing. Fifty-two pupils from the National School, escorted by five teachers, visiting the British Empire Exhibition.

The British Empire Exhibition had opened that April – on St George's Day – at Wembley, a western suburb of London. The exhibition had been conceived in 1913, before the First World War, and the eleven-year gestation had allowed the ambitions of the organisers to soar. If residents of Tickhill read *The Times*, they would have known that their fifty-two children would soon be among the 'millions' of British subjects to 'ascend the Heights of Empire', according one of many full-page advertisements. 'Spread before them is the wondrous reality of Britain's might and magnitude – her grandeur and glory.' This was no time for false modesty. 'Riches and romance, ancient civilization flowering in modern enterprise, the limitless range of activity and achievement – the scene is without parallel in the history of mankind.'

ABOVE Opened on St George's Day 1924, the British Empire Exhibition was so popular that it ran for a second year, in 1925. This shows the Indian Pavilion, intended to display a nation on the road to modernising. However, India's ambiguous position within the Empire created controversy. Having achieved partial self-rule in 1919, it was not a dependent colony, but neither was it an independent dominion – and its people felt they were not accorded the fraternal status within the Empire as were those of Canada, Australia, New Zealand or white-ruled South Africa. Moderates as well as nationalists felt entitled to self-government. The Amritsar Massacre of 1919 was another grievance. There were calls for the Indian states to boycott the exhibition.

The Tickhill party went down by train, 'speeding' south at seventy miles an hour. From King's Cross, they took the Underground, and then two trams. Finally, they saw the Twin Towers, capped by Indian domes, of the Empire Stadium – later to be famous as the Wembley Sadium, scene of FA Cup finals down the years – and 'excitement ran high' as they found 'the British Empire directly before them.' They just had time to do the Antipodes before supper. What, wondered the author of the parish magazine report, most impressed the youngsters?

> Was it the native arts and crafts of Sarawak – or was [it] the stuffed boa-constrictor which had swallowed a pig whole? Was it the Fisheries Exhibit, or the rubber tree, or the embroidery of Malaya – or the rattan-cane which went round three sides of the pavilion and was 500 odd feet? Was it the wonderful panoramic views of Australian scenes, or the frozen meat – or those slightly damaged but luscious apples we got for half-price? Perhaps none of these, but the pictures at the Cinema where (pressed for time) we had to leave it a question as to whether Jack Haines would or would not 'make good' on the Australian sheep farm and marry his guardian's daughter. But, as the girls said, 'it was sure to come out all right.'

In extent, the British Empire was at its zenith, and the exhibition sought to match it in variety in scale. As our friends from Tickhill had already found, the organising principle was profusion.

Comparisons were inevitably made with the Great Exhibition of 1851, whose Crystal Palace still stood in Hyde Park; but the whole of the 1851 site would not have been big enough to contain the Palaces of Industry and Engineering, considered to be 'the two largest buildings ever erected for exhibition purposes'. On plan, the British Empire Exhibition was eight and a half times as big the Great Exhibition; its site ran to 216 acres. The Metropolitan Line's new Wembley Park station had nineteen booking office windows to cope with the crowds. By the time the Prince of Wales closed the Exhibition on 1 November, as many as 18,000,000 people had passed through the turnstiles (paying 1s 6d a time, 9d for children). It had been so successful that it opened again the next year.

The symbol of the exhibition, the British Lion, was everywhere. The ubiquitous lion, which appeared on every poster and scrap of printed material for the Exhibition, as well as around the Exhibition grounds, reminded visitors – if they needed reminding – that the whole spectacle revolved around one country, Britain, whose manufactures and ingenuity were trumpeted even more loudly than those of her colonies. Shipbuilding, wireless, armaments, X-rays, ore testing, dyestuffs, oils, biscuit making, rubber gloves – the displays of manufactures were heroic in scale, intricate in elaboration. Meanwhile, H. M. Government Pavilion provided a subtext to the dizzying profusion of the exhibits. Its Tropical Health Section, having frightened the visitor with a corner on killer diseases, presented two views of the jungle: wild and tamed, disease-ridden and safe. The moral did not need to be underlined. Empire was good for you.

The Great Exhibition had, under the chairmanship of the earnest Prince Consort, been didactic. It had sought to inform and improve rather than to sell goods. But the exhibitions held in the second half of the nineteenth century abandoned that model in favour of commerce; they were trade shows, in which the educational element was window dressing. In need of a public to sell to, they made themselves into entertainments. The British Empire Exhibition, for example, had an amusement park. Earlier exhibitions were not quite so flagrant, but often contained an ethnographical element, which was not so far removed from a freak show. A popular draw was the native village, generally African – never mind the fact that the tribespeople might have come from widely different places and could not speak each other's language. Even the Irish were treated as curiosities to be stared at; the Franco–British Exhibition of 1908 – a celebration of the Entente Cordiale, which occupied the same site as the British Empire Exhibition – included a sham Irish village called Ballymaclinton.

By 1900, exhibitions featuring colonial people and artefacts were being staged in London and other British cities on a regular basis. A famous example was the Colonial and Indian Exhibition of 1886 at the South Kensington Museum. The Queen Empress left the seclusion of her palaces to open it. A choir sang 'God Save the Queen', with one verse in Sanskrit; and she set off down a corridor that ran, as *The Graphic* put it, 'Twixt East and West', on one side being a stage set representing Old London, on the other the monumental and very solid Gwalior Gateway, weighing seventy-two tons. The Exhibition had been organised on an Arts and Crafts programme, and the Gateway, financed by the Maharajah Jayajirao Scindia, had been carved by 2,000 artisans. The design was an amalgam of both Hindu and Muslim elements, with a preference – similar to Pugin's for the purity of Early English in the Gothic Revival – for the 'pristine excellence' of earlier styles. Wall paintings of Australian cities testified, in the patronising words of the *Illustrated London News*, 'to the wonderful progress made by our energetic and enterprising colonists'. Not only were there dioramas of jungle scenes (a 'colossal masterpiece of taxidermy') and a native bazaar in India, but also genuine Indians working at traditional crafts (in fact prisoners from the Agra jail). Where Her Majesty led, visitors followed – more than 5,000,000 of them, fascinated by the sight of cultures that had yet to be transformed by industrialisation.

To the champions of the Arts and Crafts movement, then in full swing, the scene may have seemed pre-lapsarian; there was considerable sympathy for craftwork in the colonies at the British Empire Exhibition, the Director of the United Kingdom Exhibits' section being Lawrence Weaver, a former Architectural Editor of *Country Life*. Before the Boer War, Herbert Baker and his patron Cecil Rhodes promoted local crafts in the Cape. But for the most part the Arts and Crafts style was too homely for imperial taste and, in 1896, Sir John Donnelly, Secretary for the Department of Art and Science, judged the Gwalior Gateway to be a 'beastly thing'. Not even he, however, had the heart to destroy such a costly object, and it was built into the Victoria and Albert Museum, as successor to the South Kensington Museum, where it remains: albeit hidden behind a wall.

Exhibitions were not alone in demonstrating the extent of the Empire, which was also embodies in parades. Every great occasion of state, culminating in Queen Victoria's Gold and Diamond Jubilees, her funeral, the Coronation of Edward VII and George V, summoned troops from around the Empire to take part in a parade. They came from the immensity of Australia and mere dots on the map, such as Malta; from the rock of Hong Kong and the open spaces of New Zealand; from old colonies in the West Indies and new ones in Africa. Canada, Natal, India, Ceylon, Fiji, Rhodesia, Hong Kong, the Straits Settlements, Borneo, Jamaica, Trinidad, Bermuda, Barbados, Sierra Leone, Gambia, the Gold Coast, Lagos, Northern and Southern Nigeria, Malta, Cyprus … Even today, the global reach of the Empire, as represented in the soldiery it could camp out in the Home Park at Hampton Court, seems almost bewildering. Romance fluttered in the pennons of the Bengal Cavalry and bristled in the fearsome moustaches of the Bombay Grenadiers; the tall red fezzes, khaki shorts and black skins of the King's African Rifles spoke of a continent tamed.

These messages, beamed into the popular consciousness by a magnificent and disciplined military were reinforced by largely amateur pageants of imperial themes. Frank Lascelles, 'the man who staged the Empire', as he was known, became a specialist in producing them; he put on twenty-two between 1907 and 1932. These included the Great Pageant, on the theme of London, held alongside the Festival of Empire and Imperial Exhibition at the Crystal Palace, Sydenham, as

BELOW Pageants on historical and imperial themes became a popular entertainment in the early twentieth century. This photograph shows one that was staged at the Sydenham Crystal Palace for George V's Coronation in 1911 by the actor-turned-pageant-master Frank Lascelles. The following year, Lascelles mounted a pageant of even greater spectacle and colour at Calcutta for the King's visit. Village pageants became so popular that E. F. Benson satirised the rage in his novel *Mapp and Lucia* (1931).

part of George V's coronation ceremonies in 1911. Its theme, in four parts held on four separate days, was the 'magnificence, glory and honour of the Empire and the Mother Country'. Fifteen thousand costumed volunteers rehearsed for six months to get it right. More than thirty London Boroughs and corporate organisations supplied the constituent parts – early Britons from Penge, Wars of the Roses warriors from Wimbledon. Pageants – always on an historical, Empire-linked theme – entered the national bloodstream, and were mounted by village committees as well as pageant masters of state. There was of course a pageant at the British Empire Exhibition: the Pageant of Empire, words by Rudyard Kipling, staging by the great Shakespearean actor-manager Harley Granville-Barker. And also a parade of the Dominions, India and the Colonies, accompanied by 4,000 musicians in massed bands and choirs, on 24 May: Empire Day, a holiday which, from 1904 until 1958, allowed the nation to wrap itself in the Union Jack and cheer.

Like the 1951 Festival of Britain, the British Empire Exhibition opened six years after the conclusion of a World War, and sought similarly to lift the spirits of the nation, partly by reminding Britain of what it still (for the time being at least) had, and partly by the dignified *joie de vivre* with which it was staged. Nearly half a century of parades, popular songs, journalism, Jubilees, Coronations and Empire Day bank holidays had made the Empire second nature to British subjects. They identified with it, they were proud of it, they found it glamorous and exciting. Just as Dickens's Mr Podsnap declared to the foreign gentleman at dinner that 'We Englishmen are Very Proud of our Constitution, Sir. It Was Bestowed Upon Us By Providence. No Other Country is so Favoured as This Country'. So the public of the 1920s could not help being tickled by the assumption, implicit at Wembley, that their country had been marked out by destiny as superior to the common run of nations on earth. Empire was an idea lodged in their heads. It needed expression in architecture.

BELOW Most of the cloud capp'd palaces at the British Empire Exhibition were temporary and left not a wrack behind (or, in the case of the Palaces of Industry and Engineering, limped on as warehousing, due to the high cost of demolition). But the British Empire Stadium continued to function as a sports stadium until the end of the twentieth century: the sacred home of the FA Cup until replaced by the present Wembley Stadium. Maxwell Ayrton's twin entrance towers, evocative of Indian architecture, became an instantly recognisable symbol with a wide public.

Architecture and design were carefully considered at the British Empire Exhibition. There was a house style, with a specially designed serif alphabet; to advertise the Exhibition, the best graphic artists of the day were commissioned to draw colourful posters that almost fizz with exuberance: clearly, they seem to imply, the sedate, immemorial Empire was still young and nimble enough to kick off its shoes and have a party.

But the default position, through the Exhibition, was – like the alphabet – classical. It had to be. Classicism, handed down from Rome, had become the style of Empire. Few buildings repay close scrutiny; the principal architect, John William Simpson, although knighted for his achievement at Wembley, was not of the top drawer. More remarkable than outward appearance was the system of construction that lay beneath. For everything in the Exhibition was built of the material which, in the hands of the Modern Movement, would undermine the values of Classicism completely: reinforced concrete. It was chosen for reasons of speed and cost. Nobody expected the buildings to last – although some of them did: the Wembley Stadium was used for football matches, pop concerts and other events until 2000. There is now a new stadium on its site, visible from across the capital due to the scimitar-like arc that rises above it – an arch, but not as the Empire would have known it.

Outward show was as important to the Empire as a whole as it was to the British Empire Exhibition. With or without consciously realising it, architecture always transmits values; in the second half of the nineteenth century, supporters of Empire saw that it could convey as much about purpose and resolve as the red coat on the back of a soldier or a scarlet pillar box in Bombay. As the Empire transmuted from a series of buccaneering commercial ventures into a solid and unified institution, with a government and military infrastructure to back it up, it acquired an iconography, supported by architecture. Symbols were needed and supplied. After the erection of Nelson's Column in Trafalgar Square in the mid nineteenth century, statues of imperial heroes began to stare out over public spaces in increasing numbers: Baron Napier of Magdala (famous for the telegram supposedly sent when he captured Sindh; it consisted of the one Latin word: *Peccavi* – I have sinned), Earl Roberts of Kandaha, Major General Sir Henry Havelock, suppressor of the Indian Mutiny …. Government buildings were rebuilt on a mightier scale and in imperishable materials. Public institutions, banks, City corporations and private individuals heard the call of Empire and built accordingly. The Empire created new industries and new fortunes; trade grew, commerce grew, buildings swelled in size and opulence, the metropolis of London came to feel woefully shabby, cramped and disgusting, in the light of its new purpose as the capital of the greatest Empire ever known. Britain smartened itself up; it smartened up its colonies, too. Architecture became a means of knitting the unwieldy mass of colonial possessions together.

'And so to King's Cross and northward,' writes the Tickhill parish magazine, 'homeward with tired bodies, but happy hearts and memories stored with unforgettable experiences.' The description ends with an account, not of the wonders Empire but of the expenditure incurred by the visit, which amounted to £91 10s 10d. Money was an equally pressing concern for the exhibition organisers. For despite their best efforts and its immense popularity, the British Empire Exhibition made a loss.

In this, it may have resembled the Empire itself, which had acquired its own self-fulfilling *raison d'être*, quite beyond any profit it brought to the country in hard cash. Having begun as a series of independent, sometimes piratical trading operations, it was now weighed down with the costs of administration and defence – and the taxes paid by ordinary people were almost certainly not recouped by them as benefits (although the 'plutocrats' who were as conspicuous as their consumption on the early-twentieth century scene may have done well). The year that the Exhibition opened, 1924, also saw the publication of E. M. Forster's

SCOTTISH AVENUE SHOWING TOWER AND ATLANTIC
EMPIRE EXHIBITION, SCOTLAND, 1938.   A 716

ABOVE The Glasgow Empire Exhibition
of 1938, planned by Thomas S. Tait, was
sparkling in its layout and architecture, its
Modernist structures surveyed by a blade-
like observation tower. It was the last of
a series of exhibitions – others were held
in 1888, 1901 and 1911 – which celebrated
Scottishness and Empire in the Empire's
Second City. Despite one of the wettest
summers on record, the 1938 Exhibition
attracted 12,000,000 people.

A Passage to India, in which the ruling class are shown on the edge of the abyss.
Conditions at home were reflected in the strikes that interrupted the construction
of the Exhibition. And yet even this was not the end of architecture for the Empire,
or even architectural exhibitions. Another Empire Exhibition would be held in
Glasgow in 1938 – and it was not until 1931 that Sir Edwin Lutyens and his wife
Lady Emily travelled to New Delhi for the city's official opening with Edward
Hudson – 'so moved that he can hardly keep from tears. He said to me yesterday
"Poor old Christopher Wren could never have done this!"'

Wherever the British went across the world, they built. They could not help
building. They needed forts to defend themselves, homes to shelter in, barracks
for their soldiers, prisons for miscreants and enemies, writers' buildings for bevies
of clerks, dak bungalows for travelling administrators to stay in. Trade called for
depots, or 'factories'; grain had to be stored, sugar milled, ships repaired, minerals
dug out of the earth. Religion bespoke churches – and burial grounds. For health
was a constant anxiety, which was met by a host of measures to improve sanitation;
these included the drainage of marshes, the laying of sewers and the provision of
open spaces that allowed air to circulate, as well as the development of hill stations
to which to retreat during the unsupportable heats of summer. Even so, hospitals
could not be forgotten.

Utility was not the only purpose in building, of course. After basic needs had
been met, the British wanted to make themselves as comfortable as they could in
unfamiliar, climatically hostile surroundings. Gentle walks – the limits of exercise
for most women – required esplanades, or the winding paths of the gardens that
were planted wherever the British travelled, as surely as clubs. Clubs for tennis,
yachting, polo racing; clubs for an endless consumption of cocktails, served, at

the Shanghai Club, at a bar so long that as Noel Coward said 'one could see the curvature of the earth along it'; clubs to establish solidarity among the European population and keep the natives in their place. Expectations of an ordered and civilised life demanded that the amenities of home should be replicated in paved and well-lit streets, post offices and well-appointed hotels, after the model of the legendary Raffles in Sinagpore. To Somerset Maugham, Raffles stood for 'all the fables of the exotic East', but then the hoteliers who built it were Armenian rather than British. The British wanted to convey a different idea through their railway stations, telegraph offices, courtrooms, banks, port authority buildings, insurance offices, cathedrals, museums and public statues. They stood for order, discipline and honourable business dealings. They proclaimed an Empire that was just, unified and enduring.

The legacy is both various and immense. On the Tasman Peninsula of Tasmania stand the grimly indestructible remains of the penal settlement of Port Arthur, which included prison buildings, barracks, a wharf, a hospital, stores, houses for officials, the commandant's residence, a church, bake house, carpenter's shop, shoemaker's shop, blacksmith's shop and a shipyard. In the hills of Ceylon (Sri Lanka), enjoying 'the perfection of a healthy climate', can still be found the tea (originally coffee) planters' bungalows, described with such enthusiasm by the German naturalist Ernest Haeckel in the 1880s: on his first morning in the garden of Whist Bungalow outside Colombo, he 'wandered for hours, dazed with admiration, from one plant to another, from one clump of trees to the next, incapable of deciding to which of the endless marvels before me I should direct my particular attention' in that 'paradise'. In the hills overlooked by Adam's Peak – it really was a Garden of Eden – endless miles of immaculate retaining walls, drainage channels and bridges, all of neatly squared black granite, were built to maintain the terraces of the tea gardens; many of the estates still bear names evocative of other gardens, including Kew. Ceylon became the world's biggest tea exporter, and the English national drink, helped by the trade in rubber and spices, built Colombo.

Clock towers arose all over the Empire. Recalling the towers of Victorian towns halls and public buildings in the home country, they were planted – generally at the expense of the local population – as a moderately subtle symbol of conquest, in the tradition of the towers of Mughal India. There was, of course, a clock tower on the Gordon Memorial College, remembering that great imperial martyr General Gordon – Evangelical Christian, believer in reincarnation; it was built as part of a new city of Khartoum after the defeat of the Mahdi in 1898 and survives within the University of Khartoum. The Church of England and dissenting sects constructed mission stations and chapels, parish churches and cathedrals, from Brisbane to

BELOW Port Arthur, Tasmania. The architecture of the early Empire arose according to the needs of an ad hoc assemblage of colonial possessions, acquired for reasons of expediency or trade, without much thought as to the projection of a coherent identity by the Mother Country. These buildings survive from the penal colony, where convicts farmed, worked at trades and dug coal. The object was to make labour rather than save it, as can be seen from the twelve-man treadmill and the fact that ploughing was performed by gangs of men, rather than horses.

ABOVE A tea bungalow, in Ceylon. Ceylon became the biggest exporter of Britain's national drink, tea. Bungalows became the standard Anglo-Indian dwelling space, cooled by verandahs and (without an internal courtyard) necessarily surrounded by gardens to catch the breeze. From a word that means 'belonging to Bengal', the bungalow was the only Indian-derived building type that became naturalised in Britain.

BELOW The states of Canada joined to become a dominion in 1867. It was the first dominion, a term that denoted self-government. New Parliament buildings had already been constructed, their location at Ottawa having been decided in 1857. In its crook of the Ottawa River, the ensemble of towers, spires and flying buttresses was one of the most romantic achievements of the Gothic Revival. The contrast that this Ruskinian vision made with the remorselessly Classical American capital of Washington D.C. may not have been unwelcome.

Bombay; the Arts and Crafts architect Leonard Stokes built the Roman Catholic cathedral in Georgetown, Guyana (out of concrete). The military erected – and then forgot – defences. Malta still bristles with the pill boxes built during the Second World War, and cocks a deaf ear towards incoming planes in the curving wall of concrete known as the Maghtab Sound Mirror. Nor were those structures the last to be built on British territories around the world. A new airport was opened on the Falkland Islands in 1986, four years after the war with Argentina.

The Empire also built towns, even complete new capital cities. 'I am commanded by the Queen to inform you that in the judgement of Her Majesty the City of Ottawa combines more advantages than any other place in Canada, for the permanent seat of the future government of the Province and is selected by Her Majesty accordingly.' With these gracious words the Governor General Sir Edward Head announced the site of the new Parliament buildings in Canada, and a chivalric skyline of towers and turrets arose above the Ottawa River: the official style of the Dominion, following the dictates of the English sage John Ruskin, became – curiously, now that one comes to think of it – that of the Middle Ages.

Rangoon, which got into its stride after the annexation of Upper Burma in 1886, appeared at the Victorian zenith of Empire, demonstrating the principles of imperial planning at their most fully evolved. In the mid nineteenth century, the site had been nothing but swamps and lagoons, and a fishing village which also served as a landing point for the Buddhist pilgrims visiting the dazzling Shwedagon Pagoda with its many golden domes. In the 1820s, when the British began their campaign of conquest, so little was known about the area between British India and China that it had no geographical name. In 1852, it was decided that a capital should be built for the territory that Britain had acquired in two Anglo-Burmese Wars (there would be a third in the 1880s), and with due deference to the supremacy of health, the man called upon to plan it was the Superintendent Surgeon William Montgomerie. As so often happened, his scheme was then implemented by a Bengal engineer, Lieutenant Fraser – on what a town planner of 1923 called 'a delightfully simple method'.

Rangoon's chief glory was the Strand, a broad thoroughfare that ran parallel with the riverfront. Behind it was a grid of streets, centred – Lieutenant Fraser taking his courage in both hands – on the Shule Pagoda: this salute to local culture cannot have pleased all his contemporaries. On the other hand, some street names might have been designed to summon dewy-eyed memories of school rooms at home,

RIGHT The Strand, Rangoon, in 1921. Rangoon was a city of great charm in the early twentieth century. The site had been nothing but swamps and lagoons when the British decided to make it into the capital of the newly acquired colony of Burma in 1852. Having declared that the Government of India, which administered Burma, owned the land, it then sold it in lots; this provided money to drain the swamps, fill in the lagoons and build roads. The grid was centred on a local structure: the pre-existing Shule Pagoda.

having been inspired by English history: Lancaster and York (recalling the Wars of the Roses), Hanover (after the dynasty) and Windsor (after the Castle).

Describing Rangoon in a paper read to the Royal Society of Arts in 1914, G. C. Buchanan – not present in person, because he had been forced to postpone his leave – noted Rangoon's 'imposing public buildings', such as Government House, the Secretariat and the Courts of Justice. 'It is unfortunate,' he continued, 'that, with rare exceptions, the buildings are devoid of any architectural merit.' Alas, it is difficult to dissent from this opinion. But the architecture of Rangoon was not its greatest amenity. That lay in Dalhousie Park and the Royal Lakes, 'quite the most beautiful and artistic pleasure grounds in the Indian Empire'. There was also The Strand Hotel, opened by the Sarkies family, owners of the Raffles in Singapore, in 1901.

The Sarkies had caught a wave. Although The Strand remained unpaved in the early twentieth century, other advances in urban amenity were soon made. An electric tram arrived in 1906, replacing a steam one; electric street lighting followed the next year. The first motorcar had already appeared in 1905; flying boats began arriving in the 1920s. Postcards from before the First World War, which show The Strand handsomely lined with porticos and arcades, the street empty of all but a few strolling figures, shaded by parasols if European, make it seem delightful. You would hardly have known that this was not a rather warmer version of Margate but a frontier town, until you had walked a few blocks inland. Around the Shwedagon Pagoda were the barracks, exercise grounds, parade grounds, artillery lines, elephant lines and coolie lines that made this part of the city feel more like a military outpost than a seaside resort.

To teak and rice, Burma's principal exports in the pre-War period, were added oil and rubies. Rangoon dressed its buildings in the latest Paris fashion of Art Deco, and cultivated a *douceur de vivre* that charmed those who knew it well: 'It was the most beautiful city in the world. The way we lived there, we will never live anywhere again'.

Those words were uttered by an Indian lady, whose family were among the many landowners, moneylenders, merchants, rice millers, cinema owners and business people to have come to Burma from the subcontinent under British rule and prospered (to the disgust of the Burmese). The end for them came, as Mira Kamdar remembered, quite suddenly, on 23 December 1941. Knowing that the Japanese might attack Rangoon, the British military had sent its own women and children into the mountains for safety. But they did not want to spread panic among the local population. When the warplanes appeared in the sky, many people simply looked up at them, as though they were witnessing an air show. The bombing took a terrible human toll. 'By nightfall, dogs were feasting on the corpses left uncollected on the deserted streets of the city.' Burma was lost.

RIGHT Generally, the most impressive government-funded structures from the early Empire are naval and military buildings. This range, built out of coralstone, stands on Nelson's Dockyard in Antigua. Ships sheltered in English Harbour during the hurricane season. Nelson, regarded locally as a prig for his overzealous enforcement of laws forbidding trade with the newly established United States, hated his time there (despite a romantic attachment to a young married woman). The immense value of the sugar trade meant that the route between the Caribbean and Europe had to be protected and at times of war, French and English squadrons would pursue each other across the Atlantic.

After the Second World War, Rangoon barely had time to rebuild itself before Independence in 1948. And after General Ne Win's coup in 1962, Yangon, as the city was now called, reverting to the name of the original fishing village, slept through more than half century of isolation. The awakening of recent years has been sudden, sometimes rough. A city of more than 5,000,000 people, Yangon is a hundred times bigger than old Rangoon, but many of the landmarks of the colonial era are still there – the legacy of Empire.

The earliest building of the Empire – at this stage English, if not Anjevin, rather than British – was Dublin Castle, the work of King John in the thirteenth century. Beyond Ireland and English possessions in France – gone by the end of Mary Tudor's reign in the sixteenth century – the Empire had to wait until the 1660s before a monarch directly interested himself in significant building operations overseas. Part of Catherine of Braganza's dowry, on her marriage to Charles II, was the previously Portuguese colony of Tangier. Immediately the King had received it, work began on the Mole to protect the harbour; 480 yards of it were built before it was concluded that the cost of keeping Tangier outweighed its usefulness; and in 1683, the Mole was, with difficulty, blown up, the colony being evacuated the next year. As John Evlyn wrote to Samuel Pepys, who had done very nicely out of his position as Treasurer for Tangier, in a letter (possibly unsent) of 1682: commerce 'was evidently carried on more by antient Methods, and the sedulitie of Private Men, than by any publique Encouragement'. Ancient Methods meant private enterprise, spurred, very often, by greed, supported by the Royal Navy and sometimes missionary zeal.

Trade had a galvanising effect. Over the next two centuries, the British fortified their Empire, made it safe for shipping, established themselves in as much comfort as could be afforded in unfavourable climates – and in the case of America lost part of their possessions through neglect. The Union Jack fluttered over colonnaded streets, governor's mansions, wharves and warehouses, racecourses and rowing clubs, town halls and churches of all denominations. This phase of the Empire trod lightly. Neither government nor private investors wanted to spend more than they needed on architectural display; the beautification – or not – of colonial settlements was left to the people who lived in them. And except in America and Canada, which developed settled populations, their thoughts were on home. They generally saw life overseas as the staging post to a triumphant return to their native land, laden with money. This they spent on an altogether grander style of life than they had known in the colonies; typically its background was a fine country house.

Before the coming of the railways, the only constructions that could truly be called monumental were military and naval buildings. One that survives in something like its original condition is English Harbour on Antigua, built to provide a base from which permanent squadrons could harass the French and protect English convoys.

Colonised from the 1620s, the West Indies grew spices and could be made to grow sugar cane, which made them an immensely valuable possession. Among planters, the suspicion that the Caribbean was regarded as 'the dunghill whar our England doth cast forth its rubidg' naturally rankled. Those on the richer islands built 'great houses' to display their taste, heavily dependent, usually, on patternbooks from home, whose architectural models were adapted with wider door and window openings and verandahs to take maximum advantage of any breeze. The great house was part of an agri-industrial complex that included slave quarters and factory buildings, the largest enclosed space being that of the boiling houses where sugar was extracted from the cane; often, the boiling house was more imposing, architecturally, than the church.

In 1825, the artist James Hakewill presented an idyllic impression of those on Jamaica; his *A Picturesque Tour of the Island of Jamaica* emphasises the charms of the vegetation and hilly landscape, amid which slaves only appear as exotic accents in a fertile scene. Even allowing for artistic licence, this was a misleading image of planter society, which lived in constant fear of slave revolt. Early planters from Scotland built square-planned houses with corner towers, after the model of ancient – and outmoded – defensive structures in their native land; they feared raids from Spanish planters on other islands, eager to seize slaves, as well as from the slaves themselves. Such piratical behaviour on the part of other Europeans declined, but the danger of attack from slaves – or liberated slaves – actually increased during the nineteenth century. The Caribbean was not, therefore, a place in which to linger after a planter had made his fortune, and the great houses there are not nearly as great as those built with planter money in Britain – although some families sustained a dual existence, frequently crossing the sea between homes in the West Indies and the UK. In British terms, Caribbean towns remained modest; none of them would have outshone Tunbridge Wells. The unforgiving climate and hurricanes of the tropics took a heavy toll of architectural and decorative finery. At home, returning planters put the memory of the West Indies behind them. There are even fewer references to the Caribbean in the country houses built by sugar planters than to India in those erected by nabobs; we see no chained slaves, no gilded sugar canes used as a decorative motif. The very term 'sugar planter' carried the sort of opprobrium that would later apply to 'play boy': the planters themselves had no desire to advertise the source of their wealth.

By the time of the Revolution, some American cities had shed the provincialism usually associated with the colonies. When Lord Adam Gordon, son of the Duke of Gordon, visited Philadelphia in 1765, he was bowled over. He wrote that it 'is

ABOVE Eighteenth-century Philadelphia
had ambition, according to the almanac
publisher, the heroically named Titan Leeds,
who wrote 'A Memorial to William Penn' in
1729. Travellers who were able to compare
its broad, paved streets and air of sobriety
to European cities were also favourably
impressed. William Moraley, who visited in
the year that Leeds wrote his poem, found
its 'Shops and Houses as handsome as those
at *Newcastle upon Tyne*'. Thirty years later,
the English clergyman the Rev. Andrew
Burnaby considered that its progress from 'a
wild and uncultivated desert' in the space of
eighty years 'must certainly be the object of
everyone's wonder and admiration'.

perhaps one of the wonders of the World, if you consider its Size, the Number
of Inhabitants, the regularity of its Streets, their great breadth and length, they
cutting one another all at Right Angles, their Spacious publick and private
buildings, Quays and Docks, the Magnificence and diversity of places of Worship.'
This colonial town was the rival of 'any in Europe'. John Adams found 'opulence
and splendor' in the New York of 1774, although he found it fast-talking and under-
bred. The busy port of Boston was the fourth largest city of the British Empire in
the 1740s, exceeded by only London, Bristol and Norwich.

Of these early cities, Charleston, in South Carolina, founded two years before
Philadelphia, in 1680, had the best houses. Built of brick, perhaps covered in
coloured stucco, they were ornamented with quoins, marble bands and and
Classical doorframes; although British visitors would have been more struck by
the measures taken against the heat, such as shady galleries or 'piazzas', raised
basements and high ceilings. Throughout the American colonies, local details
of this kind created idioms that – though cross-pollinated with fashions from
overseas – were special to their area; homes in the Flemish regions of New Jersey
were different from German Pennsylvania, for example. But these vernaculars
were of local creation: colonial buildings, almost entirely built by master builders
or amateurs, rather than professional architects, owed much to the example of
the Mother Country, disseminated through patternbooks, but did not reflect
an attempt on the part of Britain to exert its will. On the contrary, Americans
were all too conscious of their distance from Britain and the reluctance of the
British government to do much for them. Eleven years after Lord Adam's visit
to Philadelphia, the Declaration of Independence was signed in the city he so
admired, and America passed out of the imperial orbit altogether. So ended the
Empire's first phase.

The Empire's second phase was focused on India. Before 1800, the East India Company (EIC) made surprisingly little architectural show considering the scale of its operations. Having been founded in 1600, the EIC – John Company as it was sometimes called – combined trade with military adventurism; its private army bullied or fought the princes who had previously ruled India into accepting its conditions, initially for trade, then, from the mid eighteenth century, raising taxes. Its Residents, who began as the equivalent of ambassadors, morphed into de facto governors. Through it all, until the Indian Mutiny of 1857, the Company remained a commercial enterprise, not an arm of the British state; its wealth was such that Parliament did not want it to flow directly to the British sovereign, since that would have put him beyond its control. This left a clutch of private merchants and soldiers in possession of self-made fortunes of a sometimes staggering extent. These young men – they were mostly young and mostly men – enjoyed the fabled luxuries of the east, no doubt conscious, as the memorials in the churches of India testify all too poignantly, that life, if opulent, was often short. 'Most gentlemen and ladies in Bengal live both splendidly and pleasantly,' declared a contemporary.

But the directors saw waste in the 'expensive and extravagant way of life, particularly in equipage and show', being pursued, not least by the Governor who had 'a sett of musick at his table and a coach and six with guards and running footmen'. The majority of Britons in India were too busy making money to give much thought to their buildings. Their ambition was to dazzle their contemporaries at home with the loot they amassed (loot being an Indian word which entered the English language in the late eighteenth century) and the splendid houses they built on their return; anyone wanting a glimpse of what loot could mean need only visit Powys Castle to behold the treasures that remain from Robert Clive's plunderings: golden hookahs, bejewelled daggers, elephant armours, silken hangings and statues of Hindu gods. But until 1799, when Lord Wellesley built the Governor-General's

BELOW *Colonel Mordaunt's Cock Match* was painted by Johann Zoffany for Warren Hastings, Governor General of Bengal, in the mid 1780s. The nabobs of the East India Company could live in great opulence in India, adopting sybaritic practices that would have shocked society at home. This scene depicts a cock match between Asar-ud-daula, Nawab Wazir of Oud (standing in the centre) and Colonel John Mordaunt (on the left in white). The figures include the Nawab's engineer, the East India Company's paymaster at Lucknow, a French adventurer, the assistant to the Governor General's representative and a Lieutenant of the East India Company's Corps of Engineers. As the catalogue of the Tate Gallery, which now owns the painting, speculates, it appears to have contained some private jokes for Hastings to have enjoyed after leaving India.

residence, Government House, in Calcutta, the EIC was content to rule the subcontinent from run-of-the-mill administrative and military buildings. It was administratively a very lean organisation: a mere 250 bureaucrats with a locally recruited army of 20,000. Eighteenth-century Calcutta, although the headquarters of British India, was little more than a village or small town in British terms, its white population numbering about a thousand souls.

Lord Wellesley, brother of the future Duke of Wellington, was determined to rule India from a palace, not a counting house. When building that palace, he did not trouble himself by obtaining explicit permission from the directors, knowing their parsimony. Seat of supreme EIC authority in India, Government House spoke to two audiences. One was the native rulers, who should know that the EIC was capable of splendour – a quality greatly valued in India. The second was the European community. Following the protracted and bitter attempt to impeach Warren Hastings, former Governor General of Bengal, during which the reputation of the EIC had been dragged through the mire, the rectilinear, many-columned architecture of Government House, reworking Robert Adam's Kedleston Hall in Derbyshire, proclaimed a new purpose. It was not only imposing but, in the language of the time, 'chaste'; it signalled that a new page in a history notorious for corruption had been turned.

Although Lord Wellesley's palace was a potent symbol of the will to rule, its occupant lacked the tools to forge a common identity for the country, let alone the British Empire as a whole. They did not come until the arrival of the telegraph in 1851 and the improvements to steamships that followed in the decades thereafter. The will to impose an imperial image on the subcontinent was not summoned until the shock to the system provided by the Indian Mutiny of 1857. One response to the catastrophe was to build. The subcontinent could be cowed, yes, by sepoys, but also by architecture.

At home, the Empire was, before the Indian Mutiny, Rebellion or First War of Independence of 1857, part of the background of British life, not something that required self-conscious promotion, or even explanation. Although Sir Thomas Bertram in Jane Austen's *Mansfield Park* owns a sugar plantation in Antigua, which he has to visit to improve returns, the implications are barely explored, the subject of slavery never raised. (Unless the author made a subtle point in the title of the book, the judge who ruled that slavery could not exist in Britain – as opposed to her colonies – being Lord Mansfield.) The loss of America in 1776, the vitriol against Warren Hastings, and the noble passion of the Society for the Mitigation and Gradual Abolition of Slavery throughout the British Dominions, which led to the abolition of the slave trade in 1807, seven years before *Mansfield Park*'s publication, although not slavery itself, gave Empire a bad smell. The French Revolutionary and Napoleonic Wars were felt, principally, as a struggle with the old enemy of France, whose imperial dimension was almost coincidental. While Nelson, Wellington and their victories became obvious choices for place names, with Ramsgate demonstrating its patriotic zeal in Belle Alliance Square and a street called The Plains of Waterloo, the colonial possessions which Britain acquired as a result of the conflict were not celebrated with Grenada Terraces and Saint Lucia Crescents.

When Queen Victoria came to the throne in 1837, the great cause in architecture was the Gothic Revival. Its champions saw it as a national style. Not even the Houses of Parliament, begun in 1840, sought to present itself as an imperial symbol; the statues depict saints, kings and queen, virtues like Justice and Mercy – not Clive of India or Woolf of Quebec. Nearly all the mural paintings were allegorical or depicted events from before 1700 – *Caesar's Invasion of Britain* (Edward Armitage), *Caractus Led Through the Streets of Rome* (G. F. Watts), *The Baptism of Ethelbert* (William Dyce), for example – except for two relatively recent episodes of national deliverance: *The Death of Nelson* and *The Meeting of Wellington and Blücher on the Field of Waterloo* (Daniel Maclise). The military or commercial triumphs of the East India Company were ignored. Parliament had to wait until 1925–27 before William Rothenstein painted Sir Thomas Roe, James I's envoy to the Mughal court, appearing before the Emperor Jahangir in 1614: one nation speaking to another, rather than an Indian ruler being fleeced by an adventurer. Few of the people who saw this painting will have realised that Jahangir was incomparably richer and more powerful than the English and Scottish monarch, whose combined territories and wealth were a molehill beside the eastern mountain. They and their Victorian forebears were, however, aware of the spoils that the East India Company had brought home, and felt morally queasy about its acquisition.

In the mid century, the Battle of the Styles that followed the competition for rebuilding the Foreign Office had no imperial dimension; although George Gilbert Scott, like other architects, championed Gothic as a national style – nobody in Victorian Britain was going to get far with a style that was anything else – nobody claimed that the Classical alternative, which triumphed, evoked Empire. Nor does Empire feature in the iconography of the Albert Memorial in Hyde Park. While statuary groups of the continents stake out its corners, the Prince Consort is otherwise set amid the flowers of European civilisation, epitomised by the frieze of 169 figures, including Rubens, Beethoven and other non-native greats: a cultivated, Christian prince who saw material prosperity as flowing through world trade, but was not besotted with Empire.

In view of the riches that poured in from the Empire, as well as the novelty of the possessions under British control, one might have expected architects and their patrons to allude to the cultures from which the new wealth accrued. Yet they did so rarely. Famously, Samuel Pepys Cockerell built Sezincote in Gloucestershire, with a Mughal dome, for his brother Sir Charles, nabob and first baronet; and the Prince Regent had Nash give his Marine Pavilion at Brighton an Indian make-over, after William Porden had built an Indian stables and riding school in 1804–08, gratifying the Prince's taste for novelty and the exotic. But apart from a few garden structures, these are the only buildings of note to have been erected in the Indian style. It was not that Indian monuments were unknown: some had been published in the engravings of Thomas and William Daniell in the 1780s and 1790s, and painted by Thomas Daniell in his *Composite View of Hindoo and Moorish Architecture* for the rich connoisseur Thomas Hope, who hung it in the Indian Room he had created in his London mansion. But the Indian taste simply did not take off to the degree that chinoiserie had done from the 'China worke' owned by the Earl of Northampton in the early seventeenth century onwards.

The one architectural import from India that became truly domesticated arrived later. The first bungalow was built on the extreme south-east point of Kent around 1870. The word 'bungalow' derives from '*bangla*' being the Hindi or Mahratti for 'belonging to Bengal'. Originally, it referred to local huts, with their rippling roofs of thatch and sweep of eaves. By the end of the nineteenth century, an Anglo-Indian bungalow inhabited by a 'man of simple tastes' required a staff of fourteen local servants, whose personal characteristics and sometimes arcane functions were described by the humorous Edward Aitken in *Behind the Bungalow*, 1897. To keep a well-ordered bungalow, symbolically isolated from other Europeans, was, indeed, an index of imperial control. Translated to Britain, the bungalow operated on a different scale, with other

BELOW Thomas and William Daniell's aquatint of the Jami Masjid in Delhi, from *Oriental Scenery*, 1797. Prints like this fed the Regency taste for the exotic, which blossomed soon in John Nash's remodelling of the Prince Regent's Brighton Pavilion, with Indian-style stables by William Porden of 1804–08. And yet it is surprising, given the riches flowing into Britain from the East, and the availability of published images of Indian architecture, how few buildings were erected in this style, apart from Sezincote House in Gloucestershire, which was designed by Samuel Pepys Cockerell for his nabob brother Charles. Even fewer architectural references were made to the origin of the West Indian sugar planters' wealth, despite their appetite to build houses once they had made their fortune. Perhaps neither source was thought to be particularly reputable.

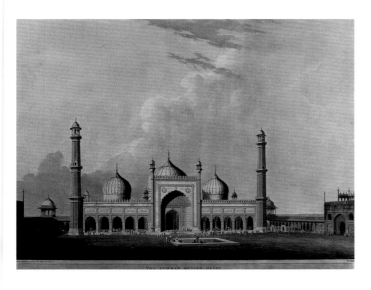

THE JUMMAH MUSJED, DELHI.

connotations. Erected at Westgate-on-Sea and Birchington, near Margate, the first examples of the form had verandahs and croquet lawns and tunnels to the beach. Less rumbustuous in tone than was the case of some seaside architecture, they were, nevertheless, arty. You could get away with things on the coast that would have raised eyebrows elsewhere. But the seaside meant not only holidays and letting one's hair down, but fresh air and health. One of the first occupants was Dante Gabriel Rossetti, invited to recuperate by the coast by his friend, the architect J. P. Seddon. Neither the timber bungalow nor the ozone did the trick on this occasion, since Rossetti died there at Easter in 1882. That did not deter the architect R. A. Briggs – Bungalow Briggs as he came to be called – who made it a mission to domesticate the bungalow across Britain. The bungalow became as British as chintz.

The bungalow was a harbinger of change. Attitudes to Empire were rapidly rethought after the Indian Mutiny, when it seemed that Britain was within an ace of losing her most prized overseas possession. The reins of governance were removed from the hands of the East India Company and taken directly into those of the British state. By the 1870s, when Queen Victoria was declared Empress, a growing call for new markets could be heard from Britain's industrial towns. Manufacturers were right to worry about their relative decline: over the next century and a half, prosperity would be pulled as though by a gravitational force from the yards and workshops of the North and Midlands to the banks and offices of the Southeast. The first industrialist to become a very senior politician, Joseph Chamberlain, the monocled Screw King of Birmingham, his buttonhole always fresh with an orchid from his own glasshouses, was among the foremost advocates of the New Imperialism, promoted as policy when he became Colonial Secretary in 1895.

Britain's Empire had previously been an ad hoc affair, acquired, in the words of the popular Victorian historian John Robert Seeley, 'in a fit of absence of mind': meaning, perhaps, that it had been driven by the predatory greed of private adventurers, protected by the Royal Navy, rather than much conscious activity on the part of the state. This vast and amorphous collection or limbs, bones, organs and skin would be turned into a single animal, whose brain would be seated in London; nerves were already in place for conveying orders – the wires of the telegraph system. Architecture was needed as a symbolic trapping, to conceal the anatomical deficiencies of the result.

The rise of the New Imperialism coincided with a change in the nature of finance. The early Empire had been backed by rich individuals, usually landowners, characterised as 'gentlemen capitalists'. In the late nineteenth century, the City of London triumphed over the landed interest. While Britain's share of world trade was falling, its financial institutions were in the ascendancy. One effect was to create an affluent middle class, many of whose sons, educated at public schools, found employment in India and the colonies. Another was to capitalise shops, offices, hotels, professional institutions and the government itself more munificently.

Inevitably the result was inflation – not of the currency, with the pound pegged to gold, but of architecture. London swelled. Its bounds expanded. Regency shops were replaced by department stores. Office buildings increased both in their size and the costliness of their materials. Universities, the Metropolitan Police, the Royal Automobile Club, the Theosophical Society, the United Grand Lodge of England (Freemasons Hall) – all desired buildings that would have struck a Georgian as overwhelming. So it was overseas. The scale of building echoed the size of the Empire itself. You cannot approach the Victoria Memorial in Calcutta, or climb the steps of the Union Buildings in Pretoria, without feeling that a mighty race has bestridden the earth. Or that was the idea; there were some who

ABOVE Such was the force of the New Imperialism of the 1880s that an Imperial Institute was conceived; this emerged about the time of the Colonial and Indian Exhibition of 1886, the competition for it being launched the next year. High hopes were held of it; better understanding of the Empire would promote trade and help manufacturing out of a recession. In the end, these aspirations were too vast and amorphous to realise, but Thomas Collcutt produced a lively addition to South Kensington, its skyline busy with gables, turrets and tower. The Queen laid the foundation stone. Although the Institute was never a success, a vigorous campaign was mounted against its demolition to make way for Imperial College in the 1950s. But only the curious tower survives in lonely grandeur.

thought the fanfare only left a ringing in the ears. This was an architecture of landmarks, and it is appropriate that the building that most typified the first years of the New Imperialism, the Imperial Institute, should survive only in its most dominant aspect: a lonely but eloquent tower.

The Imperial Institute was born of two parents, one of whom we have already met: the Colonial and Indian Exhibition of 1886. The other was Queen Victoria's Golden Jubilee, the next year. Alfred, Lord Tennyson caught the mood, imploring:

> *You, the Patriot Architect,*
> *You that shape for Eternity*
> *Raise a stately memorial,*
> *Make it regally gorgeous,*
> *Some Imperial Institute,*
> *Rich in Symbol, in ornament,*
> *Which may speak to the centuries*
> *All the centuries after us,*
> *Of this great Ceremonial,*
> *And this year of her Jubilee …*

The Poet Laureate may already have had an inkling of what was in the wind, since a competition for an Imperial Institute was launched that year. In a rush of blood to the head, *The Builder* would call it the most important building under construction in Britain. That verdict reflects its mission, which was to develop the arts, crafts and manufactures of the Empire, making cross connections where possible – part museum, part talking shop.

Clearly, the Institute had been set an impossibly grandiose task; but it typified the programme of consolidation that imperialists were now following. Big ambitions needed big architecture, in this case the 285-ft Queen's Tower. Thomas Collcutt, who designed it, had a delicate touch – too delicate perhaps to command the masses of so large a building, though certainly subtler than the gustier Baroque Revival that became standard for imperial projects in the next decade. When built, the Queen's Tower stood like a poplar tree in a hedgerow, rising above the profusion of gables, turrets and chimneystacks that formed the skyline of the main building. Its dome, pointed and double-layered, was probably intended to evoke India, although the *Building News* seemed to think it was Spanish. On this important building, Collcut was constrained to use Portland stone, but the material that he really loved was terracotta, so cheerful and suited to sculptural modelling; he did not hesitate to smother the Imperial Institute with statuary, portraying the heroes of colonial expansion, allegories of Queen Victoria's rule in the Eastern and Western hemispheres, and of the Empire.

The laying of the foundation stone was attended by twelve Indian princes, two European kings, numerous colonial representatives, the politicians of the day and a crowd of 11,000 spectators. All of which, to *The Times*, symbolised 'the mutual dependence and hearty good will upon which the greatness of the Empire depends'. Alas, the Institute could not live up to the high hopes expected of it – but not all was lost. Britain had entered an era in which symbolism had a value of its own: Collcutt's building was, in this respect, just the thing.

By 1892, London was 'the greatest of the world's cities', according to one observer. '…No man really knows the full joy of social life who has never lived in London.' To some colonials, the place was overwhelming. 'Partly beautiful, and partly fearful,' was how the heroine of Louisa Mack's *An Australian Girl in London*, 1902, found it. 'London!' she gasped. 'To be in London!' It was both new and luxurious, and ancient and grubby. Docks, bridges, underground railway trains, the flux of humanity – Henry James found himself subject to 'a kind of imaginative thrill' at the immensity of the latest civil engineering works. Although the shops on Regent Street were not as big as the department stores in the US, they offered, according to one of James's compatriots, 'an enormous stock' of articles in every conceivable style: 'That is what astonishes the American.' It could not help but think of itself as imperial, being, to quote a visitor, 'a little world in itself', where 'representatives of every nationality are congregated'.

London had responsibilities, however, and historically, they had been taken lightly. Like the Empire, the metropolis might have grown 'in a fit of absence of mind', for all the system that had lain behind its development. Paris and Vienna, Berlin and Brussels had been provided with broad, well-lit streets, with vistas aligned on showy monuments. London was visibly the bastion of private property rights. With the exception of Somerset House and the Houses of Parliament, the churches and cathedrals, most of its finest buildings were in private hands. The better areas were planned around square gardens which were maintained for the enjoyment of the keyholders. There were parks, many of them – a legacy of the Picturesque movement. But little had been done to improve the physical organisation of the city since John Nash had created Regent Street, for the benefit of the Prince Regent at the beginning of the nineteenth century. This was another Picturesque endeavour, whose route began in one park (Regent's Park) and ended in another (St James's Park). The intervening thoroughfares were ingeniously contrived so that the jinks caused by the difficulties of acquiring the land on which to build were concealed for people strolling past the stucco-fronted terraces and plaster porticos. The result had charm, but the scale had come to seem woefully inadequate. The arcade on the Regent Street quadrant – one of the clever means of disguising a change of axis – was plagued by 'nuisance' (shorthand for gentlemen relieving themselves against its pillars). A generation used to judging architecture by Pugin's True Principles and Ruskin's Lamp of Truth shuddered at the architectural as well as human indecorum: Nash's name had become synonymous with gimcrack.

Some improvements had been made by the Metropolitan Board of Works. Sewers, Embankments, and the Metropolitan Railway had been built in the 1860s; but London had clearly outgrown its administrative arrangements, some of which would have been familiar to Samuel Pepys in the seventeenth century. If it were to fit its role as a modern European capital and the seat of the world's greatest Empire, the capital needed the same powers as were already accorded to county councils. It needed to be able to raise money. The poor needed to be better housed. The populace as a whole needed democratic representation. To these ends – and not without controversy – the London County Council was summoned into existence, to take control of main drainage, fire prevention, the maintenance of parks and open spaces, the Thames bridges and tunnels, the improvement of streets, the enforcement of building regulations, the erection of artisan dwellings, the regulation and eventual ownership of the tramways, and the overseeing of municipal finance. Amid all these concerns, an urgent priority was the Strand.

The Strand exemplified the moral problem that terrified respectability. It may have been that the most wretched of the London rookeries had been cleared, even as Dickens was describing them; but the slums that remained were still bad enough: overcrowded, insanitary and the abode of 'vice'. These dens of poverty and prostitution squatted within a short saunter of places frequented by the well-to-do. This was particularly evident around the Strand, a street that, by day, fulfilled its immemorial role as a link between the commercial square mile of the City of London and the court and fashion at Westminster, but which at night (until the building of Shaftesbury Avenue, finished in 1886, and other West End

improvements at the end of the nineteenth century) lit its lamps as London's Theatreland. The street is supposed to have had more theatres and music halls than any other in London – which was saying something, because their numbers had boomed everywhere since the removal of restrictions by the Theatre Act of 1843. But theatres had always gone arm in arm with other forms of nightlife; the promenade behind the Empire Music Hall in Leicester Square was notorious for the prostitutes who used it to parade (attempting to close it caused an uproar from local cab drivers and shopkeepers who depended on audiences for their custom). Living in Villiers Street, Rudyard Kipling observed 'through all this shouting, shifting brotheldom' how 'pious British householders bored their way back from the theatre, eyes-front and fixed, as though not seeing'.

Improvement had already swept away Porridge Island, part of a rookery next to the Mews of Whitehall Palace; the Mews itself was demolished at the same time to make way for Trafalgar Square in the 1830s. The idea that it should commemorate the greatest of British sea battles took hold rather late – in 1835; it took even longer to build a monument to Nelson. While Glasgow had raised a monument to Nelson in 1806 and Edinburgh's was finished by the Battle of Waterloo, London as ever struggled to make the grand gesture, even after the idea had been put in circulation. After a competition, won by William Railton, work began quickly, but was then dogged by misfortune. The subsequent history was so unsatisfactory that Railton declined to attend the opening ceremony, when, at last, the column was finished in 1867. But the road that flowed east from Trafalgar

BELOW The Aldwych – the broad crescent to the left in this photograph – was created as part of the Strand Improvement Scheme, introduced in 1889, although it was still unfinished at the outbreak of the First World War. In time, it housed the High Commissions of Australia and India. The widened Strand sweeps to either side of Wren's St Clement Danes and Gibbs's St Mary-le-Strand – after a campaign to prevent their demolition. One advantage of the widened route is that it could accommodate trees.

OPPOSITE Admiralty Arch, London, which was used for the first time for the Coronation of George V. There was now an imperial route from Buckingham Palace eastwards to the new streets of Aldwych and Kingsway, and south along Whitehall, past the new War Office and Government Buildings. State processions could pass through Aston Webb's triumphal arch, ingeniously designed to conceal a change of axis from the Mall into Trafalgar Square.

Square remained as tawdry as ever. In 1879, it was denounced by Charles Dickens Jr. 'At present,' he wrote in his *Dictionary of London*, 'there is no street of equal importance in any capital of Europe so unworthy of its position.'

It was with these words ringing in their ears that the London County Council introduced a Strand Improvement Bill in 1889, the first year of its existence. Their target was not only the congestion of a street that was obstructed (as both they and Dickens Jr saw it) by the churches of St Clement Danes and St Mary-le-Strand, but also the area of rotting courts and alleys known as Clare Market.

These days, historians would surely deplore the clearing of Clare Market. West of Covent Garden, it was, architecturally, an example of what the City of London had been like before the Great Fire. But the Elizabethan buildings had degenerated into squalor, where the presence of a market famous for selling tripe 'stale and revolting-looking portions of the internal parts of animals, or foul-smelling remnants of inferior joints, cooked or uncooked', did nothing to improve the amenity. A report of the LCC's Housing of the Working Classes Committee of 1895 saw it as 'the largest and worst of those crowded collections of the courts and alleys to disgrace central London'. It took the LCC ten years to negotiate with the landlords of Clare Market and the north side of the Strand, but in 1899 the bill was published; demolition started forthwith. No fewer than fifty-one public houses were closed.

Five years later, *The Times* gasped at the transformation that had been wrought: 'Lofty buildings and time-honoured land-marks have been swept away, whole streets demolished, and the face of London in this locality completely transformed.' Architecturally, the Strand never produced the imperial fanfare that some observers may have hoped for; although the street was widened, the façades along it were a jumble. But now the broad and glittering Aldwych curved like a bow through the area cleared of slums; and from it, speeding north, shot the arrow of Kingsway.

The elegant *Morning Post* building, Inveresk House, designed by Mewès and Davis, raised its dome opposite Richard Norman Shaw's gutsy, more ostentatiously domed New Gaiety Theatre (demolished in 1957) – Beauty and the Beast, as one critic called them. Then came the Waldorf Hotel, backed by the millionaire William Waldorf Astor, the Aldwych Theatre, the government of India's building, India House, and the building to which the federated Australian states sent their Official Secretary, Australia House; so important was the last that, after the foundation stone was laid in 1913, construction continued throughout the First World War, until the opening ceremony in 1918. Even those buildings that were not actually commissioned for purposes of Empire seemed to radiate an imperial self-confidence and expansiveness. These were modern structures, their stone façades hung on steel frames, the whole serviced by hot water and electric lifts. Kingsway was the only London boulevard to have a tramway running beneath it. The Empire was go-ahead.

The Strand, Aldwych and Kingsway, pioneers of Beaux-Arts town planning in London, did not stand alone for long. They were joined to an even grander scheme that would create something that the capital had never had before: a grand processional – indeed imperial – route. Let us join the crowds to see it used ceremonially for the first time on a June morning in 1911.

The time is exactly 10.25 am. Rain has been falling on and off, but fortunately the golden, preposterously fairytale State coach, made in the mid eighteenth century, is closed. Fanfares sound, the National Anthem plays, and George V and Queen Mary emerge from Buckingham Palace. Eight

horses take the strain of the coach and it rumbles across the forecourt, past 200 cheering Chelsea Pensioners, to join the procession. It is Coronation day.

On its way to the Abbey, the procession does not turn abruptly right, to go through Horse Guards' Parade. Instead, it sweeps smoothly onwards, through the central of the three mighty arches that piece the sweeping Baroque façade of Admiralty Arch. It has just been finished. There was some doubt, earlier in the year, that it would be ready in time: the London County Council was squabbling with the Office of Works about who should pay to remove some obstructions on the farther side. Unlike the rest of the soot-grimed capital, the freshly erected Portland stone is still cream-coloured and pristine. This is the first time that it has been used.

As an addition to the ceremonial route, Admiralty Arch must have been

particularly gratifying to George V. Like his great-great-uncle William IV, he was
a sailor king. Purists may have criticised the structure for combining a piece of
monumental scenery with civil service accommodation – an expedient that allowed
the cost of construction to fall on the Admiralty, rather than the Office of Works.
But there was also a symbolic fitness to the arrangement. The British Navy was the
most powerful in the world. It absorbed a fifth of all government expenditure. A
quarter of a million people worked for or in the Service. 'The Admiralty built and
maintained an enormous fleet, it specified, designed and often manufactured every
variety of stores from chamber-pots to torpedoes. It fed, clothed and supervised
its officers and men from boyhood to the grave, and to a considerable extent their
wives and children with them,' writes N. A. M. Rodger in *The Admiralty*, 1979. 'The
British Empire rested on the shoulders of its seamen. Admiralty Arch was part of
an imperial conception of urban improvements that would render London more
worthy of its position as the capital of a great Empire. Its intimate connection with
British sea power could not have been more apt.

Admiralty Arch formed part of the Queen Victoria Memorial conceived to honour
the Queen-Empress by providing a proper setting for the state and panoply of
monarchy in the motor-car age. Within a month of her death in 1901, a Committee
for the Memorial had been formed, under the chairmanship of the Prime Minister,
Lord Salisbury. The new monarch, cosmopolitan Edward VII, particularly wanted
it to be architectural in character. The result included a towering monument to the
late Queen, sculpted by Thomas Brock (whose profile of her already graced the
coinage) and, in 1913, a new façade for Buckingham Palace, designed in a distinctly
French style by Sir Aston Webb. But like Admiralty Arch, these were only incidents
in one of the few examples of grand Classical town planning ever achieved in
London. Debouching via a new entrance into Trafalgar Square, it led not only to
Whitehall and Westminster Abbey but also linked with the Strand and Aldwych
to form a new route to the City of London. An imperial route. Eventually, all the
most important High Commissions of the British Empire would adorn it – Canada,
South Africa, Australia and India.

The theme of the Victoria Memorial was set in the monument outside
Buckingham Palace. Gruff and choleric, George V – a home-loving man, who liked
stamp collecting and uniforms – was not famous for his aesthetic taste. But he
responded so warmly to Brock's work that, in an uncharacteristic departure from
protocol, no doubt stage managed, he seized a sword and immediately knighted the
sculptor on the spot.

But the tribute had only just begun; it was to continue in the reconfiguration of
The Mall, Admiralty Arch and the junction of The Mall with Trafalgar Square. Those
works fell to the prolific and highly organised Sir Aston Webb.

The anonymous author of Webb's *Times* obituary in 1930 considered that it
was 'doubtful' that he was a great architect: 'The fact is that he was almost too
successful. His work was so vast that he had to surround himself with clerks
– people say, 50 at least – so that his office became more like a Government
Department than the studio of a man who had time to think and draw.' But he
was a man of supreme organisational ability – demonstrated by the remodelling
of Buckingham Palace that took place in 1913. On 5 August, the royal family left
for Balmoral; a mere thirteen weeks later it was ready for their reoccupation when
the scaffolding came down on 31 October. Dealing with government departments
and royal households requires different skills from that of the purely art architect.
Ministers respected his capabilities. Few architects other than Webb could have
convinced them to go so far beyond the original brief for the Victoria Memorial,
persuading them to create a new ceremonial route which would lead from
Buckingham Palace to Trafalgar Square, until then inaccessible from The Mall. As
the architect H. V. Lanchester commented, Webb was a 'born leader of men' who
'possessed the happy gift of seeing not only the right course to pursue but also the

ABOVE Domes, a neglected motif during the high days of the Gothic Revival, were a *leit motif* of the imperial age. Not only did they lend an air of Augustan pomp to public architecture, but they were also adopted by more modest structures, particularly theatres and musical halls. It was in this spirit that the Electric Cinema in Notting Hill was domed. Constructed in 1910, it was one of the earliest theatres built specifically for showing motion pictures, although not the first; the Electric Cinema in Birmingham had opened two months before.

best method of convincing others of the soundness of his opinions'. Those qualities were crucial to the success of the Victoria Memorial.

Opening The Mall into Trafalgar Square was a masterstroke. One of the triumphs of Admiralty Arch is that it enables an awkward change of direction to be carried out seamlessly, without people travelling the route being aware of it.

From this point, it would have been possible to go on towards the City, via the Strand and Aldwych; but as anyone in the crowd would have known, the royal coach turned into Whitehall, towards Westminster Abbey. Whitehall had been lined, for the first stage, with white masts supporting armorial shields and national flags and linked with garlands of green foliage and red berries. Then came white pillars surmounted alternately by winged griffins and figures of Victory or Fame. A triumphal arch spanned the street, a flourish of the New Zealand government; it had been designed by Frank Brangwyn and was draped in crimson and gold. Opposite Downing Street, the coach passed between two pylons erected by the Government of Ontario, as Canada's premier province. The Empire was on parade, and many in the crowd had been waiting all night to see it – or in the case of one lady with a spirit lamp and kettle, for several days. There would inevitably be a pageant: the Great Pageant at the Festival of Empire and Imperial Exhibition, with an 'all red' tour around the Dominions. (A pageant of a different kind had taken place two days before the Coronation when the Suffragettes organised an alternative Coronation Procession.) For now it was Colonial troops and British guardsmen and dancing plumes and the 'oompah, oomphah' of military bands. The king was almost certainly more interested in the colour, noise and uniforms around him than the architecture; but if he had been able to spare a thought for various new buildings along the route, he might well have noticed a connecting and conspicuously imperial theme. Domes.

Over the previous decade, London, Britain and the Empire had been domed up. On Whitehall, domes had appeared at either end of William Young's War Office, finished by his son Clyde: a bow towards Sir Christopher Wren, held to be the presiding genius of English classicism. Another pair fluttered, rather heavily, above the New Government Offices on George Street; John Bryon, the architect, was, like William Young, a Scot – and like him again, did not live to see his building finished, dying in 1901 (the New Government Offices were completed in 1908). To the King's right, as he entered Westminster Abbey, was the bravura dome of Lanchester and Rickards's newly finished Methodist Central Hall, erected, a little late, to mark the centenary of John Wesley's death. This was an extraordinary suave and worldly building, almost diametrically opposed to the chapels and meeting houses that Wesley himself had known. But this was an age in which even the Methodists carried all before them, and it felt almost as appropriate for a public building to be domed as for a lady to wear a hat. Metropolitan domes include those over the Old Bailey (E. W. Mountford, 1900–08), the Victoria and Albert Museum (although it could equally be described as a corona; Aston Webb, 1899–1909) and the elegant *Morning Post* building, on the Aldwych (Mewès and Davis, 1907); domes floated like bubbles over theatres and music halls like the Gaiety, the London Coliseum and that early picture house, the Electric Cinema, in Notting Hill, which opened in 1911. Five years earlier, one had emerged, strangely elongated in form, golden and topped by a kind of kiosk, itself domed, above the red sandstone Argyll Motor Works in West Dunbartonshire, an extravagantly plush building whose interior boasted columns in scagliola, imitating patterned marble.

Which shows that provincial taste was just as susceptible to a dome as that of London. Whereas the tower of Glasgow's Victorian university had been spikily Gothic, the suite of impressive libraries constructed across the city in the Edwardian decade was often domed. They include several endowed by the Scottish-born steel magnate Andrew Carnegie, such as the red sandstone

Hutchesontown Library in the Gorbals, whose off-centre domed tower surges unstoppably upwards, despite the efforts of the building's end turrets to anchor it in a Free Style version of the Baronial Revival; and the Dennistoun, Govanhill and Parkhead Libraries designed by James Robert Rhind, all around 1905. This rash of construction gave the trustees of Stephen Mitchell's bequest something to live up to; Mitchell, who died in 1874, had been a tobacco manufacturer – his company later became one of the founding elements of the Imperial Tobacco Company – and left the residue of his considerable estate to build a library. Eventually, this took place after a competition, won by William B. Whitie. The wait had been worth it, because Whitie produced a Palladian building of great presence, whose central dome is commanding. (In London and elsewhere, the prolific builder of libraries, as well as town halls, Henry T. Hare from Scarborough contented his clients with a panoply of carved swags and other Wrennish details, but – happily – cupolas rather than domes.)

Domes ballooned over office buildings and fire stations in Manchester, above the Laing Art Gallery in Newcastle, atop the railway station at Nottingham. Let one dome stand for them all: the Ashton Memorial outside Lancaster. It achieves the ambition, so much wished for in the imperial years, so rarely achieved: total domination of its landscape. In terms of detail, this masterpiece of John Belcher could be criticised; Pevsner, in his *Buildings of England* volume, does criticise it (not surprisingly, given his Modernist point of view). Edwardian puddings rarely went under-egged. But if we set the impurities aside (more fussiness than the dome of St Paul's), the mass is swaggeringly dramatic, the sight – even if only glimpsed from a speeding train – unforgettable. Completed in 1909, it remembers Jessie, the second wife of the linoleum manufacturer Lord Ashton.

The Ashton Memorial gives a clue as to the popularity of the dome. With the advent of steel-frame construction, which arrived from the United States not, as is often thought, with London's Ritz Hotel in 1906 but in a number of structures some years earlier, domes became cheaper to build. Their return to favour in the

BELOW Edwardian Baroque: the Ashton Memorial achieved the imperial idea of dominating its landscape, rising from the highest point of the Williamson Park and forming a spectacular monument on the route of the West Coast railway line and visible for many miles from the East. Williamson Park had been created out of a stone quarry by James Williamson, whose son continued his business making oilcloth and became the 1st Baron Ashton, Linoleum King. Built in 1907–09, the memorial remembers Ashton's second wife Jessie who helped him in his political life (he served briefly as an MP, before being awarded the peerage in return, it was believed, for party donations). The architect, John Belcher, possessed the quality so much associated with the portrait painter John Singer Sargent: swagger.

last years of the nineteenth century can be attributed, like so much else in the period, to Richard Norman Shaw. They were a feature of the muscular Baroque idiom that he pioneered from the late 1880s at Bryanston in Dorset and Chesters in Northumberland. Not only was Norman Shaw the doyen of architects, but the precedents to which he looked back in these buildings belonged to the age of Sir Christopher Wren, popularly regarded as the greatest of English architects and, as the architect of St Paul's Cathedral, a particularly national one. Of course, Wren's domes owed more to France and Italy than any indigenous tradition, for none existed; but like other Classical motifs, the one architectural idea of the dome is capable of carrying different meanings, sometimes of a contradictory nature. Edwardian architects looked to Wren, certainly, but also beyond him to Imperial Rome; domes suggested Empire in national dress.

Edwin Rickards, partner of Henry Lanchester, was one of the greatest of dome builders (as we have seen at the Westminster Central Hall); he spent much time as a young man 'wandering through the City ... amongst the monuments of Wren'. Not that Rickards confined his borrowings to Wren – but many did. These were the years of Lutyens' discovery of the High Game of Classicism, which he called the Wrenaissance. We have the novelist Arnold Bennett to thank (as well as the evidence of our eyes) for telling us that Rickards loved Paris, whither he accompanied the older but provincial Bennett on his first trip. 'His capacity for appreciation knew no fatigue,' he wrote – neither did his ability to maintain the flow of ideas into the night, when Bennett was exhausted. Rickards' Baroque may have been sanctified by Wren, but it was born in Paris, out of the Ecole des Beaux-Arts tradition. Fortunately, the effervescent Rickards found a complementary partner in Henry Lanchester, against whose 'rock-like' plan for the Cardiff City Hall his 'stream ... of genius' would break, according to *The Architect* and *Building News*, to create a building (domed) of authority and élan.

Domes were foreign to the Victorians – very foreign. Respectable Anglicans shuddered at the dome of the Brompton Oratory, so obviously a reference to Rome. The dome was not a Gothic form; indeed, Britain had been dome free until 1700. In the United States, domes had, since the construction of Benjamin Latrobe's Capitol in Washington, become a shorthand for democracy – sometimes supersized. Most state houses were domed as well as a vast number of county court houses; although the largest domed building in the US – indeed in the world – was, perhaps, appropriately a hotel: the West Baden Springs Hotel, whose dome is a wondrous 200 ft in diameter. French Lick, the curiously named promoter of the West Baden Springs Hotel, may have associated domes with *joie de vivre*; that was surely the case among theatre architects in Britain, such as Frank Matcham. But in a government, civic or corporate commission, domes were the equivalent of Elgar's more sonorous passages: they bespoke imperial self-confidence. These buildings were almost always the result of architectural competitions, and domes always looked beguiling on paper.

One dome was not always enough. The Port of Liverpool Building, which helps shape the Liverpool skyline, not only has the central dome that we see etched against the scudding Merseyside clouds, but also four sub-domes at the corners of the main building, like tent pegs to stop it blowing away. Alfred Thomas had tried the idea before on Belfast City Hall – itself having a degree of kinship with the dreadful Glasgow City Chambers. From some angles, Aston Webb's Birmingham University – famously red brick but with stone dressings – is a kind of musical variation on the theme of the dome, four or five different types being seen in one view.

Domes were the most prominent characteristic of the neo-Baroque style, and the most obviously expressive. With them were deployed the full repertoire of Classical enrichment, including rusticated quoins, banded columns, broken pediments and giant orders, sometimes with a lubricity that would have shocked 'poor old Christopher Wren'. But meaning was not left only to these abstract devices; to

ABOVE Victorian and Edwardian town halls were an index of the civic wealth and aspiration of the industrial cities. Belfast's moment of recognition had come in 1888, when Queen Victoria was, in the words of the Viceroy of Ireland, Lord Londonderry, 'graciously pleased to confer' on it 'the dignity, the honour and the title of city'. Plans to commission a city hall were set in motion, although it took a decade before work began. The chosen architect was the young Alfred Brumwell Thomas who produced a many-domed design, heavily influenced by Wren. Although overblown, Belfast City Hall had many progeny, from the City Hall in Durban, South Africa of 1910 to the Port of Liverpool Building, completed 1913. The result was equal to Belfast's place in the Empire as one of its richest cities, which not only had the biggest shipyard, but also had the biggest rope works, tobacco factory, linen spinning mill and other enterprises .

many architects, the ultimate achievement was to have their buildings enriched by sculpture. The idea is as old as the Elgin Marbles, but did not emerge only from classical thought; the union of architecture and sculpture – as well as other decorative arts – was one of the prime aims of the Arts and Crafts movement. This can be seen from the Art Workers Guild, founded under the inspiration of William Morris in 1884, which included architects, sculptors, artists and craftsmen among its ranks. One Brother of the Guild was John Belcher, whom we have already seen at the Ashton Memorial. 'We may admit as an abstract proposition, that our work will gain in value and force when it is associated with sculpture,' he told the Royal Institute of British Architects in 1892.

> But how is this to be done? In this grinding, mercenary age, when clients expect so much for their money, such an extravagance as sculpture seems out of the question – a luxury which the mere utilitarian aspect of a building will not allow … one remedy, I believe, is to associate the sculptor with ourselves in the early work; he should not be left to manipulate sundry blocks reserved for carving towards the completion of the building.

In fact, Belcher had already had the opportunity to begin a collaboration of this kind, when he joined with fellow Brother, the sculptor Hamo Thornycroft, on the Institute of Chartered Accountants building off Moorgate, in the City of London. Belcher provided a deliciously incorrect framework of giant Doric columns and banded rustication, with a cupola at one end and a kind of aedicule on the corner. Into this, Thornycroft, with the help of John Tweed, fitted twelve panels carved in high relief, depicting the Arts, Sciences and Crafts, and all the areas of life watered by the refreshing dew of accountancy: education, commerce, agriculture, shipping, railways and so on, all in contemporary rather than Classical dress. Belcher and Thornycroft's example was followed in the next decade by Collcutt (of the Imperial Institute) and George Frampton for Lloyds Register of Shipping. Architects such as

ABOVE Public sculpture was one of the means by which London upped its imperial condition at the turn of the twentieth century. Edward VII himself proposed that the Quadriga would make a fitting subject for the top of the Wellington Arch at Hyde Park Corner, when he saw it at the Royal Academy in 1891. The work was not hoisted into position until 1912. The Portuguese financier Lord Michelham paid for the work; his son was the model for the boy driving the chariot. The Quadriga was a suitable subject for Adrian Jones, an army veterinary surgeon. The result was a fitting memorial to Edward VII, the most cosmopolitan of monarchs, who personified the Entente Cordiale.

Lanchester and Rickards would also have seen a different but equally convincing union of sculpture and architecture in Paris; no French architect though would have permitted himself to break Classical rules with the abandon that they do at the Deptford Town Hall, a flamboyant building with a decidedly English charm.

Public sculpture suited the lofty, myth-making ambitions of New Imperialism. Not generally known as an aesthete, Edward VII himself proposed that a Quadriga would make a fit subject for the top of the Wellington Arch at Hyde Park corner – 'Peace descending from on High upon the Chariot of War'. (It may be that he had simply seen a group in plaster, exhibited at the Royal Academy in 1891 by Adrian Jones, and suggested the Wellington Arch as a location.)

Allegorical subjects, such as the Quadriga, were complemented by statues of royalty and heroes of Empire that occupied plinths throughout the major cities in increasing numbers. Unveiling them was a familiar and popular ceremony – so popular that the crowd attempted to storm the grandstand for dignitaries when George Frampton's Queen Victoria was unveiled in Manchester by the soldier Lord Roberts (who would himself be immortalised in statues in Whitehall, Kelvingrove in Glasgow and Calcutta) in 1901, on the grounds that such an event should not be restricted to toffs. Clerical anxiety about the number of memorials accumulating in Westminster Abbey inspired John Pollard Seddon and Edward Beckitt Lamb to propose a dizzying imperial Valhalla between the Abbey and the Houses of Parliament: both would have been dwarfed had it been built.

Sculpture carried meaning, and was therefore often the subject of controversy. The most enduring storm was that which raged over the British Medical Association, which, having occupied various structures on a corner site on the Strand and Agar Street, held a competition for new premises in 1906. The doctors wanted a headquarters that would express their authority and status more adequately; they had evolved from the Provincial Medical and Surgical Association

ABOVE Sculpture caused an outcry when Charles Holden's headquarters of the British Medical Association appeared on the Strand in 1908. The building itself was Mannerist. Windows with sculptural figures squashed into panels were combined with an almost manic vertical emphasis, created to pilasters of different heights. For the eighteen sculptural figures, the twenty-six-year-old Jacob Epstein refused to restrict his brief to famous doctors, as desired by the BMA. Instead, he produced a series of nude figures loosely on the theme of the Seven Ages of Man. Although stylised, they were anatomically too frank for some sensibilities. When the BMA left the premises in 1924, the building's new owner, the puritanical Government of Southern Rhodesia, had the statues irreparably mutilated.

to become a powerful professional body, capable, within a few years, of altering Lloyd George's Act for providing workers with state medical attention. They were, in that respect, like many professional groups elbowing their way to greater status and power within the expanding middle class, conscious of a role that spread through the Empire via numerous overseas branches. The winning architect, Charles Holden, would become familiar to commuters for the Underground stations that he designed, under the patronage of Frank Pick, the Lorenzo the Magnificent of London Transport. In contrast to Norman Shaw's Baroque (domed) New Gaiety Theatre and Mewès and Davies's dix-huitième (domed) *Morning Post* at the other end of the Strand, Holden's design was Mannerist. It used elements of Classicism but in a new way. London had become used to liberties being taken with the classical vocabulary since the emergence of architects like Charles Harrison Townsend, practising an Art Nouveauish Free Style. Holden's distinctly staccato building was more rigorous. Evidently, Holden felt that Edwardian baroque had become too plush and commonplace, and he produced a more challenging building – in doing which he was not absolutely alone: Belcher and Joass produced a distinctly etiolated composition, with attenuated columns that look as though they will snap under the weight of the masonry above them, for the jewellers Mappin and Webb on Oxford Street in 1906–08, as well as an almost febrile headquarters for the Royal Insurance Company on Piccadilly.

The sculptures were provided by twenty-six-year-old Jacob Epstein who had studied in Paris. The theme was to be, loosely, the Seven Ages of Man. The BMA wanted the figures to represent eminent doctors, but, as Epstein recalled, 'I was determined to do a series of nude figures, and surgeons with side-whiskers, no matter how eminent, could hardly have served my purpose as models.' Architect and sculptor had their way, and eighteen nudes were carved out of single blocks of stone, in situ. They were stylised but anatomically frank; the figure of Maternity, for example, was shown as pregnant. Fig leaves were dispensed with. By a quirk of fate, the building on the opposite side of Agar Street housed the National Vigilance Association; they were certainly vigilant enough to spot what was happening outside their own windows. A brewing storm burst in the *Evening Standard* in 1908. 'BOLD SCULPTURE, AMAZING FIGURES ON A STRAND BUILDING,' proclaimed a seemingly innocuous headline, before asking: 'BUT IS IT ART?' In fact, the author was less concerned about the art question than the corruption of public morals. 'They are a form of statuary which no careful father would want his daughter, or no discriminating young man his fiancée, to see.' When eleven years after the BMA left for larger premises in Tavistock Square in 1924, the building's new owner, the puritanical Government of Southern Rhodesia, agreed; they had the statues irreparably mutilated. And so they remain: evidence of the strong emotion that can be generated by sculpture.

Not that such evidence is needed. A decade after the BMA building was finished, Britain began an unprecedented, spontaneous campaign of commissioning public sculpture, sometimes of a profoundly affecting kind: the war memorials erected after the First World War. Many war memorials – each one chosen by a local committee – had no sculptural content: often they were no more than stone crosses, or even, in some cases, a memorial hall. Simplicity is often as powerful as more elaborate artistic statements. But Britain was also fortunate that, at a time when the emotionally tongue-tied nation had so much to express, a tradition of figurative sculpture existed to give substance to its innermost feelings. These works have lost none of their potency over the years.

Towering over Trinity Green, next to the Tower of London, is the immensity of Sir Edwin Cooper's Port of London Authority building: Corinthian, demonstrative, as massive as the White Cliffs of Dover, a figure of Neptune prominent in its piled-up centrepiece. This façade not only incorporates sculpture, but is effectively a sculptural element in itself: there is nothing behind this piece of braggadocio because it joins two wings of offices that are set at an oblique angle to each other. As the headquarters of a new authority to govern London's docks – the original foundation of the city's prosperity, although the capital was now losing place to Bristol and Liverpool – it felt entitled to make an imperial gesture. Here, symbolically, was the might of the British merchant marine, ships that traded, yes, around the world, but particularly among the colonies, encouraged by (in mid 1920s, soon after the building was finished) slogans such as 'Buy Empire'. Trophies representing India and Africa were carved onto the walnut panelling of the board room. Here was Empire, and it was big.

Size was an issue for architecture at the turn of the century. The scale of life had increased. This could be seen in Whitehall, whose new buildings housed hundreds more civil servants than had been thought necessary a century before. It was evident in the headquarters buildings of the professions, no longer content to muddle through in a cheap terraced house. Hotels, built, like the Savoy, after the example of palace hotels in the US, rose taller because of the introduction of lifts. Even clubs were expanding. The Royal Automobile Club on Pall Mall was at least twice the size of the Athenaeum or the Travellers on the same street: wags christened it the Really Awful Club as a result. For heaven's sake, the place had a swimming pool (in Roman style), one of the earliest in London.

The escalation can particularly be seen in shops. Benjamin Harvey started business in Knightsbridge in 1813, his daughter taking a silk buyer called Colonel Nichols into partnership – hence Harvey Nichols. Debenhams began the same year. Dickins and Jones began in 1790, John Lewis in 1864. All, despite growing, continued to do business from premises that would have been considered muddled and pokey by Edwardian standards, usually not specially constructed to suit their needs. Then came the explosion. The 1890s and 1900s saw the emergence of a new breed of super shop – the department store, beneath whose roof the shopper could find anything he or she – mostly she: the shops were generally aimed at women – could ever need. Harrods (opened 1832) led the charge with its stupendous, terracotta-enriched store on the Brompton Road, begun in 1894 (following floatation on the Stock Exchange five years earlier) and finished in 1905; it had the first escalator in London. Selfridge's, a new arrival to Oxford Street, born of the eponymous Gordon Selfridge, who had worked with Marshall Field in Chicago and employed an American architect to design the store's colossal Corinthian colonnade, was almost crushing in the triumphalism of its Ionic façade.

Department stores reflected the availability of finance to the retailer and the existence of appreciative shoppers from the expanding middle class. The character of the trade that these emporia wanted to attract can be judged from the services that they offered. Selfridge's had a Library and Silence Room, a bureau de change, a post office, a savings bank, booking offices for railway, steamship and theatre, a luncheon hall and a tea garden. Harrods actually had clubs for gentlemen and ladies (to join, apply to the secretary).

Shopping in the mid-Victorian period had been a funereal experience: assistants spoke in undertones, were reluctant to show their goods, and handed over purchases when the customer left the store with the air of bestowing a small gift. By contrast, the bustle and vitality of Whiteley's were exciting. The proprietor himself set the scene when he suggested that W. P. Frith might make 'Whiteley's at Four o'clock in the Afternoon' a subject to rival Derby Day. He told the painter: 'You might introduce the young ladies who do me the honour to assist in my establishment, many of whom are very pretty.' (William Whiteley was rather too keen on his young ladies; he was shot dead in 1907 by a man who claimed he was his unrecognised illegitimate son.)

As fashion and choice became more important, so did window shopping. Although one shopper, with the penetrating eye of an architectural historian, Hermione Hobhouse, noticed that the decorative mood adopted by different retailers such as Austen Reed was carefully chosen to match the product:

RIGHT Shops got bigger in the Edwardian period, with the building of new department stores; life became more colourful. Shopkeepers introduced more eye-catching displays and flaunted their wares through advertising; the stores themselves became landmarks. Whiteleys, on Queensway, was opened in 1911. The business had begun in 1863 when William Whiteley, the Universal Provider, opened a drapery shop on Westbourne Grove. This quickly expanded to a row of shops, then an 'an immense symposium of the arts and industries of the nation and of the world'; it employed more than 6,000 staff. Whiteley himself did not live to see Belcher and Joass's building; in 1907, he had been shot dead by a young man claiming to be his illegitimate son who felt unprovided for. Fortunately, the store offered a funeral service.

ABOVE The building of Shaftesbury Avenue, opened in 1888, destroyed the harmony of John Nash's Regent Circus South, as Piccadilly Circus used to be called. Nobody could decide how to how to reshape it, given the demand for broader streets and larger buildings in the Edwardian decade. Sadly, Norman Shaw's heroic design for the Regent Street quadrant was not realised, but his Piccadilly Hotel and County Fire Office (seen here) arose, more or less as he intended. The focus of the rectangular 'Circus' was the memorial to Lord Shaftesbury, sculpted by Gilbert, and unveiled in 1893. The god of selfless love (not, strictly speaking Eros, but his younger brother Anteros) alights on just the sole of one foot, made possible through the use of aluminium. It remains a meeting place for the capital.

Thus one bought an evening dress in a room with artificial light only, a made-to-measure suit in a Louis XV room, shoes in up-to-the-minute art deco and tropical kit in a distinguished red lacquer room in a style reminiscent of Sezincote. For sporting clothes and dressing gowns, presumably intended for cold country houses, there were two floors of Tudor rooms.

The old Regent Street, planned by John Nash in the Regency period, had come to seem cramped and dowdy by the end of the nineteenth century. Behind the showy glass fronts and mahogany counters were, according to *The Architect* in 1881, low ceilings, bad lighting and 'ventilation [that] may best be expressed in plain vulgarity by the single word sweat'. The art of window dressing had moved on; the entrance door of the shop could be recessed beneath the upper stories of the building, allowing a greater expanse of glass to intrigue the eye of the passer-by – an innovation enthusiastically endorsed by Horace Dan and E. C. Morgan in their *English Shop Fronts, Old and New* of 1907. The importance that shopkeepers placed on their displays of glass led to one of the great architectural controversies of the age, when in 1904 Richard Norman Shaw, the elderly doyen of the architectural profession, produced a scheme to rebuild the Regent Street quadrant in a muscular Baroque style, which privileged Portland stone over glass. After Norman Shaw's death in 1912, the shopkeepers defeated it; Reginald Blomfield's compromise, built after the First World War, was widely derided by critics, but hardly boycotted by the shopping public.

The debacle illustrates the struggle between adherents of the classical tradition and its nemesis, plate glass. Both those who shopped and those who sold them wanted 'bigger, brighter and better laid-out shops in main street sites', with new display techniques after the First World War: out with profusion, in with clarity. Modernist shops of the 1930s, such as the Peter Jones store on Sloane Square and Simpsons in Piccadilly, revelled in these qualities.

But the Britain of 1900 had felt itself to be modern, too. Beneath the swagger and complacency, new ideas were afoot. One of them came in noisily with the motorcar. The old settled order of the countryside was being startled out of its immemorial stupor. The horses were literally being frightened by a mode of transport that could be afforded only by the very rich. The dangerous manner in which the glossy new vehicles were driven through rural districts whose roads were little more than cart tracks seemed to typify the arrogance of the plutocracy. Old-fashioned hostesses feared the liberation given to potential house guests by the 'here today, in next week tomorrow' spirit of the motorcar, which allowed its occupants to race onto a different county after luncheon, rather than stay for a week. Edward VII enthusiastically embraced this new form of transport, as did his otherwise stick-in-the-mud son George V. Indeed, while remaining a stickler for tradition as shown in the correct wearing of uniforms, of which he had an encyclopaedic knowledge, he was captivated by technology. At West Dean Park in Sussex – a decidedly modern house, dedicated to sophisticated but not specially cultural pleasures – a marble aedicule and bronze allegorical woman commemorates the opening in Montreal of a sister institution to the King Edward VII Sanatorium at Midhurst, to which the King went every time he visited the house (its owner, the half-American, big game hunter Willie James, was executive chairman). It was done by electric telegraph. As the *Daily Telegraph* gushed:

> Over land and under ocean the current, despatched on its way by his Majesty, travelled at an inconceivable pace. Arrived at Montreal, it operated the special machinery installed there, and, influenced by the invisible power, the doors flew open for the guests to enter, the electric lights were turned on throughout the building, and, as the culminating event, the Union Jack was run up the mast and broken.

The King himself would never talk on the telephone, sharing a general prejudice against a device that was originally conceived as a purely utilitarian invention (the earliest examples were intended for use by servants, who could be told what was required without their master or mistress having to summon them by ringing a bell). But the popularity of the instrument created a new type of building: the telephone exchange. The irascible Leonard Stokes, a member of the Art Workers Guild, built twenty of them; his wife, Edith Gaine, was the daughter of the General Manager of the National Telephone Company. His masterpiece was the Gerrard Street Exchange of 1904–05, extended in 1936; now demolished, it featured an arcade on the ground floor, striped bands of stone and brick and banks of window for the telephonists at the top.

In the 1880s, Electric Avenue, in Brixton, blazed forth as a pioneer of electric lighting. The new power source required the building of a previously unknown kind of structure: the power station. The architectural question raised by the power station was never satisfactorily answered during our period, despite Giles Gilbert Scott's monumental brickwork at Battersea in the 1930s; chimneys do not make good columns. (Although his Bankside Power Station, now Tate Modern, built after the Second World War, was monumental.)

Electricity did not only power light bulbs. Leslie Green made a career from designing stations for the electric railways that ran beneath capital's streets. The Underground Electric Railway Company of London, a merger formed by the American speculator Charles Tyson Yerkes out of parts of the present Piccadilly, Bakerloo and Northern Lines, commissioned fifty of them, before his death from tuberculosis at the age of thirty-four. The use of steel beams (an innovation from the United States) made it possible to create the large spaces needed for booking halls, while the façades were clad in the famous oxblood tiles. The first escalator came to the Underground in 1911, supplementing the lifts.

Modernity could also be perceived, by its champions, in the new levels of

BELOW Turn-of-the-century London was the biggest city in the world and needed mass transport. This opportunity was spotted by the American financier Charles Yerkes, who bought most of the existing Underground network and developed it – at one point beating off another American, J. P. Morgan. His legacy can be seen in the arcaded stations, tiled in oxblood faience, many of which are still in use on the Piccadilly, Bakerloo and Northern Lines. They were designed by Leslie Green, the son of an architect who had spent some time in Paris. Green built more than fifty of them before his death from tuberculosis at the age of thirty-three.

ABOVE The Kelvingrove Art Gallery and Museum in Glasgow shows the spectacular scale and flamboyance of some out-of-London cultural buildings at the turn of the century. It was opened in 1901, during one Glasgow International Exhibition, during which the Empire's Second City displayed its wares to the world, with the funds accrued from another: the 1888 Glasgow International Exhibition. In 1892, the architects John W. Simpson and E. J. Milner Allen won the competition to design

consumption and leisure. And it required new spaces and building types, such as the palace hotel. The pace was set, in this respect, by Gilbert and Sullivan's impresario, Richard D'Oyly Carte. Impressed by the hotels in which he had stayed while visiting the United States to protect copyrights and stage productions, he erected the Savoy Hotel on the Strand. Hydraulic lifts were installed by the American Elevation Company, and the hotel was run, for the first eight years of its existence, by César Ritz; Ritz secured the most famous chef in the world, Auguste Escoffier, to preside over the kitchen. The combination successfully appealed to an age that was loosening its waistband to accommodate previously unknown levels of plutocratic luxury. Previously, respectable ladies had dined only in their own and their friends' houses. D'Oyly Carte made it possible for them to eat at the Savoy. Elsewhere, they preferred to eat by themselves, and a variety of clubs was offered to

the gallery, in a Spanish Baroque style whose red sandstone towers were inspired by the cathedral at Santiago de Compostella. A splendid organ in a case of polished walnut was installed in the central hall after the closure of the exhibition. Another striking feature of the hall is the sumptuous light fittings, which are a successful solution to the problems raised by electric lighting.

unaccompanied women: the Alexandra and Victoria Clubs were listed in Whittaker's almanac as being for 'ladies of position only'. Not that ladies of position were the only class that was causing thought. In Hampstead Garden Suburb, the fifty flats in M. H. Baillie Scott's Waterlow Court, funded by the Improved Industrial Dwellings Company, offered sanctuary to 'single genteel working ladies', with the opportunity for communal housekeeping and meals. The emancipated woman, a new and (to some) puzzling phenomenon, was beginning to emerge.

These changes were chronicled by an exuberant press, another aspect of modern life that irritated social conservatives. Newspaper circulations were soaring to meet the demand from a newly literate working class, while new techniques for the printing of photographs encouraged a boom in magazines. While sycophantic deference was the default position of some publications, others feasted their readers on salacious gossip of the kind that Edward VII's Marlborough House Set so readily supplied.

London, the imperial capital, exhibited at least as much human contrast as it had in Dr Johnson's day. The point was colourfully elaborated by Geraldine Mitton in *The Scenery of London*, 1905, where an evening spent by a young officer from a public school, involving dinner at the Carlton Club – 'Here are the best-dressed women in Europe' – is contrasted to the drabness of life at the other end of the social scale, lived under grey skies and on muddy streets. Though even the dim existences of the humble could be brightened, Mitton thought, by cultural treasure:

> Even without being aught but a nonentity it is open to all to hear the best music composed by men famed all the world over, to see the great masterpieces of painting, to attend lectures by men who are in the vanguard of science. Priceless objects of art, rare books, ancient treasures, are open free for the inspection of the poorest; these things are the real gold of the richest city in the world.

Mitton had in mind the great Victorian museum complex in South Kensington, recently enlarged by Sir Aston Webb's Victoria and Albert Museum; the British Museum, to which the Edward VII Galleries would soon be added; and Henry Wood's Promenade Concerts in the Queen's Hall (transferred to the Albert Hall after the Queen's Hall was destroyed during the Blitz).

Nor were provincial cities to be left behind. Glasgow's stupendous Kelvingrove Art Gallery and Museum was opened in 1901, combining the city's familiar red sandstone with a less familiar Spanish Baroque style; the central hall, one end of which is occupied by a pipe organ, is one of the few buildings of the era to find a satisfactory solution to the problem of electric light. On Glasgow Green, one of the poorest areas of the city, the museum, reading room and winter garden of the People's Palace had been erected after a campaign by Councillor Robert Crawford, Chairman of the Health Committee. On opening it in 1898, Lord Rosebery described it as 'a palace of pleasure and imagination around which the people may place their affections and which may give them a home on which their memory may rest' – a reformulation of the Edmund Burke's maxim that 'to make us love our country, our country ought to be lovely'. Even the Northamptonshire shoe-making town of Kettering acquired a museum and art gallery in 1913, having been given the collection of the painter Sir Alfred East, a son of Kettering, who died that year.

And just as the finer sensibilities of the poor were being raised, so too – perhaps more importantly, to those who lived in the leaky-roofed, vermin-infested slums – was their physical condition. 'Never before in the life of the globe,' observed the Reverend Richard Lovett in 1890, 'have so many human beings been compressed into so small a space.' Civic improvement had been a preoccupation of late Victorian Britain, agonised over as the consequence of the Industrial Revolution and shamed as much by journalists and writers, such as Dickens, as by philanthropists (Lord Shaftesbury) and aesthetes (John Ruskin). The new institutions which made it

possible were embodied in the town halls that arose from the mid nineteenth century, culminating in Ralph Knott's County Hall in London, seat of the London County Council (LCC).

We have seen that the LCC was established in 1889 because London had outgrown the congeries of vestries, district boards, boroughs and the Metropolitan Board of Works by which its affairs had previously been arranged. Its reforming agenda was not limited to town planning initiatives such as the Strand Improvement Scheme. Public consciousness of poverty had been sharpened by the appearance, six years earlier, of an anonymous penny pamphlet under the title 'The Bitter Cry of Outcast London'. This, as the subtitle revealed, was 'an inquiry into the condition of the abject poor', written from a Christian perspective which touched the conscience of the church-going middle class. The blame lay in

THE CONDITION IN WHICH THEY LIVE

We do not say the condition of their homes, for how can those places be called homes, compared with which the lair of a wild beast would be a comfortable and healthy spot. Few who will read these pages have any conception of what these pestilential human rookeries are, where tens of thousands are crowded together amidst horrors which call to mind what we have heard of the middle passage of the slave ship.

The immorality bred by these conditions was grimly detailed, causing, in the words of *Reynolds Newspaper*, 'a tremendous sensation and thrill of horror through the land'. Beginning with the Boundary Street area of Bethnal Green, the most glaring of the slums across London were not only systematically razed, but rebuilt on model lines. After some initial hesitation – and in the teeth of opposition from landlords and other groups – it began to increase the housing stock by the supply of municipal housing which was not merely a replacement for demolished slums.

The LCC was not alone in wanting to provide better housing for the poor. Philanthropists like Octavia Hill, one of the founders of the National Trust, wanted to do this through charitable means; the Peabody Trust was one of several housing companies seeking to provide decent accommodation for hard-working members of the working class (there was little truck with feckless individuals who were deemed to have brought their troubles on themselves). Decent, however, did not extend to architectural charm, in what were typically forbidding and barrack-like blocks. By contrast, the LCC's progressive social approach extended to architecture. The outlook of members such as the socialist Sidney Webb chimed with that of a generation of young architects, led by William Lethaby, who had inherited the ideals of William Morris and Philip Webb's devotion to sound building. The turn of the century was a high point of domestic architecture for the well-to-do, as can be seen from the 'small country houses of to-day' (as the architectural critic Lawrence Weaver dubbed them: they are not so small by modern standards) that sprang up on plots of a few acres within an easy train ride of London, as well as developments such as Hampstead Garden Suburb. Beginning with the Millbank Estate, on the site of the demolished Millbank Penitentiary (now behind Tate Britain), the architecturally sober, tree-lined estates of the LCC, whose beautifully laid brickwork looks as solid today as when it was built, also represent an exceptional achievement, very different from the disasters of public housing after the Second World War.

When Behramji Malabari visited London from India in the first year of the LCC's existence, he found already a vast difference from the cities he knew at home. 'Everything was neat and clear,' he reported –

ABOVE The London County Council's Millbank Estate, Pimlico. In 1889, the London County Council was established on an improving agenda. 'We were oppressed by the chain of circumstances that had compelled so many of the poor to live in insanitary dwellings,' remembered Owen Fleming who led the Housing Branch. The LCC's answer was conceived in the spirit of Philip Webb and W. R. Lethaby: red brick blocks, with sash windows, placed on broad, tree-lined avenues and around gardens. Their kinship with prosperous suburbs such as Bedford Park made them more acceptable to the occupants than the regimented barracks erected by, for example, the philanthropic Peabody Trust. However, to avoid an excessive charge on the rates, they were available only to those who could pay a rent.

BELOW Sir Edwin Lutyens' Viceroy's House, New Delhi, 1912–29. The plan of the city over which it presided, as well as its own architecture, expressed the eternal values of order and geometry, interpreted through the Western classical tradition. To Lutyens, this represented a strain of thought that had evolved over millennia. Little planning in the grand manner was possible in Britain, where conditions were better suited to garden suburbs (like Hampstead) and garden cities (like Letchworth).

the streets, the shops and the houses. There was no stink in the road, no filth left accumulated in any place. The glass of the shop windows looked as transparent as glass could be, and the wood, brass and iron used in the construction of shops and houses shone as much like mirror as constant scraping and scrubbing could make them do.

London, almost overwhelming in its technological development, was so far ahead of his homeland that it might seem impossible that the LCC could have a bearing on it. But like almost every innovation of the period, Empire was inescapable. Not only did municipal socialism shore up Britain's wider position in the world, by preventing decay and disturbance at its very heart, but also experiments in London were quickly transferred to colonial contexts, particularly South Africa after the Boer War; Lionel Curtis, formerly of the LCC, became one of Milner's Kindergarten, the idealist cadre of imperialists who gathered around Lord Milner as High Commissioner for South Africa and Governor of Cape Colony, and was given the responsibility for replanning Johannesburg. Returning servicemen were given preference when the LCC recruited clerks. Not that even the works of the LCC were enough to satisfy some people. When in 1912 *The Builder* published a leader under the title 'Imperial London', it argued for a complete change of attitude – with, predictably, more building, with a new Imperial Parliament House, a reconstructed Buckingham Palace as an Imperial Palace and an Imperial Way through St James's Park. The First World War put an end to such grandiosity in Britain; it could not, however, be killed in the great imperial capital that was to arise in New Delhi.

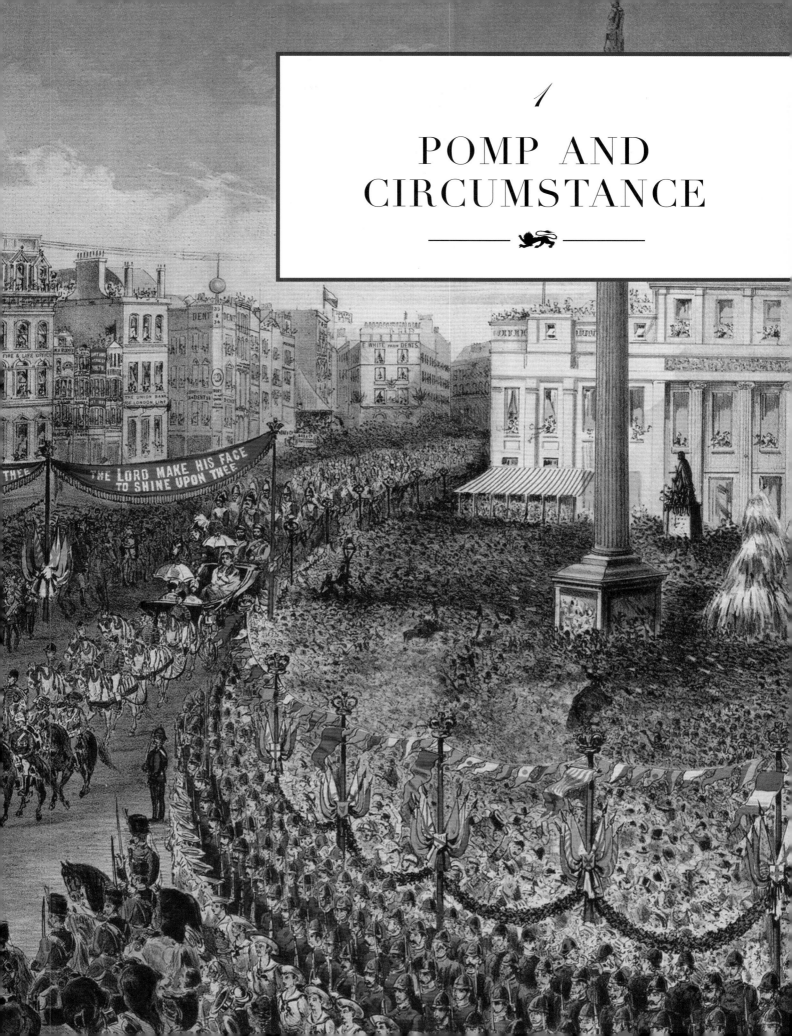

POMP AND
CIRCUMSTANCE

PREVIOUS PAGES The procession for Queen Victoria's Golden Jubilee in 1887. Early in the nineteenth century, state occasions such as George IV's coronation concentrated on their chivalric aspect; there were no soldiers from Britain's overseas territory on parade. By contrast, the processions for Queen Victoria's Golden and Diamond Jubilees, as well as subsequent state funerals and coronations, were made splendid by the dazzling array of troops from around the Empire. Their presence sent out a powerful message: Victoria was both Queen and Empress. But they took place in a capital that was poorly equipped for pomp.

After Queen Victoria became Empress of India in 1877, Britain awoke to the idea of Empire as something more than an assemblage of overseas possessions, acquired on a freelance basis; it was promoted as part of the core British identity. But this lacked architectural expression. Foggy, soot-blackened London looked dowdy – almost provincial – beside Paris and Vienna, whose glittering boulevards were lined with exuberant buildings, as rich as an Escoffier sauce. There were few new streets, even though the scale of life – as seen in bigger shops, bigger offices, bigger theatres, bigger ceremonial processions, bigger government buildings – was increasing. Conscious of being the capital of the Empire, London applied itself to improvement, in the grand, formal style of the Ecole des Beaux-Arts. Throughout Britain, new civic institutions were given town halls whose flamboyant baroque domes and allegorical sculpture evoked both Empire and local pride.

The transformation of London's ceremonial heart was achieved by a confluence of several separate initiatives. One came from the newly formed

BELOW The east front of Buckingham Palace and the Queen Victoria Memorial. Immediately after Queen Victoria's death in 1901 it was decided to remember her through a scheme that included an elaborate monument and a processional way down the Mall. Sufficient money was left over to remodel the east front of the palace. Like the rest of the architecture, this was designed by Sir Aston Webb; it was built in only thirteen weeks, while King George V was taking his summer holiday. The balcony immediately entered court ceremonial – and the hearts of the nation – as the platform on which the royal family would wave to crowds on days of rejoicing.

London County Council, established to manage the affairs of the world's biggest city; high on its progressive agenda was the need to provide decent housing for the hard-working poor. The Strand Improvement Scheme not only widened the important thoroughfare that linked government at Westminster and society in the West End with commerce in the City of London, but also eliminated a rank slum that existed in Clare Market, which, it was hoped, would have the further effect of reducing the number of prostitutes who plied their trade around the Strand's many theatres. The north side of the Strand was demolished, and while nothing much was achieved by way of architectural statement in the fronts that replaced it, a new bow of a street was created at the east end of the Strand (Aldwych), with an arrow shooting north from it in Kingsway. These new streets were modern and also self-consciously imperial, as can be seen from the names of the buildings that arose on them (Imperial Buildings, Africa House) and the Strand became home to the governments of South Africa (on Trafalgar Square), India and Australia (on Aldwych).

This scheme had not been completed before the Queen Victoria Memorial in front of Buckingham Palace got underway. The sculptural part of the memorial took the form of an immense monument, on which Queen Victoria sits beside Truth and Charity, beneath a golden figure of Peace (possibly Victory) and surrounded by nautical imagery evoking Britain's naval might. The architectural dimension, entrusted to the competent Sir Aston Webb, would, in the end, stretch from the east front of Buckingham Palace, down a reordered Mall, through Admiralty Arch and, via a new entrance, into Trafalgar Square. Here, it joined hands with the Strand Improvement Scheme, the result being a new ceremonial route from the seat of royalty to the seat of commerce. Whitehall was also substantially rebuilt, with a new War Office and government buildings and a relatively new Foreign Office.

Kaiser Wilhem II was among the guests when King George V unveiled the monument to Queen Victoria on the day after his coronation in 1911. The imperial message, heavily underscored in the King's speech and trumpeted afterwards in the press, could not have been lost on him or anyone else: in works such as this, London put itself on display. Elsewhere in the country, thanks to the reform of local government, new town halls proclaimed the effort that Britain was making to improve its cities and take control, for their own sake, of the lives of the poor. These buildings – at Deptford, Battersea, Lambeth, Cardiff, Lancaster among others – had pediments and quoins rather than (as at Alfred Waterhouse's Manchester Town Hall of a generation earlier) gables and crockets.

Appropriately for a young institution, the London County Council was housed, at County Hall, on the south bank of the River Thames, by an exceptionally young architect: Ralph Knott was still in his twenties when he won the competition to design it in 1908. It might seem that the rule-breaking Baroque façade (critics have agonised over the concavity at the centre) expresses the self-confidence of the metropolis, but as Susan D. Pennybacker discovered, the institution, however Progressive in its early phase, could hardly escape an awareness of its role as an imperial example; its employees often went on to serve in civic positions overseas, spreading the ideals of betterment and order

An echo of British civic reforms can be found in town halls from Oyo in Nigeria (1906) to Indore in India (1904), just as the desire to remember Queen Victoria outside Buckingham Palace was reflected in other statues erected after her death, from Blackburn to the Bahamas.

£1,000

THE DAILY GRAPHIC, MAY 17, 1911

THIS ISSUE OF "THE DAILY GRAPHIC" CARRIES A FREE INSURANCE OF £1,000 UNDER-
TAKEN BY THE OCEAN ACCIDENT AND GUARANTEE CORPORATION, LIMITED. (See page 2.)

£1,000

THE DAILY GRAPHIC

ONE PENNY

LONDON : WEDNESDAY, MAY 17, 1911.

No. 6688.—Vol. LXXXVI.

Registered as a Newspaper.

THE NATIONAL MEMORIAL TO "VICTORIA THE GOOD."

THE STATUE OF THE QUEEN UNVEILED BY KING GEORGE IN THE MALL YESTERDAY.—A GENERAL
VIEW OF THE CEREMONY. ("Daily Graphic" photograph.)

765

PREVIOUS PAGES LEFT The *Daily Graphic* reports on the unveiling of the Queen Victoria Memorial in 1911. During the ceremony, attended by Kaiser Wilhelm II among others, the King knighted the sculptor, Sir Thomas Brock. Brock was the sort of artist the King could do business with. An excellent shot, he loved rowing and served as a volunteer with the Artists' Rifles, and apart from the smock that he wore over spongebag trousers, looked as much like a bank manager as an artist. The Memorial is heavy both with Aberdeen granite (1,600 tons of it form the steps and pavement) and symbolism. Beside the huge figure of Queen Victoria sit Truth and Charity, while a golden angel – Peace or Victory – hovers above. Because the British Empire depended on Britannia ruling the waves, the iconography is strongly nautical; mermaids and mermen sport with hippogrifths. The art magazine *The Studio* acclaimed the result 'as a national and imperial tribute'.

PREVIOUS PAGES RIGHT Shortly before the First World War, London had been equipped with a grand processional route from Buckingham Palace to Trafalgar Square. This shows The Mall, with some of the 18,600 British and Allied troops who took part in the Empire Peace Celebrations on 19 July 1919, which was hurriedly organised after the signing of the Treaty of Versailles and took place on a Saturday so that appropriate religious services could be held the next day. 'Indian troops are coming specially from the Indian Empire for the occasion,' reported *The Times*.

OPPOSITE Admiralty Arch decked with white ensigns (the naval flag) for Queen Elizabeth II's Coronation in 1953. As well as performing a ceremonial role, the triumphal arch included residences for the Sea Lords and offices that, during the Second World War, had housed a unit responsible for novel armaments, nicknamed the Wheezers and Dodgers. Their approach resembled that of Q in the James Bond novels; it may have been no coincidence that Ian Fleming was working in an Admiralty office nearby.

ABOVE The Car of Empire, which was part of the Women's Coronation Procession in 1911. Pageants on historical or imperial themes were a popular entertainment before and after the First World War. The actor Frank Lascelles left the stage to become a pageant master, mounting twenty-two pageants between 1907 and 1932, including a Great Pageant as part of George V's coronation ceremonies in 1911. The Women's Suffrage movement also saw the value of pageants and staged one of their own a week before the coronation, in the hope that the new King would help them get their Conciliation Bill through Parliament. Altogether, 40,000 women took part, including suffragettes from India.

The Strand, London

ABOVE Entry to the Strand from Trafalgar Square, about 1905. One of the first measures introduced by the London County Council after its inception in 1889 was the Strand Improvement Scheme. Ten years earlier, Charles Dickens Jr had declared that 'at present there is no street of equal importance in any capital of Europe so unworthy of its position' as the Strand. But the scheme was was bitterly resisted by property owners, one of whom wrote to *The Times* declaring that the 'effect will be to create open war, and war to the knife, between the Council' and the people who owned, or lived in, buildings scheduled for clearance. One concern for the LCC had been the number of prostitutes attracted by the Strand's numerous theatres. In the event, the Strand was widened by demolishing most of the north side, and Aldwych and Kingsway were built. Fortunately, a campaign led by the artist

Walter Crane prevented the demolition of Wren's St Clement Danes and Gibbs's St Mary-le-Strand.

OPPOSITE A view of Southampton Row showing a tram emerging from the tunnel beneath Kingsway. To the left of the photograph is the then Central School of Art and Crafts, which was established by the London County Council in 1896. Under the directorship of the radical architect W. R. Lethaby, 900 students could learn to be goldsmiths, silversmiths, engravers, printers, lithographers, cabinetmakers, upholsterers, stained-glass artists, plasterworkers, embroiderers and weavers. The dazzling, electrically lit boulevard of Kingsway was less obviously Arts and Crafts, being both modern and imperial. Electric lifts serviced steel-framed buildings. The imperial note, set by the names of office blocks, such as Imperial Buildings, was underlined by the

sculpture that decorates them. Thus the pediment of Africa House on Kingsway contains a sculptural composition by Benjamin Clemens, featuring a big game hunter and dead elephants, among other now politically incorrect figures..

SERIES A.—No. 42   SOUTHAMPTON ROW, LONDON

OPPOSITE Sir Herbert Baker brings the Empire to London: India House (1928–30) and South Africa House (1931–33). Baker was an obvious choice for each building, having worked in harness with Lutyens at New Delhi and having designed several hundred buildings on his own account in South Africa. A member of the Art Workers Guild, Baker believed strongly in the virtues of craftsmanship and local materials. The Portland stone façade of India House, following the curve of Aldwych, is enlivened with Indian-inspired motifs, carved by Joseph Armitage (Armitage had spent six months in New Delhi with Baker supervising the crafts used in the Secretariats). Inside, the entrance hall, seen here, is dressed with red Agra sandstone and the pierced marble

balcony, or *jaali*, also came from India. Elsewhere, Indian artists painted the murals, having been sent to London and Rome for special training in fresco techniques.

ABOVE South Africa House. The bulk of Baker and A. T. Scott's building, on a sloping corner of Trafalgar Square, appears rather elephantine beside Gibbs's St Martin-in-the-Fields; look closer, though, and you will find that the mass is leavened with charming South African details, such as the flowers carved into the keystones, the heads of elephant, wildebeest, lion and antelope beneath the window sills, and a gilded springbok (all designed by Sir Charles Wheeler and carved by Joseph Armitage) over the corner entrance. Inside,

Baker used South African marbles and coloured stones, including red jasper and crocodilite. The balusters to the staircase incorporate the protea flower. A reception room on the ground floor recreates a Cape Dutch farmhouse, with beamed ceiling, terracotta tiled floor and antique Delft tiles. Throughout the public spaces, the walls are rich in mural paintings and plaster reliefs. Baker knew his South Africa. The fountain in this photograph is by Lutyens, replacing a feebler effort by Charles Barry, but in the same quatrefoil basin. The Lutyens Fountains were begun in the late 1930s and completed after the Second World War.

LEFT Among the many institutions whose scale inflated around 1900 was London's Central Criminal Court, built in 1907 by E. W. Mountford. Although handsomely appointed, the previous Old Bailey, by George Dance, had only one court. The present building, with four courtrooms, occupies the site both of it and that of the redundant Newgate Gaol next door. Dome and sculpture (the gilded 'lady of justice' among others) declared an imperial consciousness, reinforced by the Recorder of London at the opening, who told the King and Queen that he hoped that the building would not only be useful but also 'an ornament to the metropolis of your Empire'.

ABOVE The London County Council's headquarters, County Hall, by Ralph Knott. Knott was still in his twenties when he won the competition to design County Hall. Like many other competitions, the process was fraught: revisions were constantly being made on grounds of cost and Knott had to contend with the LCC's architect W. E. Riley who was a force unto himself. The façade was meant to wrap itself around a circular council chamber, but the latter was scrapped: the concavity was retained, giving the impression that a gigantic bite has been taken out of the front. Nevertheless, the building succeeds in dominating this section of the Thames, and continues to radiate, to those who know the history of the LCC, a sense of the humanity and optimism of which local government is capable, at its best.

OPPOSITE & ABOVE Deptford Town Hall (1903–05) designed by Lanchester and Rickards. By the time that Deptford acquired its town hall, the town's great days as a centre of shipbuilding had long been forgotten, and it entered the twentieth century as an industrial suburb of London. Lanchester and Rickards did their best to lift corporate spirits by a designing of building of panache, despite the limited space available to them (the site was left over from the land acquired for an adjacent public baths). Among the carvings on an already plastic façade are a relief of a battle scene and figures of Sir Francis Drake (knighted in Deptford after his return from circumnavigating the world), Admiral Robert Blake, who defeated the Dutch Admiral von Tromp, and Horatio Nelson. Rickards was the son of a Fulham washerwoman and Henry Lanchester was the son of an architect. With various partners, Lanchester worked not only in Britain, but also in Lucknow, Rangoon, Zanzibar, Cairo and Jodhpur.

ABOVE Cardiff City Hall. When the Borough of Cardiff purchased Cathays Park in 1898, the town – it was not yet a city – was relatively young. A century before, it had been bigger than a village, with a population of under 2,000. It grew because of the docks, built by the 2nd Marquess of Bute, but in Cathays Park, sold by the 3rd Marquess of Bute, it had enough space to create a new civic centre of sweeping ambition. It is not absurd to compare the vision to that of Washington DC; certainly Cathays Park evinces a similar sense of planning for centuries yet to come. Among the buildings are the National Museum by Smith and Brewer, Glamorgan County Hall by Harris and Moodie and Law Courts by Lanchester and Rickards, who were also responsible for the town hall – elevated to a city hall when Cardiff became a city at its opening in 1905. This is architecture to stake Cardiff's place in the world, the City Hall in particular being a structure of unassailable self-confidence, opulent but controlled. Maritime statuary celebrates Cardiff's trade with the world as well as Welsh heroes and national identity. The sumptuous interior is rich in coloured marble, sculpture, stained glass, plaster reliefs and bronze electroliers.

2

TO THE FAR HORIZON — AND BEYOND

In 1917, at the height of the First World War, the British government
established a Civil Aerial Transport Committee to advise on air
transport in peacetime. As the committee concluded when it
reported in 1918, the development of aviation would help answer the imperial
question which had become pressing to a country weakened by a prolonged war
of how to knit the far-flung territories of the Empire together. Cecil Rhodes had
dreamt of a railway that would run between Cairo and Cape Town, a project that
foundered equally on the challenges of the terrain and the uncertainty of its
financial viability. But an air route would eliminate at least one of those obstacles.
When, in January 1932, an Imperial Airways Handley Page HP42 left Croydon
airport, bound for Cape Town, it was at last viable.

Not all visions of better imperial communications were fulfilled. Just as the Civil
Aerial Transport Committee was at work, two leviathan-like structures were being
built on the flat landscape around Cardington, in Bedfordshire. After a two-year
gestation, something inside these colossal buildings was hatched. Local people
must have looked on in wonder as *R31*, shaped like a whale – far bigger than one
even – a vehicle of scarcely imaginable size, and as unwieldy as it was big, edged out
of its shed, between windbreaks to stop the wind blowing it onto the sharp frame
of the opening. *R31* was an airship, commissioned by the Admiralty five days before

BELOW The RMS *Empress of Britain*, built between 1928 and 1931 by the John Brown shipyard on the Clyde. Owned by the Canadian Pacific Steamship Company, she was the fastest and most luxurious ship between England and Canada. Taking a northern route across the Atlantic her hull was specially plated against ice. The owners hoped that she would lure passengers from England to Quebec rather than New York. When the St Lawrence River was frozen in the winter months, the *Empress of Britain* became a cruise ship – the first specifically designed to do so. She was torpedoed and sunk by a U-Boat in 1940.

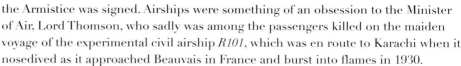

the Armistice was signed. Airships were something of an obsession to the Minister of Air, Lord Thomson, who sadly was among the passengers killed on the maiden voyage of the experimental civil airship *R101*, which was en route to Karachi when it nosedived as it approached Beauvais in France and burst into flames in 1930.

Airports would be the way of the future, and Croydon Aerodrome, built in 1926–28, was the world's first. It grew out of an airfield that had been built a little to the west, as one of a ring of defences around London against Zeppelin raids. Perhaps the imperial association dictated the style of the terminal: Classical. The airports of the coming decade favoured the modernity of smooth concrete walls, cantilevered balconies and wrap-around windows, although some features of Croydon were imitated: a similar control tower was built at Moscow.

Meanwhile, most journeys around the Empire were made by ship. Ocean liners had been steadily improving, as well as growing in size, since the introduction of the screw propeller in the 1870s. The number of passengers passing through Liverpool and Southampton brought prosperity to lodging housekeepers and inspired the building of luxury hotels for those travelling first class. And during the Edwardian decade, competition between Cunard, the White Star Line and other lines turned the liners themselves into floating showpieces of decoration. While the White Star's Olympic Class ships, including the ill-starred *Titanic* were fitted out by Adam Heaton, a company specialising in such work, Cunard commissioned Harold Peto to design the state rooms of the *Mauretania* in 1907; Peto, a former partner of Ernest George, was primarily a man of taste: his relations with Cunard were not easy. Nevertheless, the desire to employ the best architects and designers continued, the French ships *Ile de France* and *Normandie* becoming synonymous with Art Deco between the Wars. The British yard of John Brown's on Clydebank answered with the Canadian Pacific's *Empress of Japan* and *Empress of Britain*, 1930–31. The *Empress of Britain* included interiors by Frank Brangwyn, Charles Allom, Sir John Lavery, Edmund Dulac (whose Cathay Lounge took chinoiserie to new heights) and a Knockerbocker bar for cocktails – all lost when the *Britain* was bombed and sunk off Ireland in 1940. By contrast, one of the most famous British ships of her age, the *Queen Mary*, was 'teddy-bear' – that is to say, cosy and rather low-brow in taste, although a lack of aesthetic ambition did not dent its popularity. What all ships had were ingeniously fitted first-class cabins, with adjacent bathrooms where everything was provided – an improvement on many traditional homes ashore, which must have raised expectations among those who experienced them, providing a nautical equivalent of the space-conscious Mayfair flat.

At home, another transport mode – 'The poetry of motion! The REAL way to travel! The ONLY way to travel!' as Mr Toad had it in *The Wind in the Willows* – had begun to rattle rural society. The car needed a range of bespoke architectural types, from the 'motor stable' to house it, the filling station to fuel it and the Royal Automobile Club to promote its interests. It also needed new roads in and out of the major cities, creating strings of semi-detached homes characterised by the cartoonist Sir Osbert Lancaster as Bypass Variegated. Traffic jams on the South Downs and the development sprawl that accompanied popular access to the countryside between the wars created a conservation movement: Clough Williams-Ellis's *England and the Octopus* (its tentacles being the arterial roads) was published in 1928. Meanwhile, in India, one of the greatest contributions made by the Raj to the future of the country was the railway. It united the subcontinent, in a way that had never proved possible in Africa.

Southampton Docks
SOUTHERN RAILWAY

ABOVE Before 1890, Southampton's future as a port had been precarious. That year, however, the London and South-Western Railway financed the building of the huge new Empress Dock, buying the Southampton Docks Company outright two years later. By 1895, passenger traffic had increased by over seventy per cent. Over the next decade, tidal docks and dry docks were added. In 1907, the White Star Line transferred its North Atlantic Express Service to Southampton from Liverpool, and by the time that RMS *Titanic* was launched five years later, Southampton bustled as Britain's busiest passenger port. This aerial view from the 1930s features a Cunarder, perhaps being repainted.

RIGHT The dining saloon for Cabin Class on the Cunard White Star liner *Queen Mary*, the 'world's largest and fastest liner' as the publicity material boasted

in the year that she entered service, 1935. Despite the commissioning of art work from MacDonald Gill, Edward Wadsworth and others, *The Architect and Building News* characterised the general effect of the interior as 'mild, but expensive vulgarity' – or 'teddy bear', meaning cosy, in the slang of the day. Aesthetically, the *Queen Mary* – on the transatlantic run to New York – was outclassed by the Orient Line's *Orion* (1935) whose understated interiors were designed by the New Zealander Brian O'Rouke; *Orion* sailed the Australian route. In 1936, the well-travelled John de la Valette, who had organised an exhibition on British art in industry the previous year, told the Royal Society of the Arts that the *Queen Mary* 'must appear as the supreme British achievement of the two great national industries: shipbuilding and shipping'. Woods from around the Empire were used in *Queen Mary*'s decoration.

ABOVE A postcard from the 1930s showing the stupendous size of the RMS *Queen Mary*, 'Britain's Masterpiece', by comparing her to Trafalgar Square; Nelson's column and Admiralty Arch are dwarfed. Britain still thought of itself as a country that ruled the waves, and great national pride was invested in its liners.

RIGHT An illustration of the Adelphi Hotel, Liverpool from *London's Social Calendar*, 1912. In 1911, the London Midland and Scottish Railway Company, anxious about the rise of Southampton, decided to rebuild Liverpool's Adelphi Hotel. When finished, it was generally regarded as the most luxurious hotel outside London. Designed by Frank Atkinson, the façades were Beaux-Arts style. This view shows the marble-lined central court, off which French doors opened into large restaurants. The Hypostle Hall was decorated in the French Empire style; it originally led to an open-air Fountain Court, surrounded by terraces on three sides. The ballroom, which was to have comprised the fourth side, was unbuilt at the outbreak of the First World War.

LEFT The Royal Automobile Club, Pall Mall, built by the architects of the London Ritz, Charles Mewès and Arthur Davis, in 1908–11. Far bigger and more luxurious than existing clubs, it exemplified the tendency of architecture to inflate during the Edwardian decade – so much so that traditionalists thought that RAC stood for Really Awful Club. Prosperity and the development of banking meant that better capitalised businesses and institutions could build on a bigger scale. Despite its size, the RAC was also a sophisticated piece of architecture, in the soignée Louis XVI style. Here it is shown *en fête* for King George V's coronation in 1911. This photograph shows no horses in Pall Mall, appropriately enough.

ABOVE Edouard Montaut decorated the exuberant Michelin Building on London's Fulham Road (1910–11) with a series of tile panels showing exciting moments in the history of the motorcar. This one depicts the winner of a race in 1907. Another panel showed the new mode of transport being more sedately patronised by King Edward VII and the future King George V. The novelty of the Art Nouveau architecture reflected the socially rule-breaking nature of early motoring, which permitted its devotees a bewildering speed and scope of movement. Speaking at the opening of the Michelin Building, the French ambassador Paul Chambon declared that after a slow start in motoring the British Isles now had 110,000 motorcars mounted on tyres, nearly double those of France.

ABOVE A motorist fills up at Blashford in the New Forst: one of the first garages. 'Garage' – the term that the English preferred to the American 'filling station' – comes from the French verb *garer* (to store); in the earliest of motoring days, the term 'motor stable' was often used, as it had a sporty ring as well identifying where a rich man might well keep his car – in a converted coach house or stable. Like 'chauffeur' – a word that was originally applied to the man who heated up the car before it was driven – a borrowing from French seemed to add tone to an otherwise grimy activity. Britain's first roadside garage had been built at Aldermaston in 1920, only it did not sell petrol but the alternative of benzole (the cost of petrol soared to four shillings per gallon after the First World War). Here, we see that pumps have been installed after the American example. But it is still charmingly thatched in keeping with motoring's bucolic character (many people used the car as an escape from the city).

ABOVE The Blackwall Tunnel (1892–95). Before 1885, forty per cent of London's population lived east of London Bridge but had no convenient means of crossing the Thames. In that year, the City Corporation obtained permission to build Tower Bridge and in 1887, permission was granted to the Metropolitan Board of Works to construct the Blackwall Tunnel; after 1889, responsibility transferred to the London County Council and the tunnel was redesigned by its engineer, Alexander Binnie. Accommodating a roadway and two footpaths, it was to be the largest subaqueous tunnel yet built. The tunnel connected East India Dock Road on the north with the Woolwich Road on the south by a sinuous route to avoid the docks and other obstacles. A contract for the construction was signed with S. Pearson and Son at a cost of £871,000. Pearson was the firm owned by Weetman Pearson, later 1st Viscount Cowdray, an early example of a multinational company. In addition to the Blackwall Tunnel, it dug the Hudson River and the East River Tunnels in New York, as well as draining the swamps that blighted Mexico City. The last introduced Weetman Pearson to the dictator of Mexico, Porfirio Diaz, as a result of which he acquired 600,000 acres of land. The effort to find oil nearly ruined him, but when he struck it, the result was stupendous. He controlled sixty per cent of what was then the third biggest oil producer in the world. When raised to the peerage, Pearson chose supporters to his coat of arms which reflected his business life: a deep-sea diver (Pearson built docks as well as tunnels) and a Mexican peon.

RIGHT Constructed in 1926–28, Croydon Aerodrome was the first purpose-built airport in the world. Churchill used it frequently; as Minister of Munitions during the First World War, he had often flown to France from the old airfield that preceded it. Edward VIII, George VI and a galaxy of film stars and society figures were also passengers. It was to Croydon that Amy Johnson returned amid celebrations after her solo flight to Australia in 1930. Navigation in the early days was hazardous. Pilots guided themselves at night from Croydon to Paris by following a trail of fifteen beacons, flashing Morse code. It is significant that the international distress call 'mayday' (from the French *m'aidez*) was invented by the Croydon radio operator F. S. Mockford. Nineteen thirty-one saw an innovation of major importance: the chalking of a thick, white line across the grass runway to help pilots orient themselves when taking off in thick fog. The terminal presented some features, such as the through baggage hall, that were widely imitated; a similar control tower was built at Moscow. Both the concrete-built terminal and the Aerodrome Hotel were in a Classical style, much like the liner terminal at Southampton (steamships were a rival to aeroplanes). 'One gets the immediate impression,' wrote Captain Norman Macmillan, describing them in *The Air Travellers Guide to Europe*, 'that civil aviation in England has been established on a sound basis, that it is reality and not a toy to be played with by enthusiasts.'

The Airport of London, Croydon

C. E. TURNER

ROYAL AIR FORCE BALLOON BARRAGE.

OPPOSITE Royal Air Force barrage balloons above the Cardington airship sheds, near Bedford. The sheds, over 700 ft long and 145 ft high, had been constructed during the First World War to build airships, as a British answer to the German Zeppelins. At the end of the war, they were closed – only to be reopened in 1924 to construct two experimental airships: one military, one civilian. It was intended that the Imperial Airship Scheme would open a route to India. 'When complete,' wrote the Minister of Air Lord Thomson in *Air Facts and Problems*, 1927, 'these ships will provide first-class cabin accommodation for

100 passengers, with the usual accessories, restaurants, smoking-rooms and promenade decks. They will have an average speed, under standard conditions, of 63 miles an hour. At this rate, London and Bombay will be brought nearer together, in point of time, than London and Edinburgh were a century ago.' It was not to be. Alas, Cardington's *R101* nosedived and exploded into flames on its maiden flight. The optimistic Thomson was among those killed. During the Second World War, the expertise that had been acquired making airships at Cardington was redeployed towards barrage balloons and inflatable decoy tanks.

ABOVE Shoreham Airport (1934–35) designed by Stavers Tiltman. From 1934 to 1939, flying was promoted by an annual Empire Air Day at RAF stations and civil aerodromes. Shoreham Airport hosted one in the year that it opened, 1936. While Croydon was built in a reassuring classical style, Shoreham and all the other aerodromes of the 1930s – Heston, Brooklands, Ramsgate, Brimingham, Jersey – favoured the smooth concrete walls, cantilevered balconies and wrap-around windows of the Modern Movement. Modernism and flying went together.

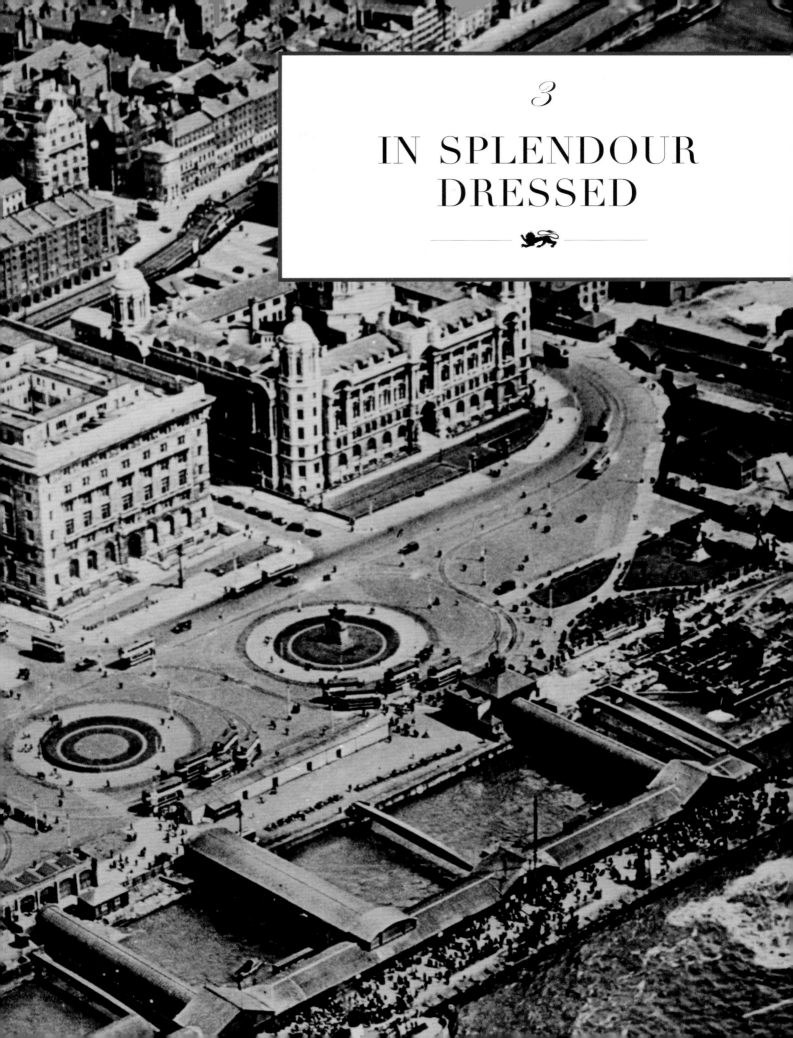

IN SPLENDOUR
DRESSED

Passengers, returning home from a stint in the Colonies, were greeted by an extraordinary architectural declaration as they approached the port of Liverpool. On the waterfront were three buildings of stupendous élan and self-confidence – the Three Graces as they would later be known. Replacing a late-eighteenth-century dock that had always been too shallow to make a profit, they comprise the Dock Offices, with central dome and domed corner turrets, designed by Frank Briggs of the Liverpool firm of Briggs and Wolstenholme; the fantastic, Mannerist Royal Liver Building by Aubrey Thomas, also from Liverpool; and between them the magnificence of the Cunard Building, a Renaissance palazzo designed in Beaux-Art style by Mewès and Davis, architects of the London Ritz. Boldly different from each other, supremely self-confident, the three structures seem to symbolise not just the city of Liverpool but also the Empire itself. As the *Liverpool Daily Post* had remarked in 1907, when the Dock Offices were completed, fifty years after the Mersey Docks and Harbour Board had been created: 'The port is not merely the port of the city of Liverpool, nor merely one of the leading ports of the kingdom; it is far more – it is a link, and an important link in the chain of empire'.

Liverpool had an imperial destiny, and it was this spirit that the buildings embodied.

Many organisations across Britain shared Liverpool's self-identity with Empire. The warehouses around London docks were fragrant with the produce of Britain's overseas territories. In 1909, the Port of London Authority came into being, building itself a wedding cake of a structure by Sir Edwin Cooper to celebrate the

event: a heady attack of imperial afflatus in stone. That building stands on Tower Green, next to the Tower of London, its bombast competing with the rhetoric of numerous other City institutions which had donned the imperial toga. Between the construction of John Belcher's Chartered Accountants building of 1890–93, with its frieze of workers and imperial personifications by Hamo Thornycroft (an idea borrowed by Thomas Collcutt for his Lloyds Register of Shipping) and the First World War, architectural sculpture became practically *de rigueur*. A favourite device was to have pairs of figures on either side of a pediment, an echo of Michelangelo's Tomb of Lorenzo de' Medici. A variant of the theme can be seen on the entrance to Electra House on Moorgate, designed by Belcher for the Eastern Telegraph and Allied Companies.

The telegraph had an obviously imperial resonance, as did many other kinds of work. C. R. W. Nevison's *Amongst the Nerves of the World*, a Futurist painting of Fleet Street in 1930, emphasises the place of the newspaper industry at the heart of a network of wires, ever buzzing with news, much of which came from the Empire. Businesses were urged to put Empire goods first, under the policy of imperial preference. The cotton spun in Lancashire came from India, and workers were unlikely to forget the fact as they walked into Empire Mill. William Lever's Lever Brothers, exporting to 134 countries, built its success on soap made with palm oil, to obtain which Lever acquired plantations in Sierra Leone and Nigeria. And yet visitors to his model village at Port Sunlight, his art gallery there, or his various homes, in a state of almost perpetual reconfiguration due to his appetite for architecture, would have deduced little of this from the architectural style, which was almost programmatically English. With only a few exceptions (the Guinness peer Lord Iveagh's Indian Hall at Elveden in Suffolk – domed of course), the rodomontade of empire found little place in the home (although two of the most prolific domestic architects, Lutyens and Baker, were also the architects of New Delhi). This was also true of the model housing estates built by the London County Council, whose style derived from the parsonage style of William Morris's friend, the architect Philip Webb. More bumptious in tone were the public bathhouses and, strangely similar in architecture, the public libraries (often the result of Andrew Carnegie's munificence) which were provided to meet the needs of cleanliness and self-improvement. The swagger feels imperial.

Quiet dignity was not the prevailing mood, and many institutions had the money and temperament to show off. Among them were the otherwise secretive Freemasons whose United Grand Lodge in Covent Garden was built between 1927 and 1933. The Theosophical Society, designed by Lutyens, was by no means so swanky: though a brick building, Lutyens nevertheless succeeded in giving it Classical bite, through his mastery of the materials (the columns are made of beautifully laid brick).

Places of worship were also built in these years. In style, they echo the sense of questing spirituality seen in what would now be called 'alternative' cults such as Theosophy. They include the Roman Catholic cathedral at Westminster, inspired by Byzantium, and the Anglican church of Holy Trinity, Sloane Street, a scrapbook of the Arts and Crafts style. Britain's first civic university at Edgbaston, a suburb of Birmingham – it was also Britain's first planned university campus – may seem far removed from matters spiritual, but this may not have been so. Some highly architectural (and uncomfortable) mahogany armchairs used for the inauguration ceremony in 1909 were borrowed from a Masonic source.

RIGHT The competition for the Institute of Chartered Accountants building, off Moorgate in the City of London, was held in 1888. That year, John Belcher, who won it, had been on holiday to Italy, and his experience there seems to have coloured the result. His building displays a prominent frieze by Hamo Thornycroft, not so much celebrating accountancy *per se* as the many different aspects of life whose prospects it could further, including manufacturing, agriculture, the sciences and India and the colonies.

BELOW Nowhere was so eloquent of Britain's imperial connections as London's docks. Their warehouses were heaped with produce from overseas territories, many of which Britain owned – cigars, dried fruits, sugar, flour, ivory, coffee, cocoa, tea, spices and much more. Here are barrels of molasses. The first of the docks, West India Docks, was built in 1799–1806 for merchants anxious that it was taking too long to offload cargoes from the West Indies, and that too much was being

pilfered when they were. They were quickly followed by the London Docks, specialising in luxuries, and the East India Docks for the East India Company. Around the dock basins were grouped cavernous but elegantly classical brick warehouses. The importance of shipping to Britain, as an island, can be seen from the attention that the docks received from the Luftwaffe during the Second World War. They were one of the most heavily bombed targets.

OPPOSITE Sir Edwin Cooper's Port of London Authority (PLA) building. The PLA began life in 1910 to co-ordinate dock activity after competition between private interests in the docks and an inadequate shipping channel had caused delays. Cooper, a Yorkshireman, won the competition for the headquarters with an unashamed piece of bombast, rich in imperial allusions. Begun in 1912, it was not opened until 1922, having been delayed by the First World War. Cooper also designed port buildings at Tilbury and the Lloyds of London office.

OPPOSITE King George V and Queen Mary go down Park Street, having just opened Sir George Oatley's Wills Memorial Building, part of Bristol University, in 1925. In the background is the Wills Tower, a tour de force of the late Gothic Revival, heroically perpendicular in style. It was commissioned in 1912 by George Alfred and Henry Herbert Wills in memory of their father Henry Overton Wills III, who had been a benefactor, as well as its first chancellor. The Wills fortune derived from the tobacco business started by the original Henry Overton Wills in the eighteenth century.

RIGHT Thornton Manor, built by William Hesketh Lever, 1st Viscount Leverhulme from the early 1890s until 1914. Leverhulme loved architecture. His son remembered his mother as saying that 'she seldom experienced the sensation of living for very long in a house free from the presence of workmen'. The architects Douglas and Fordham, Grayson and Ould, J. J. Talbot and J. Lomax-Simpson all worked on the property, although a significant role was also taken by Leverhulme. Thornton Manor was used to entertain staff to dinners and 'at homes' for Port Sunlight organisations.

BELOW Lord Leverhulme built a multinational business based on soap (nearly all the soap used throughout the British Empire was made in Britain). To avoid paying port dues and to control production, he built a port and factory at Port Sunlight. This was accompanied by model workers' housing. Leverhulme himself drew the grid of generously proportioned boulevards on which the terraces, in vernacular revival or Jacobean styles, were surrounded by their own spacious gardens, as well as parks and recreation grounds. This illustration shows Park Road, named, like other streets, after places that the sentimental Leverhulme remembered from his Bolton childhood.

ottage Homes, Park Road, Port Sunlight.

OPPOSITE The India Cotton Mill, Darwen, Lancashire. By 1860, Lancashire mills were producing half the world's cotton and, at the turn of the twentieth century, they made eight billion yards of cloth a year. Until the 'cotton famine' caused by the blockade of Confederate ports during the American Civil War, most of Lancashire's raw cotton came from the Southern States of America, but the name of this mill, built in 1867, just after the end of the conflict, indicates a new source of supply: India. Three hundred feet high, the chimney expresses an epic self-confidence: the foundation stone on which it rests is said to have been the largest single block quarried since Cleopatra's Needle. A member of the Shorrock family, which owned the mill, described the impression that the campanile-like chimney made: 'This noble structure is one of the finest towers in the world, and will, in all likelihood, survive the cotton trade of this country.' It has done. Like most of the mills that once formed Lancashire's main source of employment, the India Cotton Mill no longer spins or weaves cotton; it is now a business centre.

ABOVE The architecture of the Carreras Factory that was built in Camden, London, in 1926, celebrates the discovery in Egypt, then occupied by the British, of Tutankhamun's tomb, after which the Egyptian style became wildly fashionable. The Carreras tobacco company had been established in London by a Spanish immigrant in the mid nineteenth century, to take advantage of the immense Victorian appetite for cigars. By the 1920s, it had been floated on the Stock Exchange and was locked in competition with American rivals, such as Philip Morris, as well as Imperial Tobacco (which had reached a trading agreement with American Tobacco). Building on the gardens of Mornington Crescent, Carreras adopted the flamboyant Art Deco style that was more often associated with British subsidiaries of American companies, such as Hoover, Firestone and Gillette. The architects were M. E. and O. H. Collins, helped by A. G. Porri. While black cats are prominent – a reference to the company's Black Cat brand – the official name of the building was the Arcadia Works. That owes

its origin to J. M. Barrie, who let it be known that tobacco smoked by the Arcadian club in *My Lady Nicotine* was, as he told Carreras in a letter of 1897, 'your Craven Mixture – and no other'. The Craven in question, also commemorated in Craven A cigarettes, was the Earl of Craven, another Carreras devotee. One of the products of the British Empire was tobacco, and India constituted an important market for cigarettes.

ABOVE Lutyens was asked to design a London headquarters for the Theosophical Society in 1911 because his wife, Lady Emily, was deeply involved in the movement. The years between 1900 and the First World War were characterised by questing spirituality, which ran beyond the confines of the established Church. Lady Emily became a Theosophist in 1910, believing fervently in the coming of a World Teacher – previous World Teachers had been Sri Krishna and Jesus. Annie Besant, the President of the Theosophical Society, called Lutyens Vishvakarman, the architect of the gods in Hindu mythology.

ABOVE The Freemasons' Hall in London, originally known as the Masonic Peace Hall, was built in 1927–33 as a memorial to the British Freemasons who died during the First World War. Lutyens, then President of the Royal Institute of British Architects, chaired the competition held for it in 1925, the chosen architects being H. V. Ashley and F. Winton Newman. The building is most remarkable for its opulent finishes: the bronze doors opening onto the Grand Temple each weigh 1.25 tons. Historians view Freemasonry as having had a close association with the Empire. It provided men (not women) with a ready means of association in distant parts of the globe, and inspired a greater sense of solidarity in places where the European presence was small.

RIGHT An early twentieth-century view of Fleet Street, with the offices of the *Daily Mail*, *Liverpool Post* and *Morning Advertiser*. Fleet Street had been associated with the press since the sixteenth century, when Wynkyn de Worde, William Caxton's apprentice, printed from Shoe Lane. London's first daily newspaper was published here in 1702. But editors had to wait for mass literacy before they could sell their newspapers in quantity. That time arrived in the late nineteenth century, and with it a 'new journalism', which offered less parliamentary coverage, more human interest and a brighter look. The *Daily Mail* pioneered this approach and was selling a million copies a day by 1900. Sales were built by appealing to popular sentiment, not least by enthusiastically trumpeting the Empire.

RIGHT C. R. W. Nevinson had been a war artist. However, he was the son of a journalist and, after the First World War, turned to journalism himself as a refuge from the cold reception of his peacetime paintings. He therefore knew Fleet Street, the subject of this work of 1930, well. He called it *Among the Nerves of the World*, the nerves in question being the telegraph wires which connected British newspapers with their correspondents around the globe. The style reflects that of Gino Severini and other Italian Futurists whom he had met in Paris before the War. The electric telegraph helped knit the Empire together. Given the sardonic nature of Nevinson's own newspaper contributions, the title may echo the 'nerve cases' he had observed among patients during his time as a Red Cross orderly with the Royal Army Medical Corps in France and Flanders in 1915–16.

OPPOSITE In the lobby of the *Daily Express* Building in Fleet Street (1930–32) are two plaster reliefs (just visible at the back) by the sculptor Eric Aumonier, representing Britain and Empire. They express the fiercely patriotic and imperialist tone demanded by the newspaper's proprietor, Lord Beaverbrook – the first Minister of Information in the wartime Cabinet. The architecture of the building, designed by Ellis and Clarke with the help of the engineer Sir Owen Williams, was suavely *moderne*.

BELOW The Mitchell Library, Glasgow (1905–11). The Edwardian period saw a boom in library building, thanks to the munificence of the Scottish-born steel magnate Andrew Carnegie. The Mitchell Library, however, owed its existence not to Carnegie but another benefactor, the tobacco manufacturer Stephen Mitchell, who had died in 1874. William B. Whitie won the competition to design the building in 1905. Unlike the Gothic Revival University Library of 1870 or the unscholarly classical City Chambers (1888), he produced a disciplined Palladian design, surmounted by a dome; on top of the dome is a figure of literature. It is said to be the largest public reference library in the world. The Mitchell Library has been showcased by the demolition of neighbouring buildings and the sinking of the M8 motorway in front of it.

OPPOSITE Vincent Harris won the competition to design a library extension to the Manchester Town Hall in 1926 and it was opened, without any disruption to the service to the public, despite the transference of a million books, manuscripts, files and periodicals, in 1934. From its circular shape (and whiteness against the Manchester smoke-blackened streetscape), it became known as the Corporation Wedding Cake – alternatively, the St Peter's Square Gasometer. Scholars, however, would have seen an echo of the Colossem of imperial Rome, as well as circular libraries, such as the Radcliffe Camera in Oxford, the round reading room at the British Museum in London, the Library of Congress in Washington and, more recently, the influential Stockholm Public Library.

ABOVE Birmingham University, designed
by Sir Aston Webb. In the mid nineteenth
century, Britain found itself at a strange
disadvantage: there were more universities
throughout the Empire than there were at
home. Founded in 1900 out of an existing
college, Birmingham University helped answer
that deficiency. It grew out of the vision
of the industrialist and Colonial Secretary
Joseph Chamberlain, who wished to enhance
Birmingham's prestige and establish facilities
that would meet the demands of the twentieth
century, including competition from Germany.
It was the first university to incorporate a
medical school: a priority for Chamberlain who
not only had wide experience of sanitation
issues in Britain, but was also acutely aware of
the death rate of Britons serving in the African
colonies, who often became ill or died before
they could complete their tour. Another first
was the creation of a university campus. The
red brick of Aston Webb's buildings would
be taken to describe a whole category of
higher learning: the red brick university.

ABOVE The Library at the Glasgow School of Art. In 1896, the Glasgow firm of Honeyman and Keppie won the competition for this building with a design from the hand of one of their junior draughtsmen, Charles Rennie Mackintosh. Funds were tight and the school was constructed in two phases, the first in 1897–99 and the second in 1907–09, the Library being part of the second campaign. The Art Nouveau style in which Mackintosh worked never took hold much in England, but his name became famous on the Continent. As his friend and fellow Scot, the town planner Sir Patrick Geddes, remarked, there 'Mackintosh' was 'almost as accepted a descriptive term in architecture – and this not only in Germany, but from Belgium to Hungary' as it was in reference to a rubberised raincoat in Britain. Through Geddes, Mackintosh appears to have been inspired to contribute designs for a street in Lucknow, then under reconstruction: on the face of it, an unlikely foray into the Empire for a less than obviously imperial architect, which was not, alas, realised.

LEFT Westminster Cathedral, London. Built in the 1880s, the Brompton Oratory, until then London's largest Roman Catholic Church since the Reformation, had been obviously Roman in style. In 1895–1903, John Francis Bentley was rather more subtle in the Roman Catholic Westminster Cathedral: this phenomenon of beautifully-laid brick evokes Byzantium, the Eastern Empire where the imperial tradition continued unbroken until 1453. The style was partly chosen to distinguish the cathedral from Westminster Abbey, a few hundred yards away; in addition, W. R. Lethaby had recently published *The Church of Sancta Sophia, Constantinople; a study of Byzantine building*, calling Hagia Sophia 'the most interesting building on the world's surface'.

OPPOSITE Like Westminster Cathedral – and with similarly streaky-bacon bands of brick and stone – Holy Trinity, Sloane Street, turns its eyes abroad: John Dando Sedding's inspiration for the turrets is the cathedral at Girona in Spain: a dash of spice added to a Perpendicular stew, by an architect wanting 'to take up the threads of the Gothic tradition and weave them into the weft of modern need and thought'. Built in 1889–90, it replaced what had come to seem an embarrassingly gimcrack early-Gothic Revival building of 1828, which did little for the reputation of the Cadogan Estate on which it stands. Earl Cadogan paid for the new church, and an affluent Anglo-Catholic congregation enabled Sedding – and his partner Henry Wilson, after Sedding's death in 1891 – to commission stained glass, ironwork and other fittings. Edward Burne-Jones designed the east window, with forty-eight figures of prophets, saints and apostles; Harry Bates was responsible for the main altar; the altar reredos is by John Tweedsmuir; F. W. Pomeroy contributed the chancel stalls and screen. This union of the fine and decorative arts represents a rare achievement of the Arts and Crafts ideal. Fortunately, the church survived the bombs that landed on and around it during the Second World War sufficiently to be restored.

ABOVE The swimming pool at the Royal Automobile Club, Pall Mall. The Pompeian style, with columns covered in mosaic, evokes the tradition of bathing in Roman times – a contrast to the naturalist pools designed for some country houses, whose owners had probably begun swimming in ponds and rivers. Charles Mewès, of Mewès and Davis, had already designed a Pompeian swimming bath for the Etablissement Hydromineral at Contréxeville in 1899–1900: swimming was still regarded as much as a therapy as a sport or relaxation. After the First World War, reference to the Ancient World would be taken to a further extreme by the gilded, witty Sir Philip Sassoon at Port Lympne, in Kent, whose swimming pool-cum-fountain is reminiscent of cinema epics such as *Intolerance*.

ABOVE The Festival of Britain, which took place in 1951, was designed to pick up the nation's spirits after the Second World War. Most of it was located on the South Bank of the Thames in London, amid surroundings that were light, cheerful and modern (of which the only building to remain, altered in the 1960s, is the Festival Hall). The fare was educational and improving, although for the most part silence was kept on the subject of Empire: India had received independence four years earlier. There was, however, another side: the Pleasure Gardens in Battersea Park, a Victorian park that had been given over to allotments and cricket pitches. Tastes which found the science and stripped-down architecture of the South Bank a little austere could, as seen here, 'relax and have fun – elegant fun', as James Gardner, one of the architects involved, later put it. The slightly patronising tone did not deter a generation that had become increasingly used to the State, in shapes such as that of the LCC, organising their lives – a trend necessarily exaggerated by war and its aftermath.

4

TA-RA-RA
BOOM DE-AY

For many people, life at the turn of the twentieth century was harsh. Working hours were long, and often physically demanding; the comforts of home might be meagre. Warmth and glitter, as well as drink and company, could be found in the richly ornamented, gas-lit gin palaces that had, in cities, all but ousted the domesticity of old-fashioned pubs by the mid Victorian period. And out of the public house had grown another kind of escape: the music hall. By the 1890s, shows no longer took place in front of diners seated at tables, as they had done at the old song and supper rooms, variety saloons and tavern concert rooms (although another antecedent of the music hall, the pleasure garden in the manner of Vauxhall, had not quite died: the Rosherville Pleasure Gardens at Gravesend, did not close until 1911). A boom in theatre-building provided an alternative space – opulent, swaggering, yet, as the paintings of Walter Sickert reveal, conducive to a boisterous intimacy between the patrons watching a show and the performers taking part in it. Between 1879 and 1912, the theatre specialist Frank 'Matchless' Matcham built more than 150 and C. J. Phipps seventy-two.

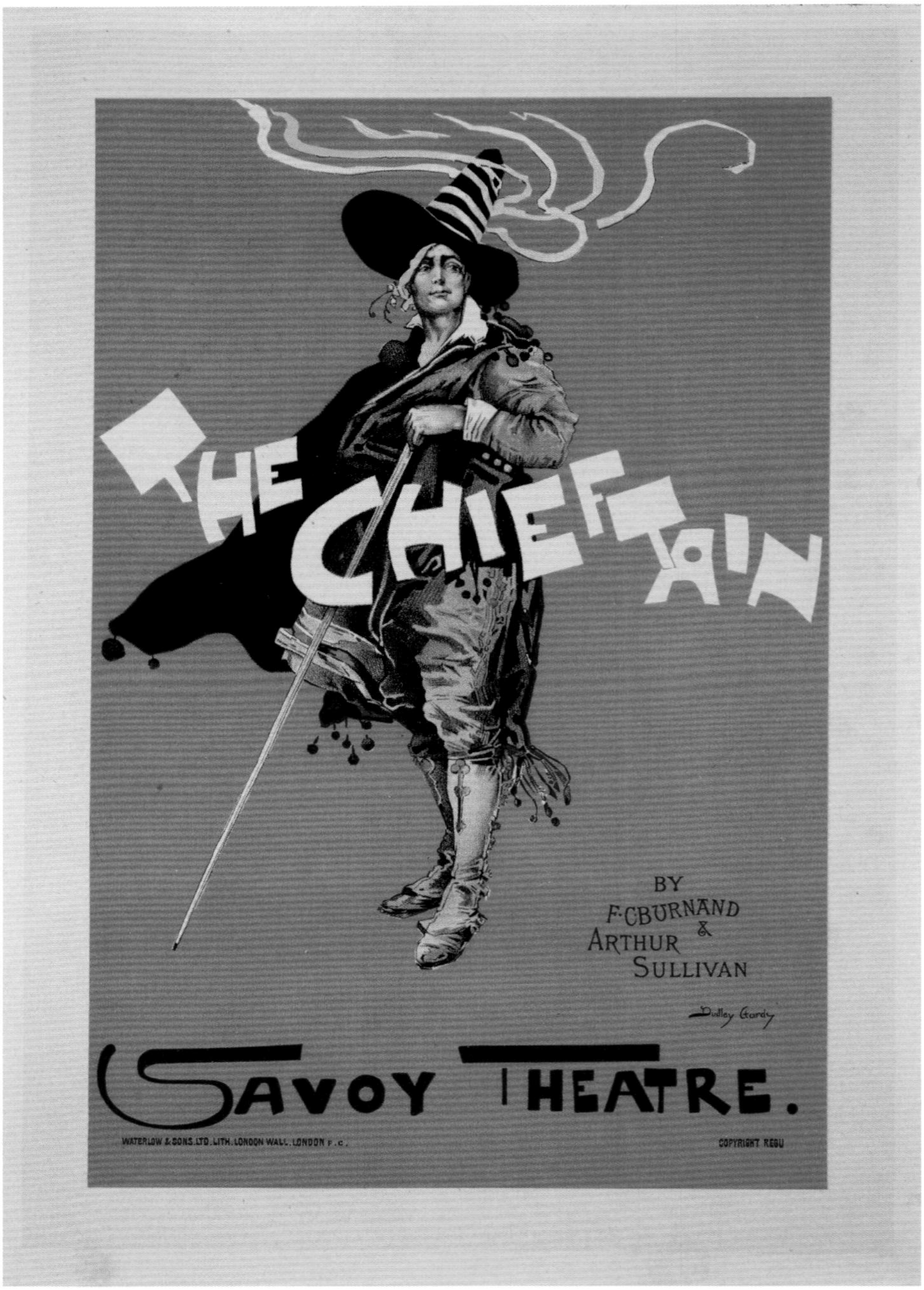

The theatre is an urban form of entertainment. Its success reflected the growing scale of Britain's towns and cities, which was where seventy per cent of the population now lived. Audiences could travel by railway, not only to shows but also to other attractions that drew large crowds, such as football matches, racetracks and the seaside, where the Blackpool Tower opened in 1894. This was in part a working-class phenomenon. But the appeal of the halls was not limited to a single tranche of society. Rough and bawdy though the first independent music halls built in London had been in the 1860s, turn-of-the-century promoters evolved the offering into a more decorous form of variety theatre. Patriotism was a potent ingredient at both ends of the social scale. G. W. Hunt's celebrated 'Jingo' song, performed by The Great MacDermott – 'We don't want to fight, but by jingo if we do, We've got the ships, we've got the men, we've got the money too'

THE CHIEFTAIN

BY
F. C. BURNAND
&
ARTHUR
SULLIVAN

SAVOY THEATRE.

Department stores such as Harrods (1901–5) were a new phenomenon. They reflected the expansionism of the age, where growing wealth stimulated an appetite for luxury. Just as the chain store began to develop, allowing businessmen such as Julius Drewe of the Home and Colonial Stores to sell items across a number of outlets in bulk, so other retailers, operating from individual premises, sought not to appeal to the many but to extract the maximum possible from the customers that they had. They could take possession of every aspect of their lives. Harrods, for example, offered clubs, one for either sex. The ladies' club was in the 'Adams' style with green-silk chairs 'tastefully decorated with appliqué embroidery', according to publicity material of 1909; while the gentleman's club was masculine in Early Georgian style. Refreshed by their clubs, shoppers could then go about their purchases, perhaps in the cornucopia of the famous food hall (Harrods had originally been a grocer's, rather than a draper's or furnisher's), 'immersed', as the publicity material had it, 'in an atmosphere of luxury and pleasure'. No wonder the store adopted the telegraphic address EVERYTHING, LONDON.

OPPOSITE Richard D'Oyly Carte built the Savoy Theatre in 1881 on the success of Gilbert and Sullivan's operettas. It claimed to be the first public building in the world lit entirely by electricity; to reassure nervous patrons, Carte broke a light bulb on stage to show that it did not prove an imminent fire risk. This poster of 1895 advertises a work by Sullivan without Gilbert; its run of 97 performances was mediocre compared to the real Savoy operas.

– gave a new word to the language: Jingoism. 'Wild enthusiasm' greeted Arthur Sullivan's setting of Kipling's imperialistic 'The Absent-Minded Beggar', first performed at the Alhambra Theatre in 1899.

The operettas that Sullivan composed with W. S. Gilbert, with their comfortable assumptions about the desirability of being British above all other nationalities, Roosian, Proosian or perhaps Itali-an, had an equal appeal across the social spectrum – although some of the doubles entendres may have been more widely understood in the gallery than in the stalls. From 1881, they were staged in Richard D'Oyly Carte's Savoy Theatre, rebuilt in Art Deco style by his son Rupert. The site of the theatre had once been part of the medieval Savoy Palace, but was now a scruffy piece of land; the theatre that arose on it, however, was the most sophisticated of its age, claiming to be the first public building in the world lit entirely by electricity. To protect copyrights and mount his own translatlantic productions, Carte visited the United States. There he was impressed by a new style of building: the luxury hotel. It was unfamiliar to London. Carte determined to build one next to this theatre. The combination successfully appealed to an age, adapting itself to hitherto unknown standards of plutocratic luxury. The extreme starchiness of Victorian social conventions were softening. Previously, respectable ladies had dined in only their own and their friends' houses. Carte made it possible for them to eat at the Savoy. New standards of cosmopolitanism were being set, soon to be imitated by other establishments, patronised by the rich, who were offered, at restaurants such as the Criterion, a décor that was as sumptuous as the food.

Less prosperous diners could patronise the teashops and corner houses of J. Lyons and Company, the first of which opened in 1894. Lyons became a restaurant chain, just as Sainsbury developed into a chain of grocery shops. While these outlets extended their reach through multiplication, others attracted consumers through scale. Unparalleled numbers of shoppers flocked to the palaces of retail that were opening in the smartest districts of the big cities: depending on a public with money to spare and a desire to show off, the new department stores turned the activity of shopping into a day out, where customers could relax, read books and eat meals, while equipping their homes with everything they could possibly need – or feel that they needed.

To this list must be added museums. When the People's Palace museum, reading room and winter garden was opened in a poor area of Glasgow in 1898, Lord Rosebery described it as 'a palace of pleasure and imagination around which the people may place their affections and which may give them a home on which their memory may rest.' That was the spirit which inspired philanthropists to create the Cartwright Hall in Bradford and the Horniman Museum in South London. To the social reformer Henrietta Barnett, for the poor to have access to pictures was as important as the provision of libraries: 'Art may do much to keep alive a nation's fading higher life when other influences fail adequately to nourish it.'

Covered in a filigree of carved vegetation, whose fronds seem on the point of breaking free of the stone, the Whitechapel Art Gallery, built in 1899–1901 to house the Barnetts' annual exhibitions in the East End of London, provided an architectural symbol of rebirth. Founded in a strong sense of moral purpose, the belief in the value of cultural self-improvement would, from 1922, animate John Reith's BBC.

LEFT Widening the Strand and building Aldwych in the first years of the twentieth century destroyed many theatres (not least the Rickety Twins, as the Globe and Opera Comique were known from their questionable soundness); but others quickly took their place. Such was the demand that W. R. Sprague, a prolific theatre architect, built a brace of them, to either side of the Aldwych Hotel (twinning of this kind was not unknown in those theatre-hungry times). Externally, it is in a heavily swagged and irreverent Baroque; the auditorium, shown here, though not in its original colours, is more elegant, the columns, wreaths and trophies being well made out of plaster, beneath a coffered dome. The theatre was commissioned by the actor-manager Seymour Hicks, who appeared, opposite his wife Ellaline Terriss, in the musical *Blue Bell*. It later became celebrated for Ben Travers's Aldwych farces.

ABOVE Richard D'Oyly Carte built the Savoy Theatre in 1881: he was an impresario before becoming an hotelier, and the Savoy Hotel came later. But the theatre never stays still, and his son Rupert D'Oyly Carte commissioned Basil Ionides to remodel the interior of the building originally designed by C. J. Phipps. He created one of the most memorable (and best preserved) Art Deco interiors in London. Mirror-lined walls and fluted plaster, coloured gold, combine with inlaid marble floors to create, as Christopher Hussey described at the time, 'the first really outstanding example of modern decoration applied to a public place on a commercial basis'.

ABOVE The London Coliseum was opened in 1904 as one of the mightiest of variety theatres, huge in scale and sumptuously decorated. Frank Matcham, the greatest theatre architect of his or perhaps any other day, gave it a terracotta façade and a turning globe on top of a round tower supported by paired columns.

Not only did it seat more than 2,300 people but the decoration also included figures of men holding lions on a leash and women decorating the proscenium arch. The ambition was to attract middle-class, family audiences with tea rooms and bars – amenities which combined 'the social advantages of the refined and elegant surroundings of a Club; the comfort and attractiveness of a Café, besides being the Theatre de Luxe of London and the pleasantest family resort imaginable'. In this incarnation the Coliseum was a complete failure, closing after two years. The theatre is now home to the English National Opera.

ABOVE Matchless Matcham, Magnificent Matcham, You can't Match 'im – Frank Matcham's sobriquets reveal the position which he occupied as the king of theatre architects at the turn of the twentieth century. The buoyancy of his personality communicated itself both to his buildings and his clients, and he was never daunted by the often awkward sites that the latter put before him, generally in London or the industrial towns. Buxton, the Derbyshire spa that had been developed by the Dukes of Devonshire, was a different proposition; the site, abutting the conservatory-like winter gardens and overlooking the Pavilion Gardens, was open, and the nature of the building – an Opera House as opposed to music hall – bespoke the expectations of management and clientele. They wanted a jewel, quite small in scale (it originally seated

1,250) but charmingly formed. And they got one. Although Matcham was incapable of being less than gutsy, the limited scale prevents coarseness. The effect of the bobble-hat domes (leaded and ribbed) above the entrance front, the cavalier use of the architectural orders and the ironwork canopy is irrepressibly jolly, without making too loud a guffaw. Inside, the shell canopies over boxes, trophies of musical instruments over the proscenium arch and allegorical panels representing the arts (largely in a state of undress) are festive but intimate; no oompah-pah here.

LEFT The Criterion restaurant on Piccadilly, which opened in 1884, was one of a number of establishments that hoped to attract respectable women (there were plenty of the other kind around Piccadilly) as well as men. Not only did Sherlock Holmes meet Dr Watson here, but it also hosted meetings of suffragettes. Theatre-going was popular and part of a night out that would probably include dinner. Just as the Savoy Hotel had sprung from the Savoy Theatre, so, in the previous decade, the Criterion Theatre (Thomas Verity, 1870) spawned the Criterion Hotel, with a number of restaurants, refreshment places and smoking rooms catering to different incomes, including the glittering American or Long Bar, decorated with marble inlays and a gold ceiling.

GUESTS ARRIVING FOR SUPPER AT THE SAVOY

THE "OPERA SUPPER   served in the Restaurant and on the Terrace from
11 p.m., à prix fixé   .   6/-

The Hotel and Restaurant Tariff for Meals is as follows:

THÉ ou CAFÉ COMPLET   .   .   2/-
ENGLISH AND AMERICAN BREAKFASTS, served in the Café Parisien
8 a.m. to 11 a.m. 3/6
DÉJEUNERS AND LUNCHEONS, served in the Restaurant from 11 a.m., à prix fixé   5/-
(Guests taking this luncheon have   free choice of dishes from the à la carte menu).
AFTERNOON TEA and Refreshments served in the Foyer and Jardin d'Hiver
DINNERS à la carte served in the Restaurant and on the Terrace
Visitors' Servants' Board, 6/- per day, rooms extra according to location

AULD LANG SYNE

LEFT & OPPOSITE A new feature of the imperial scene was the luxurious palace hotel. The Savoy Hotel was one of the first to open, in 1889. The impresario Richard D'Oyly Carte, whose Savoy Theatre became synonymous with Gilbert and Sullivan's operettas, was inspired to build it after seeing hotels in the United States. With César Ritz acting as manager and Auguste Escoffier in the kitchen, aristocrats and society figures lent it their names. Lady de Grey, whose husband was on Carte's restaurant committee, hosted a banquet there for her female friends. Such publicity coups (as well as flattering lighting) caused a social revolution: ladies could dine at restaurants without scandal. The example of the Savoy was emulated by the Hotel Cecil, the biggest hotel in Europe, which opened next door.

BELOW An illustration of the Thames front of the Savoy Hotel, showing the elaborate services that were required to make a model hotel run on ball bearings. One of Carte's innovations had been hydraulic lifts, making it possible to build higher. The hotel was originally entered from the Thames side.

The Reading Room

Telegraphic Address:
"METROPOLE LONDON."
Telephone_
8130, Gerrard.

The Dining Saloon

ABOVE & OPPOSITE Whether in Singapore or Rangoon, Paris or London, luxury hotels reflected the cosmopolitanism of the age. One of the suavest of brands was the Metropole, belonging to a group with hotels in Cannes and Monte Carlo. The London Metropole stood on Northumberland Avenue, a street ploughed through the old town palace of the Dukes of Northumberland in the 1880s. It was from here that, in 1896, a motor car rally left for the Metropole in Brighton: the first London to Brighton Run. The man behind these hotels was the solicitor-turned-hotelier Frederick Gordon. Gordon's career began in the City, where he turned fifteenth-century Crosby Hall into a series of dining rooms and established the Frascati restaurants for businessmen. His first hotel, the Grand in Trafalgar Square, was described, when the Lord Mayor opened it in 1881, as 'almost distressing in its magnificence'. Gordon Hotels did not expand into the Empire, but Maples, the furnisher and decorator with whom they worked (an association which helped set Maples on its feet), made a point of doing so: one destination for its furniture was the Viceregal Lodge at Simla.

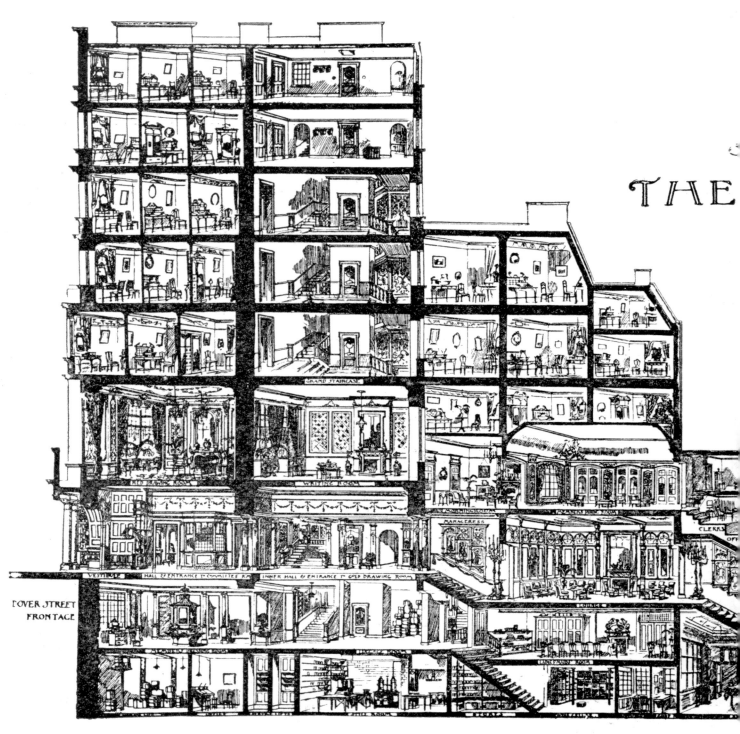

THE

DOVER STREET
FRONTAGE

BELOW A cut-away image of the Empress Club. 'Not very many years ago ladies' clubs were comparatively unknown,' wrote Sheila E. Braine in 1901; 'now-a-days, almost every up-to-date London woman belongs to one, butterfly of fashion and working bee alike.' The club of clubs, in terms of smartness for ladies, was the Empress, founded in 1897. Women could (daringly) smoke here, interview a cook, write letters in the library, study the tape machine for news, or listen to concerts; it was a space away from the traditional apparatus of social life dominated by men. There were seventy bedrooms and several dozen staff. Another socially élite institution, given the cost of motoring, was the Ladies Automobile Club, founded in 1903 when the RAC refused to admit women. The provision of women-only facilities was welcomed not just by titled individuals but by the increasing numbers of females who went out to work.

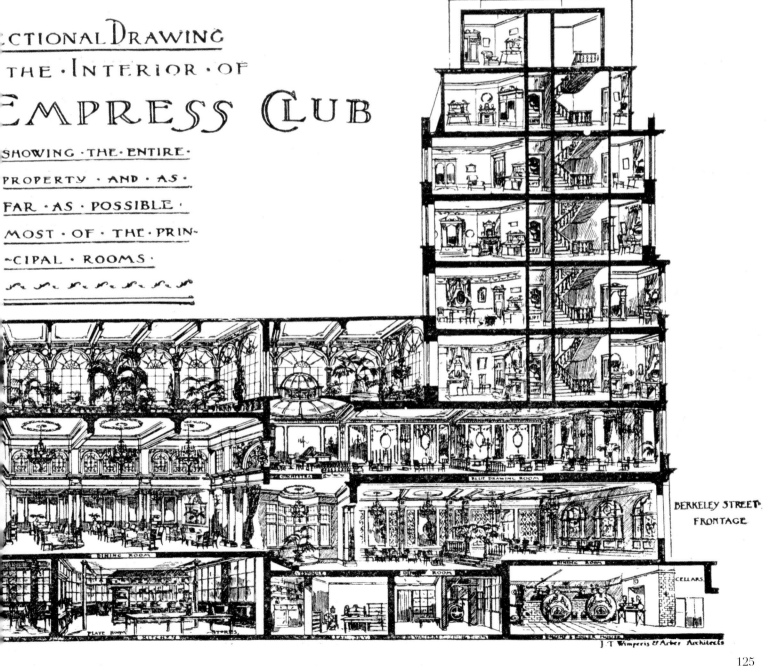

SECTIONAL DRAWING OF THE · INTERIOR · OF · EMPRESS CLUB

SHOWING · THE · ENTIRE · PROPERTY · AND · AS · FAR · AS · POSSIBLE · MOST · OF · THE · PRIN- ~CIPAL · ROOMS ·

BERKELEY STREET FRONTAGE

J. T. Wimperis & Arber Architects

ABOVE Tennis championships at
Wimbledon, 1926. Like soccer, cricket,
rugby, boxing, polo, cross-country riding,
mountaineering and some types of Alpine
ski-ing, tennis was one of the many sports
invented or codified by the English. It
emerged in the 1870s. The invention of the
lawn mower meant that grass could be cut

to a smooth sward and the vulcanisation of
rubber made balls that bounced. For many
people, life in the Empire would have been
intolerable without sport. The Tennis Club
was the centre of much social life.

OPPOSITE The Bath Club was founded
in 1894 by two members of the Carlton

Club who found that no London club had
a swimming bath. The premises that it
occupied at 34 Dover Street had previously
belonged to the Marquess of Abergavenny,
whose drawing-room was converted into the
swimming bath shown in the illustration, in
which King Edward VII presides over some
races. Women could belong to the Bath Club

"Mountview Ca[...]
LYONS' OXFORD CORN[...]
Oxford Street & Tottenham Court Ro[...]

HOUSE
London, W.1.

LEFT Sir Joseph Nathaniel Lyons, the son of an itinerant Jewish watch salesman, began life as an optician's apprentice, his spare time being spent painting watercolours and writing novelettes. Through a vague relationship, the Salmon and Gluckstein families, previously tobacco merchants, engaged him to front a catering company to serve an honest cup of tea in clean surroundings. The venture was piloted at exhibitions, but transferred to the high street and, after the first teashop was opened in Piccadilly in 1894, he soon had a chain of eating places across London. Customers were served by waitresses known as Nippies. At its 1930s peak, J. Lyons and Company employed 30,000 staff at its Hammersmith manufacturing plant alone. After 1907, the company opened a number of multi-storey outlets called Corner Houses or Maison Lyonses; the photograph shows the Corner House at the junction of Oxford Street and Tottenham Court Road, otherwise known as Mountview Café, around 1930. Each of the restaurants in these buildings had a different decorative theme and its own musicians. In the Edwardian period, London was the biggest city in the world and naturally lent itself to the development of mass catering. The Oxford Street Lyons Corner House is remembered as the first place in London which served the American delicacy of baked beans on toast.

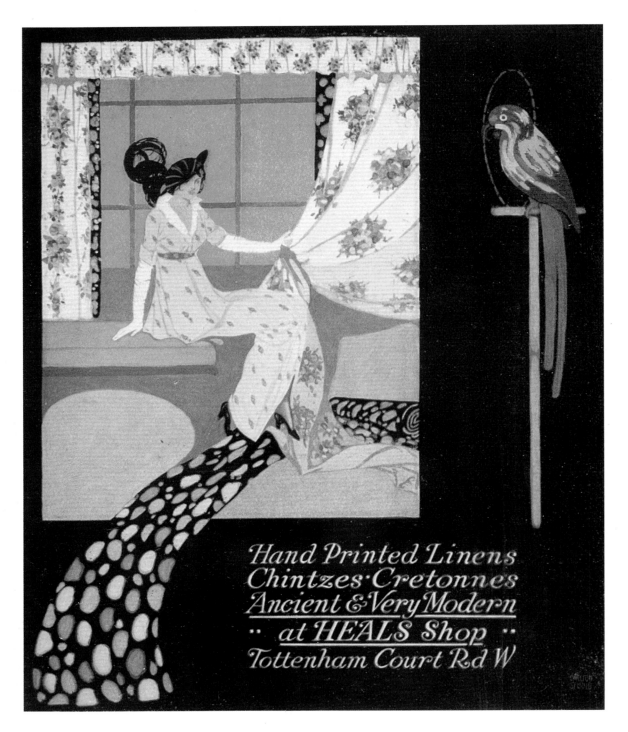

Hand Printed Linens
Chintzes·Cretonnes
Ancient & Very Modern
·· at HEALS Shop ··
Tottenham Court Rd W

ABOVE This advertisement of 1914 shows the charm with which the furniture store Heal's brought the Arts and Crafts aesthetic (the chintz is hand-printed) before a wider public than that which could afford specially commissioned work. Heal's had begun its existence, north of Oxford Sreet, more than a century before, making bedding. The firm took its Arts and Crafts direction from Ambrose Heal, who became chairman in 1906; nine years later, he was one of the prime movers behind the Design and Industries Assocation, under the slogan 'Nothing Needs to be Ugly'.

Among Heal's customers were members of the Bloomsbury Group, who were also shown in the Mansard Gallery, where objects and paintings were chosen by the architect Edward Maufe's wife Prudence. Feminine grace was, as this poster suggests, Heal's stock in trade.

OPPOSITE A detail of the opulent mosaic that decorated the central dome and pendentives of the shopkeeper Sir Ernest Debenham's house on Addison Road, Kensington. Outside, the roof was green, the walls blue and cream, having been designed by Halsey Ricardo, a champion of structural polychromy. Ricardo was a friend of Debenham and created one of the most extraordinary dwellings of the age. The house is also rich in tiles provided by William de Morgan, Ricardo's one-time partner, who described his ceramics as offering 'pools of colour into which one can dive and scarce plumb the full depth'. Since de Morgan had retired to Italy, the commission was a swansong for the firm, using old stock which may have helped Ricardo retrieve some of an investment that had not been returned.

Umbrella Section.

ABOVE The Umbrella Section at Selfridges, taken when the store opened in 1909. Gordon Selfridge was in the titanic mould of entrepreneur. A rising talent in the Marshal Field store in Chicago, he had been unable to persuade Field to open a shop in London. He therefore did so himself. The façade of swaggering giant columns was designed by a Chicago architect, with a Beaux-Arts bravura which expressed the spirit of the whole enterprise. Selfridge's ideas were considerably in advance of his British rivals. He brought over Marshall Field's chief window dresser from Chicago to glamorise the shop front. Twelve hundred people worked in the operation. They were, however, not there only to sell. Selfridge offered a library and quiet rooms, where customers could relax and meet each other. The public loved it. Other shopkeepers, however, did not. Harrods chose the very week of Selfridge's opening to celebrate its diamond jubilee, while Dickens and Jones marked their centenary – six years after the event.

OPPOSITE John Sainsbury opened his first shop in the unpromising London street of Drury Lane in 1869. The story thereafter is not only one of expansion but of new business methods, introduced to serve Britain's metropolis and other cities. By 1920, the Sainsbury family had 129 shops, vertically integrated with their own farms to offer shoppers the keenest price. Advertising, lighting and display were all considered. This shop window, photographed in 1914, trumpets the 'daily arrivals of pure rich butter', at a time when dairy products were often contaminated and had been identified as a health risk.

ABOVE The Army and Navy Stores (on the right) in Victoria Street, London. This shop did not look like other department stores: indeed its Gothic Revival premises were in part those of an old distillery, which did not have display windows. But then the business operated in a different way, too. It had been founded in 1871 as the Army and Navy Co-Operative Society for the benefit of military and naval officers and their families. Originally, the idea had been to provide cases of wine at wholesale prices, but this soon extended to anything that might be needed at home or abroad: it was to the Army and Navy that the future newspaper editor Bill Deedes went when he was sent to cover the Abyssinian crisis, buying solar topi, camp bed, metal uniform cases, cedarwood trunk, emergency rations and a tropical medicine cabinet (he was the model for William Boot in Evelyn Waugh's *Scoop*). Branches of the Army and Navy were opened across India, in Karachi, Bombay, Calcutta, Delhi, Simla and Ranchi. As an example of middle-class co-operation, the Army and Navy Stores had been preceded by the Civil Service Supply Association, selling 'anything from a blotting-pad to a bicycle or a billiard table – from ginger beer to carte blanche champagne'.

ABOVE Aston Webb's Cromwell Road façade of the Victoria & Albert Museum, London. In 1857, Henry Cole, the Director of the South Kensington Museum, forerunner to the V&A, described the success of opening the museum two nights a week. 'The working man comes to this Museum from his one or two dimly lighted cheerless dwelling rooms, in his fustian jacket, with his shirt collar a little trimmed up [with his wife and family] ... The looks of surprise and pleasure of the whole party when they first observe the brilliant lighting inside the Museum' suggested that even such high-brow entertainment as Cole offered could 'furnish a powerful antidote to the gin palace'. Although gas-lit, however, Cole's museum was inadequately housed in an awkward series of structures. In 1891, Aston Webb won the competition to reorganise it, with a scheme that appealed to the assessors because of its bold,

free-flowing plan, based around a number of large courts. It was not until 1899 that Queen Victoria laid the foundation stone, bestowing on the museum its present name; completion took a further decade. Built from red brick with stone dressings, Webb's front runs for 700 ft, with, as its centrepiece, a three-storey octagon topped by a small cupola – strangely reminiscent of Queen Victoria's crown. The statuary on the façade represents English painters, sculptors, craftsmen and architects. Inside, collections from around the world could not but help reflect imperial values, with works from India, the jewel in the crown of Empire, being given pride of place. When, in 1908, the contents of the V&A were redisplayed according to methods of production rather than place of origin, a visit from Lord Curzon ensured that the Indian collection, much of it inherited from the East India Company, was exempted.

ABOVE Sir Henry Tate had a fortune from Tate and Lyle, made from refining West Indian sugar cane. A collector of paintings, he offered to give sixty-five works to the nation in 1892. They were narrative, mostly Victorian and included masterpieces such as Sir John Everett Millais' *Ophelia*. Tate further offered to house the collection in a new art gallery, an offer which foundered for some time through lack of an appropriate site. It took several years and a new government to come up with one on the north Bank of the Thames, previously occupied by the Millbank Penitentiary. Work on the building began in 1895 and it was opened two years later. Domes were in the air and an early scheme by the architect Sidney Smith shows a proliferation of them – full domes on the main block and pavilions, the former of which has additional half domes and cupolas. This proposal was rationalised to a central block fronted by a giant Corinthia portico, flanked by wings; a dome is there but barely perceptible from the outside. Figures of Britannia and the Lion and the Unicorn stand above the pediment, as befits the first gallery dedicated to exclusively British art.

OPPOSITE Frederick Horniman left school at the age of fourteen to join his father in a business based on the invention of a tea-packing machine. By 1891, W. H. and F. J. Horniman & Co had become the biggest tea firm in the world. Business success allowed his passion for natural history to blossom and agents and missionaries were commissioned to supply material that would interest him. He turned his old house in Forest Hill into a museum. Within three years its limitations caused him to commission another from Charles Harrison Townsend, architect of the Whitechapel Art Gallery. Both the Whitechapel Art Gallery and, in particular, the Horniman Museum are masterpieces turn-of-the-century Free Style, the nearest English architects got to Art Nouveau, dipping freely into the traditions of the past for whatever ornament appealed to them, which were then beautifully crafted Both museums opened in 1901.

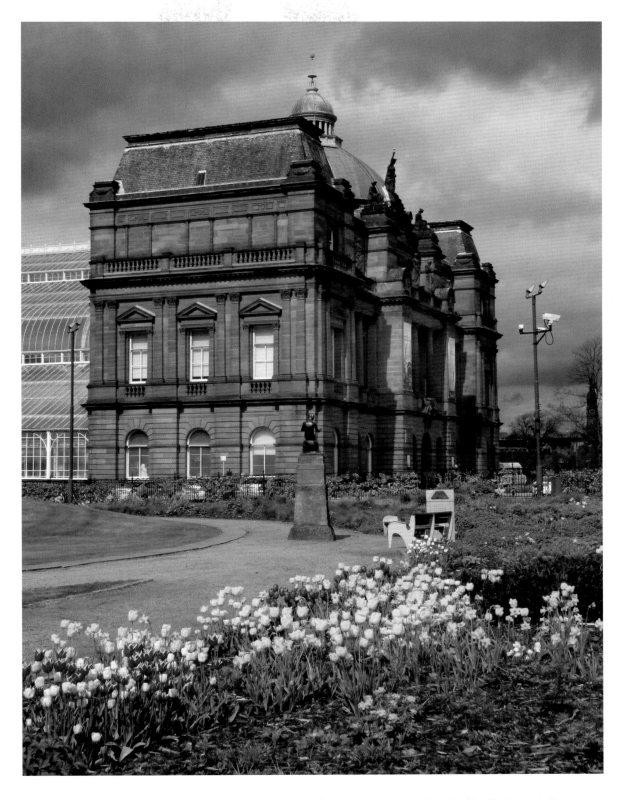

OPPOSITE An early design for Charles Harrison Townsend's Whitechapel Art Gallery, 1899. The shabbily dressed figures in the foreground of this drawing suggest the East Enders whom this gallery was to serve. It was a philanthropic venture, to open the minds and spirits of the poor to a dimension beyond work. The upper part of the façade is covered in a filigree tree of life to suggest growth. Money was never found for the mosaic by Walter Crane depicting the Sphere and Message of Art. The gallery abutted a library built by the newspaper editor Passmore Edwards.

ABOVE In 1898, the People's Palace – a museum, reading room and winter garden – opened on Glasgow Green. It had been designed by the City Engineer, A. B. MacDonald; the front in a flamboyant Renaissance style, with Art Nouveau touches inside. Lord Rosebery described it as 'a palace of pleasure and imagination' for the poor.

OPPOSITE John Reith, a Scottish son of the manse, had no experience of broadcasting when he was appointed general manager of the British Broadcasting Corporation in 1922 – but then nobody had. It was a new organisation. Previously, Reith had worked as an engineer. He revelled in the opportunities given by the as yet unformed BBC. This caricature shows him leaning on the transmitter mast above Broadcasting House and bending it in the process: an apt metaphor for the effect he had in shaping the BBC, bearing down on it with relentless and autocratic high-mindedness. From an early point, Reith had hoped to broadcast to the Empire, but the Treasury would not pay for it. In 1932, the BBC launched the service itself, out of its own funds, immediately receiving the imprimatur of George V, who used it to make his first Christmas broadcast. The Empire Service had been conceived to forestall American competition, although it was soon contesting the airwaves with broadcasts from Nazi Germany. No concession was made to the more relaxed broadcasting styles of, for example, Canada, Australia or New Zealand, nor was it thought necessary to win over listeners by deviating from the purity of Oxford English. Some thought it might become a service only for homesick ex-patriots, but to Reith its mission was a civilising one – and there was only one way of doing it. His way.

RIGHT Broadcasting House itself came into operation in the same year as the Empire Service. George Val Myer's architecture was faintly Art Deco, although clad in Portland stone. The more radical element was provided by Eric Gill, who sculpted Prospero and Ariel (the magician and attendant spirit from Shakespeare's *The Tempest*), Ariel being shown as a naked boy: the work was installed by the artist himself, dressed, despite the ladder, in his characteristic smock with no underwear. The photograph shows work on the transmitter mast, next to the spire of All Souls, Langham Place.

5

AT THE GOING DOWN OF THE SUN

In July 1914, a Bosnian nationalist assassinated the heir to the Austro-Hungarian Empire; soon that Empire, joined by the German and Ottoman Empires, was at war with the British, French and Russian Empires – only two of which would survive the next five years intact. On the Western Front, Indian, Canadian, Australian and South African troops fought in the trenches, while British Tommies were despatched to Palestine, Gallipoli, Macedonia, East Africa and Archangel. Everywhere that they went, they left cemeteries, peaceful and well-ordered, with serried ranks of identical limestone headstones that are planted in the style of an English garden; the sight of one of these instantly recognisable places powerfully evokes the scale of the conflict and the immensity of the human loss.

Architecturally, the war memorial, in all its different forms, is perhaps the most potent symbol to survive from the imperial past. There are said to be 100,000 war memorials in Britain alone. After 1918, communities and institutions of every kind wanted to record the sacrifice of those linked to them through kinship, place, work or worship. War memorials are everywhere: in town halls and regimental messes, outside schools and at village crossroads, on the walls of railways stations and in college chapels. They are so much part of the landscape of our lives that many people hurry past them without a glance. And yet almost none existed before 1914, and each one is unique.

Until the Crimean War, only officers were remembered with memorials, erected in the aisles of cathedrals and parish churches; as with Nelson, the body of the warrior might be bought back to be interred at home, while ordinary servicemen were buried in mass graves or at sea. Sentiment had changed by the time of the Second Boer War, 1899–1902, whose memorials (usually regimental) sometimes list all those who fell. Only very rarely were the men from a particular locality honoured. The rise of community memorials followed the convulsive reaction to the scale of loss during the First World War: previous wars had been fought by a professional army in far-flung places, and hardly affected life at home; this one put millions of civilians under arms and left hardly a person unaffected in some way.

Early in the First World War, wayside shrines began spontaneously appearing at crossroads. They were a folk expression of deep feeling that would have no parallel in Britain until the death of Diana, Princess of Wales in 1997; they can be compared also to the shrines of flowers, candles, poems and art that were raised in public spaces around Manhattan after the collapse of the Twin Towers in 2001. Before the end of 1915, a Civic Arts Association had been founded to promote the best standards of appropriateness and design in the building work that would have to be done after the War, memorials being a particular consideration. A Society for the Raising of Wayside Crosses was formed so that the dead would be remembered 'in almost every village'. The very first war memorial, inscribed with a community's roll of honour, was put up in the town's municipal cemetery by the Mayor of Rawtenstall, in Lancashire, Carrie Whitehead, 'that it might be some comfort to those who lost men very dear to them'. It takes the form of a simple cross, above a plinth.

Crosses would become the most familiar form of memorial but they were not inevitable. There are also monumental arches, cottage hospitals, bus shelters, park benches, wall tablets, parks, recreation grounds, bowling greens, scholarships for the children of the dead and relief funds. In some parishes feelings ran high:

PREVIOUS PAGES The Cenotaph, Whitehall, with the cupolas of the War Office to the right. In the classical world, a cenotaph was a monument built to remember someone who was buried elsewhere. This was appropriate, given that at an early stage in the First World War, it was decided that all who died should be buried where they fell: there was equality in death. In addition to this idea, Lutyens conceived a monument whose effect relies purely on geometry. It is devoid of religious imagery. Not a conventional churchgoer himself, he was conscious that among the hundreds of thousands of British and Empire soldiers who had died were many who belonged to other faiths or none. The mourners who laid wreaths at its foot may have been unaware of its great mathematical refinement, but it contains not a single straight line. So it was both obscure in meaning and austere in form; yet the Cenotaph was immediately recognised by the nation and the Empire as a powerful and appropriate focus for its grief.

advocates of religious imagery fell out with those who thought that the memory of working people would be better honoured by a village hall; Shaldon in Devon went for a clock – to the irritation of the vicar, who had hoped to reroof the church. Methodists did not want the ceremonies associated with the memorial to be controlled by Church of England vicars. Villages usually came to a decision within a couple of years, but it could take considerably longer in the case of the larger towns, where harmony might be difficult to find between the many interests and ancient political rivalries; Liverpool's war memorial was not ready until 1930, by which date the relief felt at the end of war had been replaced by the bitterness of disappointment with the peace. Nearly always, community war memorials were devised by committees, who raised the money themselves and could do with it as they wished.

The great national monument in London was the Cenotaph. In the classical world, a cenotaph, as someone had once explained to the architect Edwin Lutyens after remarking that a massive stone seat in a Surrey garden looked like the Cenotaph of Sigismunda, is 'a monument erected to a deceased person whose body is buried elsewhere': this was supremely appropriate to the memorial in Whitehall, given the government's decision that no family would be allowed to repatriate the bodies of its sons; there would be equality in death.

However, in the debate over the form by which remembrance should be symbolised in the many Imperial War Graves Commission cemeteries, Lutyens lost ground to Herbert Baker and others who favoured a more overt approach. It was decided, by a committee chaired by the Director of the British Museum, Frederic Kenyon, who happened also to be a Colonel and could therefore pull rank, that every cemetery would contain a Cross of Sacrifice, designed by Sir Reginald Blomfield. The cross incorporates an inverted sword, inspired by one hanging in Blomfield's house in Sussex.

LEFT There are thought to be around 100,000 war memorials in Britain. Every village, town, place of work, school, college and institution wanted to remember its dead, in the hope that 1914–18 would prove the war to end wars. Local committees decided on the form of the memorial and the roll of honour. Each one is therefore unique. This memorial at Stoke Bishop, outside Bristol, in the late Gothic style, was dedicated in May 1920. The sword and shield are a reference to St George, who was often evoked in chivalric terms.

BELOW The Cenotaph was originally commissioned for the Peace Celebrations on 19 July 1919. Lutyens had less than a fortnight to get it ready, and the design took only a few hours to realise (although this sketch shows Lutyens exploring the possibly of placing an urn on top of it). The Celebrations included a procession, made up of contingents of every unit of each of the Allied nations that took part in the War. J. M. Barrie wrote to his friend Lutyens: 'The cenotaph grows in beauty as one strolls down alone o'nights to look at it … I stand cogitating why and how it is so noble a thing.'

RIGHT The temporary Cenotaph, imitating stone, was unveiled on the morning of the July 1919 Peace Celebrations. 'Sir Edwin Lutyens's design is so grave, severe, and beautiful that one might well wish it were indeed of stone and permanent,' wrote *The Times*. This sentiment was so general that a new version was carved out of Portland stone, seen here, at the unveiling on Armistice Day 1920. Afterwards, the Prime Minister David Lloyd George thanked Lutyens, writing that 'The Cenotaph by its very simplicity fittingly expresses the memory in which the people hold all those who so bravely fought and died for the country'.

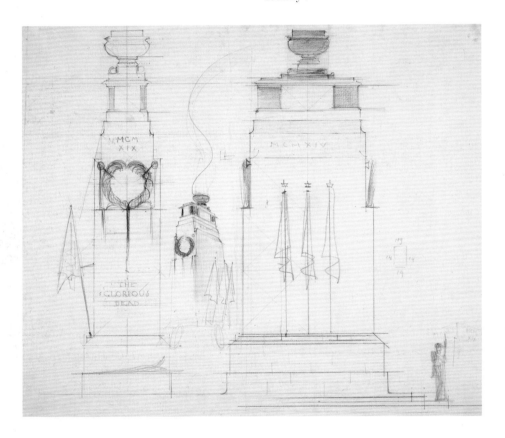

LEFT Every village in Britain wanted to remember its loss during the First World War, hoping that remembrance would prevent it happening again. Estate villages, in the ownership of a squire, were usually better provided for, as was the case at Sledmere in East Yorkshire. Two memorials were erected there. One, a tribute to local men, had originally been designed in 1895 by the church architect Temple Moore, as a pastiche of an Eleanor Cross. It was converted to a war memorial by the addition of a brass plaque. Nearby is the zanily primitive memorial to the Waggoner's

Company. The inscription reads: 'Lieutenant Colonel Sir Mark SYKES Baronet MP designed this monument and set it up as a remembrance of the calling and services rendered in the great war 1914–1919 by the Wolds Waggoners Reserve. A corps of 1000 drivers raised by him on the Yorkshire Wolds Farms in the year 1912.'

ABOVE In December 1914, more than 340 wounded Indian soldiers were taken to hospitals in Brighton. They were just a few of the million and a half troops from the subcontinent who fought in the First World

War. Some of the contingent died. While the twenty-one Muslims were taken to the mosque in Woking to be buried in a new cemetery, the fifty-three Sikhs and Hindus were cremated on the South Downs. It was quickly decided to erect a memorial to the dead. The India Office shared the cost of building it with Brighton Corporation, and the result was the *Chattri*, designed by the Government of India architectural student E. C. Henriques under guidance from Colonel Sir Swinton Jacob – a *chattri* being a domed pavilion, which marks a funerary site in India.

OPPOSITE The figure of the Driver from the Royal Artillery Memorial on Hyde Park Corner, a war memorial which combines *verismo* (the centrepiece is a representation of a 9.2-inch howitzer and a dead gunner lies on the ground) with monumentality. The sculptor was Charles Sargeant Jagger, a Yorkshireman who, having won the Prix de Rome, should have travelled to Italy, but instead enlisted in 1914, winning the MC with the Worcestershire Regiment. His style – epic but sombre – was perfectly suited to war memorials such as that on Paddington Station and this one, on Hyde Park Corner. Nearly 5,000 members of the Royal Artillery

were killed. The memorial received a mixed reception when it was unveiled in 1925, Lord Curzon declaring that 'nothing more hideous could ever be conceived'.

ABOVE The bigger the city, the more difficult it was, often, to get different factions to agree on the form that a war memorial should take. Liverpool's war memorial was not unveiled until 11 November 1930. Thousands of people attended the ceremony, though the two-minute silence at 11 o'clock was too fraught with emotion for some of them to bear: 350 of them had to be treated by ambulance

men. As in Whitehall, it was a Cenotaph – here, an austere stone slab, in the Modernist tradition of the Liverpool School of Architecture. Unlike Lutyens' monument, it was not free of figurative sculpture. On either side is a frieze by Herbert Tyson Smith, showing a march past of almost automaton-like soldiers on one panel, and a parade of mourners in everyday clothes on the other. The relief at victory in 1919 had been replaced by cynicism as the hopes of returning servicemen were disappointed by the Depression. The Liverpool Cenotaph caught the mood of a disillusioned time.

151

TO THE MEN OF CAMBRIDGESHIRE
THE ISLE OF ELY, THE BOROUGH
AND UNIVERSITY OF CAMBRIDGE
WHO SERVED IN THE GREAT WAR
1914 - 1919

1914

OPPOSITE The Cambridge war memorial shows a young soldier striding home from the front, helmet at the end of one outstretched arm, his rifle garlanded with a wreath. But his eyes are turned to the railway station, looking for his comrades who will never return. *The Homecoming* was created by the remarkable Dr Robert Tait McKenzie, a Canadian doctor and sculptor. The memorial's base was designed by George Hubbard. As well as the sculpture, Cambridge created a chapel to the Cambridgeshire Regiment in Ely Cathedral and donated a fund to Addenbrooke's Hospital. McKenzie's figure was planned to have been larger and sited on Parker's Piece, but the necessary money could not be raised and it was decided to reduce its size and that prompted a move of site, since a smaller figure would not have commanded a large open space.

ABOVE The Glenelg war memorial could hardly have a more dramatic site, beside the crossing to the Isle of Skye. It takes the form of a sculptural group by Louis Deuchars, in which a Highland soldier is garlanded by Victory while another female makes a supplicating gesture at Victory's feet; these figures stand on a pedestal by Sir Robert Lorimer, architect of the National Scottish Memorial in Edinburgh Castle. It is astonishing to come across such a theatrical work on this remote shore. The money to erect it came from Lady Scott, owner of the local estate, who wanted to commemorate her son and other local men who had died. At the head of the roll of honour is the name of Major Valentine Fleming, father of James Bond's creator Ian, who often stayed at Glenelg.

OPPOSITE Most war memorials across Britain took the form of a cross – whether a Celtic cross, a calvary with a figure of the Christ crucified, an elaborate Gothic cross or, as here at Branscombe in Devon, a plain one by a church. Devon has a tradition of granite crosses: they were put up by monasteries to guide travellers across Dartmoor. But not everybody wanted a war memorial in the form of a monument; at a time of rural poverty, voices were often raised in favour of more practical forms of memorial, such as village halls. Then, should the cross be actually in the churchyard? If so, the vicar would take control of the remembrance ceremonies, which chapel-goers could not endure. Diplomatically perhaps, the Branscombe cross is just outside the churchyard wall.

ABOVE After the First World War, the Imperial War Graves Commission (IWGC) was created to commemorate the British and Empire dead where they had fallen. Previously, they had been buried in battlefield graveyards; the bodies were exhumed and each one was given a uniform limestone headstone, set in surroundings that resembled a garden at home. Each cemetery, whether big or small, contained identical elements. This cemetery is Tyne Cot, the largest of the IWGC's cemeteries, called after the name that the Northumberland Fusiliers gave to a barn near Passchendaele, which had been fortified with German pillboxes. The largest of the pillboxes later became a British dressing station. This was retained when the cemetery was built, and it was George V's suggestion that the cross should be placed on top of it.

LEFT The Vimy Monument, designed in 1921 and erected 1925–36. While Britain's Imperial War Graves Commission cemeteries were Classical in style, Canada's national memorial in France was Expressionist – as dramatic as some of the films of the period. Twenty sculpted figures enact a mysterious drama of Christian sacrifice, giving honour to the dead, around two immense 'pylons' rising like jagged blades 120 ft into the air. The pylons were essentially an expressive device which, when struck with sunlight, would give something of a cathedral effect. At the outbreak of the First World War, Canada had a professional army of around 3,000 men, with a part-time militia of 74,000. By 1918, they had 600,000 men and women under arms. This postcard shows their memorial that stands on Vimy Ridge, part of the Arras front, which had been taken by the Germans at the beginning of the war, then retaken by the Canadians as part of the Battle of Arras in April 1917. It was designed by Walter Allward, who claimed to have been inspired by a dream of a battlefield that had haunted him during the war. Like Lutyens's Thiepval Arch to the 72,000 men of the British and South African Armies, whose bodies were never recovered from the battlefield of the Somme, the Vimy Memorial can be seen for miles in the sweeping landscape of Northern France.

6
WIDER STILL
AND WIDER

PREVIOUS PAGES The North Block of Herbert Baker's Secretariat Buildings, New Delhi. Baker already had experience of building monumental architecture on rising sites from his work in South Africa, before designing the Secretariats in 1912. On Raisina Hill, the grand simplicity of the Secretariats, built to house the small caste of imperial civil servants sometimes known as the heaven-born, seems half Acropolis, half fortress, as they ascend above cliff-like red sandstone walls. The scale was epic: each of the matching Secretariat buildings was as big as the Houses of Parliament in London. Baker's daring was equal to the commission: he did now allow himself to be constrained by the rules of the existing classical tradition, and – unlike Lutyens – relished the introduction of local elements, however misplaced, such as the *chhatris* (usually a funerary monument) on the top of the towers. The Secretariats were opened in 1926. The North Block now houses India's Ministries of Finance and Home Affairs.

Few sites say more about the hopes – and fears – of early British India than the Park Street Cemetery in Calcutta. The once-sharp edges of the urns and obelisks have been softened by heavy encrustations of moss; far from the chill conventionally associated with graveyards in Gothic fiction, the air is sultry and rings with the calls of tropical birds. The tombs are many; the lives of those buried beneath them were often short.

Early and sudden death was a risk that the small band of Europeans had to take in their pursuit of a fortune. Only about half the servants of the East India Company who went east ever returned home. Mortality among ordinary traders and soldiers was probably higher. When the foundations were begun for the Council Hall of a new Legislative Assembly in Bombay in 1928, the Indian workmen promptly downed tools: they had struck an old charnel ground called Mendham's Point. The sides of the trenches presented a millefeuille of bones. John Burnell, an early-eighteenth-century resident of Bombay, described it as 'a cormorant paunch never satisfied with the daily supplies it receives, but is still gaping for more'. Conveniently it lay next to the hospital, which was 'enough to make a man die with the thoughts of going into it, for it stands hardly fifty yards off a high grave. Then the concert of some hundreds of jackals every night shall awake him to his meditation, to think what a dainty morsel he is likely to make them'.

Burnell may have wanted to make his reader's flesh creep, but hardly exaggerated the grisly toll taken by malaria and other diseases. In 1702, Sir John Gayer wrote to the East India Company in London to complain that the quantity of soldiers being sent out was too small to meet the needs of defence: 'This number sometime will not satisfy the craving of Mendham's Point above halfe one month.' Poor Europeans were thrown into mass graves without coffins. Nabobs were commemorated with domes, obelisks and urns.

Funerary monuments were a form of private display, which, like the opulent houses in which the rich lived, reflected the fortunes that individuals went to India to assemble; in this they contrasted with the stinginess of the Company's own buildings in the early years. They emphasised the difference between European practice and that of the local Hindu population, which cremated their dead – while seeking to rival the tombs of the Mughal princes, who were Muslim. They could also make a political point within the European context. This seems to have been the case with the tomb to Job Charnock, who is traditionally regarded as having founded the city of Calcutta, previously a collection of huts. The chief agent in Bengal, Charnock had supposedly witnessed a funeral on the Ganges during which the fifteen-year-old widow had been about to commit sati. She was so beautiful that he rescued her, renamed her Maria, and lived with her for the next twenty-five years. When she died, he buried her, according to Christian practice, but sacrificed a cock on her tomb at each anniversary of her death, in a misinterpretation of a 'pagan' rite.

Job Charnock was not the only Briton to sympathise with Indian ways: the Company general Charles 'Hindoo' Stuart horrified his fellow officers by adopting Hindu practices, to the point of being buried with his idols. But such examples were rare. Generally, the city of the dead, with its Classical monuments, reflected, in a more dolorous form, the city of the living. The White Towns of the Europeans in India – so-called to distinguish them from the native Black Towns beyond the wall or ditch – were not merely white as regards the inhabitants: so were the buildings within them. Their peeling white plaster walls echoed the bleached marble of the ancient sites around the Mediterranean from which their language ultimately derived. While the typical Black Town was a spontaneous growth, hurried up piecemeal as the needs of the servants and traders who made their living from the British arose, White Towns were planned. Although each responded to the geography of its situation – Bombay was built on an island, Madras by an inlet on a long, sandy beach whose surf was much feared by those having to cross it to put ashore – the larger ones share certain features. The basic element, for Europeans, was the cantonment. At its core would be a fort, beside which administrative buildings and bungalows were laid out on streets set at right angles to each other: the civil lines. There would be a church – probably a simple Gothic box with a spire, in the manner of New England churches (decidedly less curvaceous than the Baroque style of Portuguese places of worship). A hospital was, as we have seen, essential. Almost as important was the club, with, in the nineteenth century, its polo grounds, croquet lawns and tennis courts. Barrack blocks and officers' accommodation occupied the 'military lines'. Crowded with humanity, the railway station bore the settlement's name followed by 'CANTT' – although the native quarter, into which Europeans rarely ventured, may not have had one.

Public extravagance met by Company funds was deplored. In 1640, Andrew Cogan was upbraided for building the fort at Madras at a time when the Company's 'stock was so small'. And, in 1770, Patrick Ross was suspended for introducing 'the various Ornaments which now appear in the Elevations of the Arsenal and Hospital, though the Orders of the Board were that those Buildings should be as plain as they could consistently be made'. A certain amount of display was allowed to the Governor; the newly-constructed presidential mansion at Calcutta struck the sailor Alexander Hamilton, writing his *A New Account of the East Indies*, 1727, as 'the best and most regular Piece of Architecture that I ever saw in India'. But the purse-strings were not often loosened, and although Lord Wellesley succeeded in building a palace for himself and subsequent governors, as described in the Introduction, it was without proper authorisation from London. From the beginning, a high value was placed on gardens. They were a consolation to memsahibs who would rather have been in the Home Country, the object being, with the planting of English seeds and fruit, to make them as little like India as possible; as time went on, nothing seemed nicer than a well-watered lawn. Strolls in the cool of the evening could be taken on an Esplanade or similar walk.

Most of the Europeans in an Indian White Town were young men, and they behaved as young men often do when they are far from home; drink, gambling and prostitutes were constant temptations. But the streets amid which they lived might be elegant. When the artist William Hodges came to Calcutta in the 1780s, he described the scene:

> The streets are broad: the lines of buildings surrounding two sides of the esplanade of the fort, is magnificent; and it adds greatly to the superb appearance, that the houses are detached from each other, and insulated in a great space. The buildings are all on a large scale, from the necessity of having a free circulation of air, in a climate the heat of which is extreme. The general approach to the houses is by a flight of steps, with great projecting porticoes, or surrounded by colonnades or arcades, which gave them the appearance of Grecian temples.

Classicism, a modular style of repeating elements, suited the military engineers and amateurs who often provided the designs for a White Town in the eighteenth and early nineteenth centuries.

By contrast, the Black Town was a muddle of lanes, huts, bazaars, hovels and ordure, amid which the occasional opulent dwelling would rise in defiance of its chaotic surroundings. But in the midst of their ease and over-indulgence, the inhabitants of the White Town were haunted by the twin spectres of uprising and death. At Calcutta, this can be seen in the history of the great open space known as the Maidan. Originally, it was occupied by a dense jungle, on the edge of which was a village, stalked by the Bengal tiger. After the Battle of Plassey in 1757, the jungle was cleared to build Fort William. The gunners needed a clear line of sight for their artillery. Later administrators believed that the ventilation provided by the open ground of the Maidan was essential to the health of the city. In time it became a place of resort and racing meetings: in E. M. Forster's *A Passage to India*, it is on the Maidan that Dr Aziz tries his hand at polo on a friend's pony. To safety and sanitation was added a third imperative after the Indian Mutiny of 1857: loyalty (as can be seen in the rebuilding of Lucknow).

Classicism prevailed as the organising principle throughout India until the middle years of the nineteenth century. By chance, change coincided with the end of the East India Company, whose rule, after the Indian Mutiny of 1857, was assumed by the British Crown under the Government of India Act, 1858. The importance of architecture as an expression of Empire had been recognised before the Mutiny, when the Public Works Department was created in 1853, but the rate and scale of building accelerated after 1857 – shortly before the Gothic Revival would arrive, in all its earnestness, at Bombay.

In the 1860s, Bombay was booming. Money poured into the principal port for the cotton-growing areas of Gudjarat and central India after the blockade of the Confederacy during the American Civil War stopped exports from the American South. Then the opening of the Suez Canal in 1869 made Bombay the port of preference for European trade. Soon the city had burst out of its prime neo-Classical skin to become what Gavin Stamp has called the 'the finest Gothic Revival city in the world with a remarkable concentration of Gothic public buildings'. The new Bombay was not white, but multi-coloured from the building stones that lay close at hand – buff or red sandstone, and blue basalt. The great Sir George Gilbert Scott himself sent out designs for the University Library and Rajabai Tower – named by the Cotton King who founded the Bombay Stock Exchange, Premchand Roychand, who paid for it, after his mother. Scott himself never came, but other British architects did. One of them was Frederick William Stevens, who took the examination to enter the Indian Public Works Department as soon as he had finished his articles with the architect and antiquarian Charles Davis in Bath; after three years he set up on his own, to design such stupendous Indo-Gothic works as the Victoria Terminus for the Great Indian Peninsular Railway and the Municipal Buildings in Bombay. Watson's Esplanade Hotel, 1867–71, was not merely designed by a British architect, Rowland Ordish, but was prefabricated at the Phoenix Works, in Derby, and sent out in the form of a kit of cast-iron parts.

Championed by the governor of Bombay, Sir Bartle Frere, Bombay acquired new broad streets, which improved not only the look of the city but also its sanitation; Elphinstone Circle (now Horniman Circle) embraced a park whose land had previously been used for the dumping of coconut shells. The construction of such a circus, essentially an ornament as opposed to a thoroughfare, shows the civic ambition that had taken hold of the authorities. A Ramparts Removal Committee was formed to reshape the city from a defensive bastion into an industrial, commercial and financial centre. In much the same way that London was being modernised with the construction of sewers and the Underground, Bombay was transformed by the draining of swamps, the building of bridges, the reclamation of land and the destruction of the old rampart gateways, on the site of which was placed the Frere Fountain (now Flora Fountain). To Frere himself, whose term as Governor ended in 1867, the work had hardly begun. As he told a London meeting in 1870, 'the whole of what the English government has done for the adornment of the capitals of India may be summed up by saying that very few public buildings have been erected which would be considered in any small seaport town in the country to be above ordinary merit'.

It was clear that India needed a public face; it was less obvious what that should look like. There were two views. One stuck to the idea that British India should imitate home. 'We ought, like the Romans and the Mohammedans, to take our national style with us,' announced the architect T. Roger Smith. This would set an example and awe Indians by difference. But others believed that, like the Mughal Emperors, India's new rulers should adapt their own style to what they found locally. By this method, different ingredients and flavours would be blended into a single eclectic curry – analogous, perhaps, to kedgeree or other Anglo-Indian dishes inspired, but rather different from, Indian originals.

No less a figure than Lord Napier, Governor of Madras, believed, in 1869, that 'the next five or ten years' would decide 'whether we are to have a style suited to the requirements of this country, or whether we are to be the mere copyists of every bubble which breaks on the surface of European art, and import our architecture, with our beer and our hats, by every mail-steamer which leaves the shores of England'.

Napier himself commissioned the Government Architect R. F. Chisholm to design a new building for the Madras Board of Revenue in the 'Mussulman style'. By the middle of the 1870s, Mussulman, meaning Muslim or, in a term familiarly used at the time, Saracenic, had been merged with 'Hindoo', in a decorative coat of many colours that was hung onto bones of essentially European structure and planning. The earliest expression of the resulting Indo-Saracenic style was the Mayo College at Ajmere, with verandahs, numerous *chhatris* and a clock tower that could be mistaken for a minaret. This was followed by such masterpieces as the Law Courts at Madras, 1888–92, and the Gateway of India at Bombay: the ceremonial entrance to the subcontinent which, finished in 1921, soon enough became the place of exit for the last British troops at Independence. It was also the style of choice for architecturally exuberant maharajahs in palaces such as the preposterous Laxhmi Vilas at Baroda, supposedly the most costly private building of the nineteenth century, and the Ambas Vilas at Mysore. Equally splendid but more touching is the Taj Mahal Hotel, by Bombay's Apollo Bunder, next to the Gateway of India. The Taj represents a deliberate fusion of eastern and western principles, combining, as Aldous Huxley put it rather unkindly in 1926, the 'style of the South Kensington Natural History Museum with that of an Indian pavilion at an International Exhibition'.

Such buildings called for ornament, and Lockwood Kipling, Principal of the Mayo College of Art, was on hand to supply it. This marked a difference from Britain. At home, the Arts and Crafts Movement, coloured by socialism, was not seen as a style of Empire. In India, by contrast, crafts were part of the fusion which the British sought to achieve, demonstrating that their rule could bring harmony out of what had previously between discord between opposing cultures.

The discussion, however, was not closed. Calcutta clung to Classicism in buildings such as the Post Office on Dalhousie Square, 1864–68. It would be the recipient of the colossal Victoria Memorial, a project dear to the Viceroy Lord Curzon, who championed the architecture of the Roman Empire as the appropriate correlative of the Raj.

The question of style was still in debate when New Delhi was commissioned. Lutyens believed in the eternal values of Classicism, as manifested in the works of Sir Christopher Wren; his was an essentially abstract vision which nodded playfully towards local traditions – Lutyens invented a Delhi order whose capitals have bells at the corners – but which relied on geometry rather than decoration. Lutyens was unable to respond to what he regarded as the chaos of Hindu architecture with its riotous carving. A building of the scale of his Viceroy's House, bigger than Versailles, awes the spectator through the calm of its almost unadorned surfaces rather than hectic ornament. Over it is a dome which to Robert Grant Irving, the greatest historian of New Delhi, 'expresses the very essence of art for empire's sake. It broods over the city, astoundingly animate, like the topeed head of a British soldier, district officer, missionary, or Viceroy, while great arms below grasp to subdue in their embrace an alien land and culture.' In the endeavour of city-making Lutyens was yoked with the truly imperial architect Herbert Baker, much of whose prolific career had been spent in, or associated with, South Africa. Baker's two Secretariat buildings, each about the size of the Houses of Parliament in London, rise above the King's Way or Rajpath by which they are approached as though they are immense defensive bastions, but the skyline is enlivened with Mughal open pavilions or *chhattris*, which also surround the dome, and more Mughal detail appears in the otherwise Renaissance courtyards.

Famously, a dispute about the gradient of the Rajpath leading up to the Viceroy's House, which meant that for part of the way its dome almost disappears from view, led Lutyens to declare that he had met his Bakerloo. That, however, is in the end a fault of detail. For once, architects of the Empire were able to create a city on a virgin site, with all the avenues and focal points that their Beaux-Arts imaginations could desire. They could make of New Delhi an imperial capital of a kind that London could never be: ordered, rational and immense.

Until now, little has been said about domestic architecture, either at home or abroad. We have seen that in Britain, very few people who had made fortunes in far-flung parts of the Empire chose to reflect the source of their wealth. Imperialism was a public expression. Distinctive house types emerged in India, notably the colonial bungalow, with its verandahs and large garden (the garden was necessary so that air could circulate around the verandahs; most Indians did not sit out on verandahs, but in courtyards, which meant their dwellings could be built on streets). It was, however, in South Africa that the private house excelled as a self-consciously imperial statement, because of the friendship of Cecil Rhodes, that titan of Empire, and the architect Herbert Baker. The colonial home was to Rhodes what display was to Lord Curzon.

'I like the look of that young man,' Rhodes, then Prime Minister of Cape Colony in what is now South Africa, is supposed to have said on first meeting Baker, 'he doesn't talk too much.' Baker was then at the start of his architectural career. The son of a gentleman farmer and MP, Baker had been brought up in the lovely Owletts, a red-brick house of the reign of Charles II in Kent, the experience of which instilled a love of craftsmanship and materials. After a public school education at Tonbridge, a talent for drawing suggested that architecture would be a suitable profession. He laboured for many years in the office of George and Peto, where he became chief assistant and met the brilliant young Lutyens, who dazzled the office during the few months that he spent there. Posterity has consigned Baker to a place in Lutyens' shadow, and admirers of Sir John Soane can hardly forgive him for the desecration of his Bank of England, built during the Regency and enlarged in the 1930s. That judgment is not, however, entirely fair. A literary and quietly idealistic man, he loved traditional forms, 'made living in expression', as he put it in his book *Architecture and Personalities*, with reference to the war memorial cloister at Winchester College, 'with symbols, heraldry and sculpture'; he also stuck to the principles of the Arts and Crafts movement. Brought up in an eccentrically Spartan household, Lutyens seemed not to need or even to notice comfort; Baker's interest in local materials and furniture was sympathetic to the lives of his clients. The debacle of New Delhi shows that his feeling for landscape was certainly as acute as Lutyens', if not, on occasion, more so; the great, open canvas of South Africa could have been made for him.

After George and Peto, Baker opened an office in Gravesend. Gravesend was not, however, big enough to hold his ambition, and in 1891 he sailed to South Africa, supposedly to inspect his cousin Lionel's fruit farm. The meeting with Rhodes came by chance. In the context of the twenty-first century, Rhodes is a controversial, sometimes repellant figure, but his imperialistic vision and personal charisma were seductive to his own age, and his status – almost that of a divinity – in South Africa and the country named after him, Rhodesia, ensured that, once he had taken Baker under his wing, the young architect had unrivalled opportunities to build. Seats of government, railway stations, medical institutes, commercial offices, churches, colleges … all flowed into his practice, as well as houses for the administrators of Empire: three hundred in the Transvaal alone.

Rhodes, having learnt that the young man had been studying the region's colonial architecture, immediately asked him to restore Groote Schuur, an eighteenth-century house that had originally been a granary, which he had bought. Rhodes was away conquering Matabeleland while the first phase of work was being done. He evidently liked the result because he gave Baker a further commission to extend it. As Baker describes in *Cecil Rhodes by His Architect*, there was a corner in Rhodes's grand vision of the world and its future for architecture: 'He abhorred the small and the mean and any commercial things made with the machine and not with hands and brain. He had an instinct and the right feeling for personal craftsmanship and good honest material.' Rhodes demanded that the work which Baker had already executed in deal was replaced by teak, the Javanese wood that had been used by the old builders (Baker sourced his supply from Burma). Strangely, the principles of the Arts and Crafts Movement had morphed into a manifesto for an architecture of Empire.

The first Groote Schuur, filled, not with imported antiques, but with furniture that had been made by the first settlers, sometimes out of the local stinkwood (so called from the smell that it has when it is first cut), burnt to the ground while Rhodes was away, a year after the notorious Jameson Raid. Rhodes took his loss philosophically, and decided to rebuild, out of sentiment, on the original site, even though nearby woodland, which he could not buy, kept off the refreshing breezes and obscured the view of Table Mountain, all of which Rhodes owned. Satisfying Rhodes's taste for breadth and simplicity, the new Groote Schuur was for the most part a severe, white-walled building, except, as Weaver described in *Country Life*, 'for touches of traditional gaiety in the curved gables and window pediments and in the spirally modelled chimneys'. Because of the fire, hand-made tiles were used for the roofs, rather than the original thatch. If Arts and Crafts architects in the Mother Country were attracted by indoor-outdoor spaces, the balmy climate of Table Mountain made them all the more desirable in Baker's South African work. A feature of early houses had been the *stoep*: a raised terrace, sometimes culminating in plaster benches with high, curly backs at the ends. There had been one at the front of the first Groote Schuur and Baker added another, wider and longer one at the back, which 'became in day-time and fine weather the chief "living-room" of the house'. Stoeps were equally prominent in the new building. Inside, teak is used both for the heavily beamed ceilings and the simple panelling of the walls, set off by pewter plates. Groote Schuur was left to the nation of South Africa on Rhodes's death.

At home, Baker could not shake off the curly gables of his Cape Dutch style, which reappear at Port Lympne: permissible in an area of Kent that had been influenced by Holland in the seventeenth century.

Rhodes died in 1902. By then, Baker had already impressed Alfred, Lord Milner, Governor of Cape Colony and High Commissioner of South Africa. Milner invited him to establish an office in the Transvaal to help with the effort of reconstruction after the Second Boer War that had recently ended. House building was a particular concern because of the need to attract settlers from Britain, who would, it was

BELOW The Gateway of India and the Taj Mahal Hotel, Bombay (now Mumbai). The Gateway was built to commemorate the landing of George V and Queen Mary at the Apollo Bunder en route to the 1911 Durbar, and was the ceremonial entrance to the subcontinent. Designed by the Consulting Architect to the Government of Bombay, George Wittet, it is in the Indo-Saracenic style, combining a European triumphal arch with Indian decoration. Finished in 1921, it became the exit for the last British troops at Independence, little more than a quarter of a century later. Behind the Gateway stands another Indo-Saracenic icon, the Taj Mahal Hotel. It was designed by a British architect named Chambers, having been

hoped, come to outnumber the Boer population. Baker himself described the pleasures of Parktown, the superbly placed Johannesburg suburb, originally discovered by Lady Phillips, who persuaded her husband, the buccaneering Sir Lionel Phillips (sentenced to death for his part in the Jameson Raid, although this was commuted to banishment) to build a house there: "We lived in the pure air".

The Phillipses' first house had been a prefabricated Swiss chalet; this Baker replaced in 1909 with Villa Arcadia. As the name suggests, the clients particularly wanted an Italianate villa, and Baker was well equipped to satisfy them, as he had been sent on a study tour to Italy by Rhodes. The house commands a grand panorama 'embracing a distance of forty miles' (as A. M. Adams commented in *Country Life*, 21 January 1922) and thirty acres of garden. Sadly, in view of Baker's enthusiasm for local craftsmanship, the antique furniture and ironwork was brought over from Europe, including the organ built into an end of the library, 'Sir Lionel Phillips being a musician of talent and a great Bach enthusiast'.

Other houses drew on Baker's memories of Kent, as can be seen from the chimneys, though with columned loggias and vaulted or beamed *stoeps* for outdoor living. In the Orange Free State, where the young Duke of Westminster

commissioned by a member of the Parsee community who did well from relations with the British, Jamsetji Nusserwanji Tata; it was Tata's revenge for having been excluded from the nearby Watson's Esplanade Hotel.

was establishing a colony for ex-servicemen, the Big House is built of squared, random, rubble stone which suggests the Cotswolds, as does the low-sweeping roof – except that the red tiles came from Marseilles.

The Union Buildings at Pretoria of 1910–12 must be regarded as Baker's masterpiece in South Africa, on grounds of their size. But the inward curving segment of the main front, surmounted by Wren-like, but under-scaled domes, and accompanied by some not-very-commanding Classical detail, is weak; yet it is magnificently placed, halfway up a slope. Perhaps Baker had in mind those Italian villas whose terraced gardens can be seen above their roofs, climbing up the hillside. Or was he thinking of the cities of the ancient Mediterranean – Athens, Segesta, Corinth – the nobility of whose architecture gains from the contrast that it makes with rude natural surroundings? Baker had an affinity for such places. He may not have been the greatest architect of the early twentieth century but perhaps he was the one whose work most fully expressed his generation's ideal of Empire.

RIGHT Job Charnock's Mausoleum, Calcutta. Charnock, the East India Company's chief agent in Bengal in the late seventeenth century, has traditionally been taken as the founder of Calcutta, although that honour is now disputed by some Indian historians. It was some years after Charnock's death in 1693 that his son-in-law Sir Charles Eyres erected this mausoleum behind St John's Church.

BELOW The South Park Street Cemetery, Calcutta. Only about a third of the British who came to make their fortune in India under the East India Company went home again. Many died young, to be interred in cemeteries at Calcutta and elsewhere. Unlike the Dutch tombs at Surat from the mid seventeenth century, those in the South Park Street Cemetery, opened in 1767, are mostly neo-Classical. Among those who are buried there are diplomats, army officers, naval captains, botanists, architects and Walter Savage Landor's muse, Rose Aylmer, who sailed to India in 1798 and died of cholera two years later, aged twenty.

BELOW Bombay improved: a photograph of Carnac Road, 1881. Arthur Travers Crawford, the first Municipal Commissioner and Collector of Bombay, was not good at handling money; his official budgets always overran and his personal finances were so suspect that he had to be sent home in the 1870s. By then, through what was later called his 'wise but hasty expenditure', he had helped to transform the city by cleansing streets, building new ones, improving drains, supplying water and erecting the Crawford Market, seen on the left of this photograph, to provide a salubrious bazaar. The architect of the market was William Emerson, a pupil of William Burges in London, whose influence can be seen, for example, in the twining reptiles on the lamp standards. The bas-reliefs depicting Indian village life on the outside of Crawford Market were designed by Lockwood Kipling. Carnac Road was later renamed Lokmanya Tilak Road.

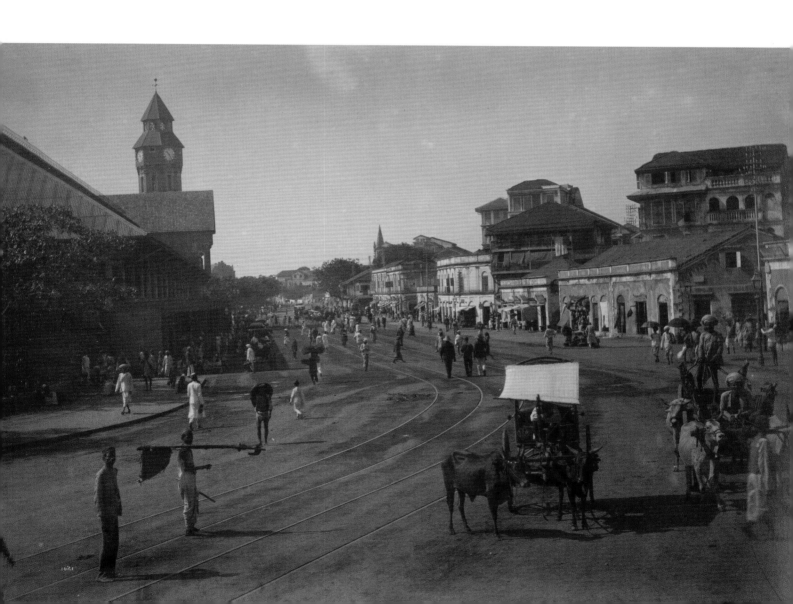

ABOVE The gleaming white neo-Classical architecture of Lord Wellesley's Government House (1798–1800) declares his intention to govern India from a palace, rather than a counting-house. Captain Charles Wyatt, a nephew of the suave Georgian architect James Wyatt and cousin of Sir Jeffrey Wyattville, was inspired by Robert Adam's Kedleston Hall in Derbyshire. The gateways by which it was reached echo that at Syon House, the Duke of Northumberland's house outside London. This was not highly original in design terms, but made a point: after the scandals of Warren Hastings, government would raise its head from the trough. This lithograph by William Wood of 1833 shows Esplanade Row. Esplanades, for walking, were an essential provision for the British and their ladies, although Wood presumably shows it in the heat of the day, since only Indians and donkeys are in occupation of it. To the left of Government House is the Treasury on Council House Street, built by the Reverend Mr Johnson in 1780.

OPPOSITE Elphinstone (now Horniman) Circle was begun during the cotton boom in India, caused by the Union blockade of Confederate ports during the American Civil War which prevented cotton exports and prompted the need for a new source for Lancashire mills. The design of a circus, on what had been Bombay Green in the Fort area of the city, showed that the civic imagination rose above the purely utilitarian. When laying the foundation stone of the circle in 1864, the Governor of Bombay, Sir Bartle Frere, warned, 'No prudent man can expect such a tide of prosperity to continue without check.' His words were prophetic: a stock market crash came the next year. But the financial reverse was only temporary. The opening of the Suez Canal in 1869 made Bombay the port of preference for European trade. Bombay was transformed by the draining of swamps, the building of bridges, the reclamation of land and the destruction of the old rampart gateways, on the site of which was placed the Frere Fountain (now Flora Fountain).

ABOVE Victoria Terminus, Bombay, in a photograph of around 1912. 'Those two thin strips of iron, representing as they do the mightiest and the most fruitful conquest of science, stretch hundreds and hundreds of miles,' wrote George Otto Trevelyan, describing a railway journey in the 1860s. '… The gay bullock-litter bearing to her wedding the bride of four years old; the train of pilgrims, their turbans and cummerbunds stained with pink, carrying back the water of the sacred stream to their distant homes; the filthy, debauched beggar, whom all the neighbourhood pamper like a bacon-hog and revere as a Saint Simeon – these are sights which have very little in common with Didcot or Crewe Junction.' Bringing the railway was one of the greatest of the Raj's achievements in India, celebrated in all the major towns with a terminus of dizzying size and architectural exuberance. Victoria Terminus was the largest modern building on the subcontinent when it was opened in 1888 after an unprecedented (for India) ten years of building: a work of such bravura that it has proved impervious to the official change of name, being still, to most people, simply VT. Pointed arches are combined with Gujarati trelliswork; surfaces bristle with crocodiles and monkeys as well as heraldic shields.

ABOVE While Bombay was becoming polychrome and Gothic, Calcutta, the City of Palaces, stuck to white stucco and Classicism, reminiscent of St Petersburg or Nash's London. The General Post Office, with no fewer than three colonnades and a dome where it turns the corner, was built in 1864–68. The architect, Walter Granville, was then Consulting Architect to the Government of India and Special Architect to the Government of Bengal, charged with the design of important buildings in Calcutta, such as the senate house of the new university, now demolished. Before the construction of Granville's building, the General Post Office had, since it was established in 1727, shifted home a dozen times. However, the mutiny gave added weight to the campaign for a permanent location: communications were of strategic importance. The site chosen had a symbolic resonance, being the spot on which the infamous Black Hole of Calcutta had been situated. The General Post Office is seen here from across Dalhousie (now Benoy-Badal-Dinesh Bagh) Square, in which is the Lal Dighi, or 'Red Tank', a body of water that reflects the buildings above.

BELOW The Rajabai Tower, with the Frere (Flora) Fountain to the right. During its brief existence in the 1860s, *The Bombay Builder* lamented (rather unkindly) the absence of architectural talent in the city: 'Bombay has at the present moment a chance of becoming at least in part a splendid city, a second Indian City Of Palaces …Who is there in the Public Works Department who has the smallest artistic power? Or who even knows anything at all about architecture?' In one respect, they were right: very few buildings in Bombay were designed by architects whose names would have meant anything in Britain.

The exception is the university, designed by Sir George Gilbert Scot, although he never actually came here. It was paid for by Premchand Roychand, who founded the Bombay Stock Exchange and made a fortune during the cotton boom; the Rajabai Tower is named after his mother. If famous architects' names were sometimes lacking, civic ambition was not. The Frere Fountain stands on the site of a demolished gateway in the old ramparts. A Ramparts Removal Committee supervised the destruction of Bombay's now redundant defences in order to re-imagine it as an industrial, commercial and financial centre.

BELOW The Victoria Memorial, Calcutta. On Queen Victoria's death in 1901, Calcutta threw itself into mourning. Huge crowds gathered in the Maidan and grieved all day without food. Before long, Lord Curzon saw an architectural opportunity. Curzon, as he declared in an Empire Day speech in 1906, was convinced that Britain's Empire 'is one of the guiding factors in the development of mankind … part of the dispensation of a higher Power which for some good purpose – it cannot possibly be for an evil one – has committed the fortunes of all these hundreds of millions of human beings to the custody of a single branch of the human family'. He also loved architecture. He built big and he built to last. Typically, Curzon had no doubt that the Victoria Memorial should be a British product, without the dilution of local stylistic references. His choice of architect was Sir William Emerson, who by then was President of the Royal Institute of British Architects. He produced a building of spectacular scale and presence, a cliff of white marble in front of which the late Queen sits in an immense and as yet immovable effigy (Curzon's statue is at the back). It is not a building of great subtlety, but it says a lot about Curzon's idea of Empire – and something about why the British, through an unwillingness to compromise until too late, lost India. Inside, the memorial was intended to serve as a repository of Anglo-Indian art and relics, which would remember, in Curzon's words, 'the mighty deeds that had been wrought on Indian soil', inculcating 'the lessons for the sake of posterity'.

BELOW George V and Queen Mary with some of the Indian princes at the Coronation Durbar, Delhi, 12 December 1911. 'Durbar' means *meeting* and three of them were called to announce great imperial events. The 1877 Durbar told the gathered princes and maharajahs that Queen Victoria was now their Empress. In 1903, when Lord Curzon was Viceroy, the Durbar celebrated the accession of Edward VII. Eight years later, George V became the first (and last) monarch to attend a Durbar, and revealed that the capital of India would be moved from Calcutta to Delhi. The Durbar on December 12 was held in the open air, so that the greatest possible number of people could see it.

OPPOSITE The courtyard in the South Block of Herbert Baker's Secretariats. Delhi's strategic location – equidistant from Calcutta, Bombay and Karachi – gave it an irresistible advantage. New Delhi arose on a site to the south of Delhi's Coronation Park. The Viceroy's House, 630 ft wide, was built on a platform that, Acropolis-like, also accommodated two majestic Secretariat buildings by Sir Herbert Baker, which preserved the spirit of the Durbar: the architecture cannot fail to impress visitors with the ordering of scale and space. Here was calm, here was confidence: Pax Britannica in stone.

BELOW The long sweep of the east front of Lutyens' Viceroy's House, New Delhi. Through the use of verandahs, courtyards and deep cornices (jutting 8 ft from the building and borrowed from Mughal practice), the architect adapted the Western classical tradition to the climate of the East. In a building that is bigger than Versailles, the restraint with which the surfaces are handled, with little surface decoration but grandly repeating elements, preserves unity in the composition. The rather flat profile of the dome hints at Indian precedent. Originally, fountains played on the roof. The overwhelming impression is one of controlled majesty. A visitor whose ear was deaf to politics and mind closed to history might think, 'Here have trod the great ones of the earth.'

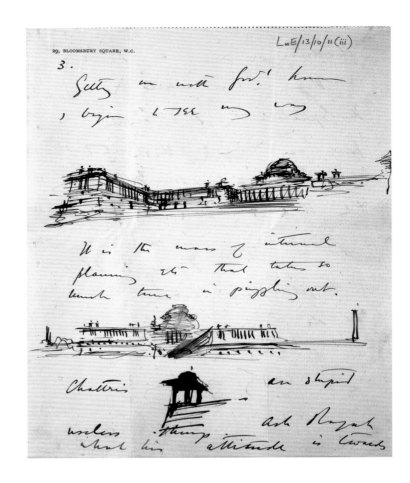

OPPOSITE Lutyens's evolving thoughts about the New Delhi can be followed in the letters to his wife, Lady Emily, such as this one, from September 1913. 'Getting on with Viceroy's House,' he tells her, 'begin to see my way. It is the mass of internal planning that takes so much time in puzzling out.' He had evidently been considering the expansion of his Classical vocabulary with Indian borrowings, since at the bottom of the page is the silhouette of a *chhatri*: 'Chattris are stupid useless thing,' he observes. In the end, he changed his mind, including four around his dome. He also devised what he called the Delhi order, whose capital includes palm leaves and pendant bells.

BELOW The Council Chamber, where the three houses of the Indian parliament would meet, is a circular colosseum, within which, at an equal distance around the diameter, are three semi-circular chambers. The idea – Lutyens' – had been that these arrangements would shelter beneath a central dome. Baker, the architect of the building, was unconvinced, but, as a sportsman, felt he had to respect the umpire's decision, given by the New Capital Committee. It was never popular. Baker himself dubbed the plan the 'merrie-go-round'. To his friend, Sir William Marris, Home Secretary in the Government of India, the oddly spaced chambers would always be 'fantastic & undignified – like

elephants dancing'. The architectural critic Robert Byron was scathing: 'It resembles a Spanish bull-ring, lying like a mill-wheel dropped accidentally on its side.' Poor Baker. However, he could be proud of the internal courtyards, such as this one, from which the dome was visible (it is not always from outside). The photograph dates from 1927.

GROOTE SCHUUR, C. P.

ABOVE Groote Schuur. In 1891, Herbert Baker sailed for South Africa. The idea had been for him to inspect a fruit farm but he soon met Cecil Rhodes, the Prime Minister of Cape Colony. This was a glorious opening for a young architect. Rhodes, who had already made a fortune in the buccaneering, dangerous society of the Kimberley diamond mines, and had personally taken control of swathes of tribal Africa to exploit their gold and minerals, believed that he was planting civilisation in a dark continent. His boundless energy embraced architecture. Rhodes had an educated taste and believed strongly in the virtues of craftsmanship. Baker created the country house of Groote Schuur (Big Barn), on the pattern of the old Dutch farmhouses which client and architect both admired. There, Rhodes dispensed hospitality in the manner of a bluff country squire. In his insistence on hand-work, Rhodes outdid Baker himself, asking him, as Baker recalled in a memoir of Rhodes, 'to replace all imported ironmongery, the things he hated, such as hinges and metal work for doors and windows – even the screws in those places where they could be seen; and craftsmen had to be found and taught to hammer in iron or cast in brass and bronze, as in the golden days of the crafts before the hostile influences of machinery.' The house burnt down soon after it was finished, but Rhodes immediately rebuilt it. This image from the 1920s comes from a cigarette card issued with Army Club Cigarettes.

ABOVE Immediately upon Rhodes's death, aged forty-eight, in 1902, plans were made to commemorate him. Admirers felt that the memorial should reflect the titanic character of the man; one proposal was a giant statue in Cape Town, on the lines of the Statue of Liberty. This was reduced to a statue of more conventional size in the Company Gardens. The Rhodes Memorial Committee, however, was determined to do more than this, and in 1905 settled on a site called Devil's Peak on the Groote Schuur estate, on the shoulder of Table Mountain, for a larger piece of work. This was, appropriately, entrusted to Baker, who quickly formed a scheme. It was to be the first of several projects – including the Union Buildings in Pretoria and the Secretariat Buildings in New Delhi – which took dramatic advantage of a sloping site. The structure takes the form of a propylaeum, raised on a base in the manner of the Acropolis in Athens. In the centre of it is G. F. Watts' statue *Physical Energy*, showing a horseman twisting to shade his eyes from the sun. (Watts was presumably not an equestrian himself, or he would have known that a horse only adopts the posture he chose, with both rear legs back, when it is urinating.) Rhodes is a controversial figure, and always was, but in the evening light, it is still possible to catch something of his epic, if misplaced, vision on the plinth of Baker's memorial.

ABOVE The South African Institute for Medical Research, 1913. Rhodes's death in 1902 coincided with the beginnings of reconstruction after the Boer War, and Baker was recruited by the colonial administrator Lord Milner to work in the Transvaal. Typically, the first laboratories in the Transvaal had been set up to assay gold. After the Boer War, a bacteriological section was developed to combat diseases among the large numbers of black workers in the mines. Better facilities were needed. The government donated a site next to the Johannesburg General Hospital, a little outside the city. 'Between the wings of the building you can see the refreshing sight of a court of green turf and orange trees through the white columns of a central loggia,' wrote Baker in *Architecture and Personalities*. 'The whole building is crowned with a high dome, the finial of which is a globe supported by a spiral of three serpents, emblems of Aesculapius; and here expressing poisons and their antitoxins which are the basis of so much of the work of the Institute.'

OPPOSITE One of Baker's first jobs on moving to the Transvaal in 1902 was to build an Anglican church in the prime Randlords' enclave of Parktown. To call Parktown a suburb underplays its spectacular position. As Baker described it, the landscape and atmospheric effects were not only delicious but sublime, if not mythic in character: 'There, perched high, 5,700 feet above the sea, we lived in the pure air from all the winds that blew, and above the frosts of winter that settled in the plains below.' To stand up to its setting, St George's Church is in a stern Romanesque style, softened by the warmth of the rough, irregularly-sized stone. It began as a barn-like church hall in 1904, to which a chancel and bell tower were added in 1910. Baker's workload both in South Africa and India was prodigious, and he took a number of partners, including, for St George's, Ernest Sloper and Francis Masey.

OPPOSITE Northwards is one of many houses that Baker built in Parktown in the first decade of the twentieth century, including his own Stonehouse. Most are built of rugged stone (quartzite, quarried on site, in the case of Northwards), with passages of white render, in Baker's Arts-and-Crafts style, with occasional allusions to Cape Dutch. In the dry, hot climate of South Africa it was natural to develop the English taste for living in the open air – encouraged by the discovery that sunlight is an antidote to tuberculosis. Northwards' one-time chatelaine was Josephine Dale Lace, known as José. José came from Richmond in the Karoo, but became an actress in London. She met John Dale Lace, owner of the Lace Diamond Mine. A marriage took place, but José refused to consummate it: she was still in love with the 2nd Baron Grimthorpe, a volatile banker, philanderer and former MP, by whom she would have a child (later maintaining that it was Edward VII's). At her request, Lace divorced her, but since Grimthorpe would not propose, she married Lace again, this time in Cape Town, and Lace adopted her son. She became a figure of legendary extravagance, driven in a carriage pulled by zebras. But the money ran out and after a fire at Northwards in 1911, the Laces sold the house and disappeared, only returning to Johannesburg after the First World War to live in modest circumstances.

ABOVE Baker built Roedean School in the suburb of Houghton, next to Parktown, in 1904. It had been founded the year before by Theresa Lawrence and Katherine Margaret Earle, two women in their early thirties who had been educated at Cambridge University. Lawrence, a sister of the Lawrence triumvirate – Penelope, Dorothy and Millicent – had started the original Roedean in Sussex in 1885, specifically to prepare girls to go to the newly opened women's colleges at Cambridge: Girton and Newnham. If there was a bluestocking, Suffragist air to the Sussex Roedean, there was also a spirit of Empire-ready boldness: yet another sister, Sylvia (there were fourteen Lawrence siblings altogether), designed the school uniform, known as a 'djibbah', reputedly inspired by the dress of North African tribesmen. The African Roedean was built in surroundings that encouraged pupils to spend time out of doors, often on horseback. Baker's economical, white-rendered buildings are designed to take advantage of the health-giving sunlight and fresh air, with loggias, verandahs and covered walks.

FOLLOWING PAGES Among Baker's many buildings in South Africa are Pretoria Railway Station, the Rhodes University at Grahamstown, the Union Club in Johannesburg, offices, banks, cathedrals in Cape Town and Johannesburg, workers villages, the Rhodes Fruit Farm and many houses. The crowning achievement, however, is the Union Buildings at Pretoria, housing the parliament of the Union of South Africa which was formed in 1910 when the Boer Republics joined Cape Colony and Natal Colony. Magnificently positioned, the central loggia sweeps inwards (like the façade of County Hall in London) and domed towers arise above each of the wings, in the manner of the Seaman's Hospital at Greenwich. The deliberate lack of any central emphasis (except the equestrian statue of Louis Botha, the first Prime Minister, unveiled in 1946) might be criticised as Mannerist, but the fourteen million bricks and half a million tons of stone that went into the construction of the Buildings achieve a building of undeniable presence.

RIGHT The Memorial to the Honoured
Dead at Kimberley is a great monument of
Empire, raised after the morally questionable
2nd Anglo-Boer War. It remembers the 27
soldiers and militiamen who fell during
the four-month siege of Kimberley that
began in 1899. Cecil Rhodes himself had
been present during the siege, hoping that
his charisma would lend protection to the
town whose diamond mines his De Beers
company controlled. Rhodes had helped
to precipitate the war through the noisy
anti-Boer propaganda of his newspapers.
Ruthless in putting De Beers' interests
ahead of any others, he quarrelled with
the military commander at Kimberley,
Lieutenant Colonel Robert Kekewich, to
the point that he tried to punch him. The
De Beers engineers demonstrated their
resourcefulness by improvising a refrigerator
for cattle which had to be slaughtered and
a large gun called Long Cecil. As soon as
the siege was lifted, Rhodes commissioned
Herbert Baker to design a memorial, sending
him to Italy to gather inspiration from the
ancient world. Among the monuments
that the architect studied there was the
Tomb of Theron at Agrigento in Sicily, to
an Olympian victor. The Memorial to the
Honoured Dead is a variant of this, with
an open peristyle of Corinthian columns
made of yellowish sandstone above a
browny-red base: the stone came from the
Matopo Hills in Rhodesia where Rhodes,
who died of heart failure aged 49, would,
before very long, be buried. The memorial's
uncompromising form suggests both a
temple and a fort. Long Cecil was placed
at its base, and an inscription composed by
Rudyard Kipling, who spent every winter
for eight years as Rhodes's guest at The
Woolsack, a writer's retreat designed by
Baker; bronze reliefs were made by Kipling's
father, Lockwood. Local opinion insisted that
the Memorial to the Honoured Dead should
be dedicated on the fifth anniversary of the
death of the popular Major Henry Scott-
Turner, a dashing officer of the Black Watch
who was killed leading a raid. A memorial
in front of the Dutch Reformed church
remembers the women and children who
were interned in the concentration camp
which the British established at Kimberley
after the siege.

INDEX

FURTHER READING

BOOKS

Architectural Design, Vol. 48, no 5–6, 1978, 'London 1900'
Architecture and Personalities by Herbert Baker (Country Life, 1944)
Architecture and Social Reform in Late-Victorian London by Deborah E. B.Weiner (Manchester University Press, 1994)
Architecture of the British Empire, Robert Fermor-Hesketh (ed) (Vendome, 1986)
Behind the Bungalow by Edward Hamilton Aitken (Various publishers, 1889) (6th edition 1897)
British Architecture in India 1857–1947 by Gavin Stamp (1981)
Buildings of Empire by Ashley Jackson (OUP, 2013)
Cambridge Illustrated History of the British Empire, The, P. J. Marshall (ed) (CUP, 1996)
Cecil Rhodes. By his architect by Herbert Baker (OUP, 1934)
Edwardian Architecture by Alistair Service (1977)
Edwardian Architecture: A Biographical Dictionary by A. Stuart Gray (University of Iowa Press, 1986)
Edwardian Country House, The by Clive Aslet (Frances Lincoln, 2012)
European Architecture in India 1750–1850 by Sten Nilsson (Taplinger, 1969)
Farewell the Trumpets by Jan Morris (Faber, 2012, new ed.)
Frank Matcham, Theatre Architect, Brian Walker (ed) (Blackstaff, 1980)
Heaven's Command by Jan Morris (Faber, 2012, new ed.)
Herbert Baker: Architecture and Idealism, 1892–1913 – The South African Years by Michael Keath (Ashanti, 1992)
Herbert Baker in South Africa by Doreen E.Greig (Purnell, 1970)
Imperial Gothic by G. A. Bremner (Yale University Press, 2013)
Imperial London by M. H. Port (Yale University Press, 1995)
Imperial Vision, An by Thomas R.Metcalf (OUP, 1989)
Imperialism and Music: Britain, 1876–1953 by Jeffrey Richards (Manchester University Press, 2001)
Indian Summer by Robert Grant Irving (1981)
Influences in Victorian Art and Architecture, Sarah Macready and F.H.Thompson (ed) (Society of Antiquaries of London, 1985) (For chapter Raymond Head, 'Bagshot Park and Indian Crafts', pp139–49)
Late Victorian Britain, 1875–1901 by J. F. C. Harrison (Routledge, 2014, new ed.)
Letters of Edwin Lutyens, The, Clayre Percy and Jane Ridley (eds) (HarperCollins, 1985)
Life of Sir Edwin Lutyens, The by Christopher Hussey (ACC, 1984)
Lion Roars at Wembley by Donald R.Knight and Alan D.Sabey (Don. R. Knight, 1984)
London 1900 by Jonathan Schneer (Yale University Press, 1999)
Modernity and Meaning in Victorian London by Joseph de Sapio (Palgrave Macmillan, 2014)
Oxford History of the British Empire, The: Vol. III: *The Nineteenth Century*, Andrew Porter (ed) (OUP, 1999)
Pax Britannica by Jan Morris (Faber, 2012, new ed.)
Splendours of the Raj by Philip Davies (John Murray, 1985)
Stones of Empire by Jan Morris, with Simon Winchester (OUP, 1983, 2005)
Victoria and Abdul by Shrabani Basu (The History Press, 2010)
Vision for London, 1889–1914, A by Susan D. Pennybacker (Routledge, 2014, new ed.)

ARTICLES

Bremner, G. Alex: 'Nation and Empire in the Government Architecture of Mid-Victorian London: The Foreign and India Office', *The Historical Journal*, Vol. 48, No. 3 (September 2005), pp. 703–42
Bremner, G. Alex: '"Some Imperial Institute": Architecture, Symbolism, and the Ideal of Empire in Late Victorian Britain, 1887–93', *Journal of the Society of Architectural Historians*, Vol. 62, No. 1 (March 2003)
Chamberlain, M. E.: 'The New Imperialism', Historical Association pamphlet 73, 1970
English, Jim: 'Empire Day in Britain, 1904–1958', *The Historical Journal*, Vol. 49, No. 1 (March 2006), pp. 247–76
de Figueiredo, Peter: 'Symbols of Empire: the Buildings of the Liverpool Waterfront', *Architectural History*, Vol. 46 (2003)
Forsyth, Alastair: 'Floating Palaces: British Liners of the 1930s', *Thirties Society Journal*, No. 4 (1984), pp. 10–15
Mallins, Edward: 'Indian Influences on English Houses and Gardens at the Beginning of the Nineteenth Century', *Garden History*, Vol. 8, No. 1 (Spring, 1980), pp. 46–66
Marshall, P. J.: 'The White Town of Calcutta under the Rule of the East India Company', *Modern Asian Studies*, Vol. 34, No. 2 (May, 2000)
Miers, Mary: 'Osborne House, Isle of Wight', *Country Life* (29 March 2001), pp. 86–91
Sekules, Veronica: 'The Ship-Owner as an Art Patron: Sir Colin Anderson and the Orient Line, 1930–1960', *The Journal of the Decorative Arts Society*, No. 10 (1986), pp. 22–33
Tarapor, Mahrukh: 'John Lockwood Kipling & the Arts and Crafts Movement in India', AA Files, No. 3 (January 1983), pp. 12–21.
Tarapor, Mahrukh: 'John Lockwood Kipling and British Art Education in India', *Victorian Studies*, Vol. 2, No. 1, Victorian Imperialism (Autumn, 1980), pp. 53–81.
Weinhardt, Carl J., Jr.: 'The Indian Taste', *The Metropolitan Museum of Art Bulletin*, New Series, Vol. 16, No. 7 (March 1958), pp. 208–16

PICTURE CREDITS